SILENCE AND PRAISE

SILENCE AND PRAISE

RHETORICAL COSMOLOGY AND POLITICAL THEOLOGY IN THE BOOK OF REVELATION

RYAN LEIF HANSEN

Fortress Press
Minneapolis

SILENCE AND PRAISE

Rhetorical Cosmology and Political Theology in the Book of Revelation

Copyright © 2014 Fortress Press. All rights reserved. Except for brief quotations in critical articles or reviews, no part of this book may be reproduced in any manner without prior written permission from the publisher. Visit http://www.augsburgfortress.org/copyrights/ or write to Permissions, Augsburg Fortress, Box 1209, Minneapolis, MN 55440.

Cover design: Alisha Lofgren

Library of Congress Cataloging-in-Publication Data is available
Print ISBN: 978-1-4514-7011-6
eBook ISBN: 978-1-4514-8442-7

The paper used in this publication meets the minimum requirements of American National Standard for Information Sciences — Permanence of Paper for Printed Library Materials, ANSI Z329.48-1984.

Manufactured in the U.S.A.

This book was produced using PressBooks.com, and PDF rendering was done by PrinceXML.

CONTENTS

Acknowledgements	vii
Introduction	1
1. "The Apocalyptic Technique": How John's Apocalypse Makes Meaning	13
2. The War of Worldcraft: John's Cosmic Rhetoric Against Roman Imperial Cult Discourse	49
3. The Three Cycles of Seven as Object of Interpretation	69
4. Silence: The Prayerful Endurance and Non-Participation of the Saints	83
5. Praise: Narrating the Emergence of God's Reign and the New Creation	107
6. Silence and Praise: Economic Non-Participation and Narrating the New Creation	133
7. Toward an Apocalyptic Political Theology	157
Bibliography	169
Index of Subjects and Names	181

Acknowledgements

A project like this can only be undertaken with the help of many kind mentors, friends, colleagues, and family members. I owe a large debt of gratitude to my teachers, especially Dr. K. K. Yeo, Dr. D. Stephen Long, Dr. Brent Waters, and Dr. Osvaldo Vena. Also of immense help were the countless conversations and encouragements afforded to me by my fellow students, especially Rev. Dr. Rusty Brian, Dr. Brandon Winstead, Rev. Dr. Brent Peterson, Rev. Jimmy Cooper, and Jonathan Dodrill. I have also been enriched by many conversations with my friend and fellow scholar Andy Guffey. I owe a special thank you to my New Testament colleague Dr. René Such Schreiner, whose friendship and insight into the biblical text I have come to value immensely. The team at Fortress Press has been extremely helpful and professional, and I am honored to be included in the Emerging Scholars series. Thanks to Neil Elliott, Marissa Wold, Amy Sleper, and Carolyn Halvorson. Thanks are due to my family, especially my parents, Jon and Shawn Del Hansen, my sister Thea Ardrey, my grandparents. Finally, thanks to my beloved wife, Karen Elizabeth, my constant support and friend, and mother to our son, Emmett. Karen, your sacrifice and patience have made this work possible, and I dedicate this work to you.

Introduction

> The black sky was underpinned with long silver streaks that looked like scaffolding and depth on depth behind it were thousands of stars that all seemed to be moving very slowly as if they were about some vast construction work that involved the whole order of the universe and would take all time to complete. No one was paying attention to the sky.
>
> —Flannery O'Connor, *Wise Blood*[1]

Each year around Christmas time, choirs in churches and various concert halls around the globe sing a song derived from one of Revelation's best known passages, "The reign of the world has become the reign of our Lord and of his Messiah, and he shall reign forever and ever" (Rev. 11:15).[2] Swirling around in this "Hallelujah" chorus is a convergence of praise, politics, and—submerged beneath the beauty of Handel's score—cosmic upheaval. Taken out of the choral setting and placed back into its context in the Apocalypse, this statement functions as the pinnacle of John's[3] vision. This text served as my entry point into John's work as I began to explore the way politics and worship function and relate to each other in the book of Revelation. It communicates in hymn form the overthrow of a kingdom, but also the unmaking of a world, sitting as it does at the climax of a cycle of seven divine judgments upon the created order. But this cycle is not the only of its kind in Revelation. It is part of a wider vision of recapitulative visions of divine judgment on the cosmos. The trumpets cycle can hardly be understood fully apart from the cycle of seals that precedes it (6:1—8:5) and the cycle of bowls (16:1-21; 18:1—19:8) that follows it. Each of these cycles finishes with a liturgical flourish. Therefore, the question

---

1. Flannery O'Connor, *Wise Blood* (New York: Farrar, Straus, and Giroux, 1962), 37.
2. Unless otherwise attributed, all biblical translations are the author's.
3. The argument of this book does not stand or fall on the question of authorship or date, but a few comments regarding those subjects are appropriate here. I understand the author to be John of Patmos, a prophet among the churches to which he writes in Asia Minor. It is difficult to say whether or not this John can be identified with John the Gospel writer. He does demonstrate some of the same literary mastery and theological interests, but there are significant differences and difficulties as well. Perhaps it is best to not say too much and just suggest that at the very least John of Patmos shared the same theological atmosphere as John the Theologian. I agree with most scholars that the work was written somewhere around the end of the first century CE.

of worship and the political in the Apocalypse would have to deal with the climax of each cycle. As I began to look into the climaxes of each cycle, I came to realize that the question of the political required one to look into the question of the cosmological, for that is really what is at the heart of John's vision in the three cycles of seven: not only the judgment and proper reign of the world, but more radically, the unmaking and making new of the entire world. This means one of John's central concerns is cosmology.

In a recent essay on the cosmological thought of the Apocalypse, Sean McDonough writes, "A careful book-length treatise on the subject is still a *desideratum*."[4] This study is, unfortunately, not the supplement to that lacuna. This is not due, one can hope, to a specific deficiency in the work presented here. It is rather the case that this study points to the extreme difficulty bordering on impossibility of explicating something approaching "the cosmology of the Apocalypse." John's view of the reality of the universe does not easily lend itself to this kind of inquiry. The world John lives in and the world that John narrates does not have that kind of stability.[5] As I will argue in this study, John's concern with cosmology is not to parse out the deep structure of a mysterious cosmological reality. Instead, his task is one of portraying the dismantling of the cosmic reality, which in his opinion has become so marred and disfigured by idolatry and overrun by the cosmically construed reign of Caesar that it must be brought to its end. Once it has been deconstructed or unmade, God's creation can then be made new to conform to the divine intent and purpose for creation. Cosmology, therefore, is decidedly political.[6] John presents for his audience, not a meditation on a sturdy and stable cosmos, but rather a *rhetorical* cosmology.

The rest of this study will be given to explicating what is meant by "rhetorical cosmology," but for the time being I refer to rhetorical cosmology as a discourse that participates in and constructs a particular world system. I

---

4. Sean M. McDonough, "Revelation: The Climax of Cosmology," in *Cosmology and New Testament Theology*, ed. Jonathan T. Pennington and Sean M. McDonough, Library of New Testament Studies 355 (London and New York: T & T Clark, 2008), 178 n. 1.

5. See Steven J. Friesen, *Imperial Cults and the Apocalypse of John: Reading Revelation in the Ruins* (Oxford: Oxford University Press, 2001), 163–166.

6. John's vision of creation contains implications not merely for the natural world, but also for the political realm. For him, creation has as much to do with how people live together as it does birds, mountains, rocks, and trees. Ragan Sutterfield pointedly observes, "When we think and talk about creation, we tend to think that there are two distinct things, us and it. We go to a National Park and talk about how wonderful it is to be in creation, but we don't say that in the midst of a crowd on a New York City subway," Ragan Sutterfield, *Farming as a Spiritual Discipline* (Indianapolis: Englewood Review of Books, 2009), Kindle electronic edition, Chapter 1, Location 76.

say both "participates in" and "constructs" because I understand cosmology to be more than just a "symbolic universe" or a "worldview." The world does not exist because it is subjectively imagined into existence. The cosmic reality is a given entity—it is there regardless of an individual or group's subjective construction and configuration of it. But rhetorical cosmology is also a discourse that constructs a world system because the material of the world is given to be inhabited in a number of possible ways, given to be governed in one fashion or another. Cosmological discourse also constructs because it creates a public space within which to participate in the cosmos so inhabited or governed. This indicates the intimate relation between cosmology and politics, a connection that will be clarified throughout this study.

As I began to tease out the connections between the theological and political that I was seeing in the cosmological, I could not find anyone who had put them together in the way I was seeing, or who had done so with the requisite attention to the theological and political matters that I see as integral to the climactic conclusions of the Apocalypse's cycles. Before looking at the theology of the transition from the reign of the world to the reign of God, I needed to investigate the socio-political, rhetorical, and historical issues involved in order to understand the cosmological implications of John's vision. Here I think it is beneficial to examine some previous scholarship on the cosmology of the Apocalypse, in order to position my own study and justify its existence. Previous approaches to the cosmology of the Apocalypse may be generally gathered into three overarching groups—(1) cosmology as a revelation of the deep structure and inner workings of God's creation, (2) cosmology as literal or literal-like description of the dissolution of the world, and (3) cosmology as the "symbolic universe" or "worldview" of the text.

Cosmology as revelation of the deep structure and inner-workings of the world can take a few different forms. First, one can assume a continuity between much cosmological thought of earlier apocalyptic literature and what takes place in John's vision. If this is the case, then John is seeking to explicate the hidden elements of cosmic reality that have either been obscured or are visible only to a chosen few. 1 Enoch 1–5 and 72–82 exhibits this cosmological approach, examining the inner-workings of God's creation and the heavenly beings in charge of keeping them functioning correctly. Usually included in this understanding of apocalyptic cosmology is a list of things that are revealed to the seer, demonstrating the abundance of information about the world privileged to him (see also Job 38–39).[7]

---

7. This element of apocalyptic literary thought is discussed in Michael E. Stone, "Lists of Revealed Things in the Apocalyptic Literature," in *Magnalia Dei: The Mighty Acts of God: Essays on the Bible and*

A slightly different way of this same approach is to understand apocalyptic cosmological thought as "astral prophecy," a vision of the sky conceived of as a strategy for "obtaining information from the world of God(s)."[8] Bruce Malina argues that when John looked up to the heavens what he saw was a literal vision in the sky.[9] The cosmic bodies provided information about divine activity that affected the earth and its inhabitants.[10] The planets and cosmic bodies provided a seer with material to interpret in order to discern the impact of sky phenomena on earthly matters.[11] Therefore, this mode of apocalyptic cosmology is not strictly "eschatological." Rather, it is concerned with "existing, present things . . . What is happening at present? What has caused or is causing present conditions?"[12]

The main problem with this approach is that it does not seem to be what John is doing with cosmological thought. He is not intent of revealing the deep structures of the cosmos so as to somehow reveal the divine plan in all of it. He is, rather, pointing to the work of God as bringing that cosmos to an end. We receive, in fact, a surprising lack of revelation about the world of God and the heavens (when compared to other apocalypses). At most, we receive the set and stage directions, and then move very rapidly to the action. There seems to be less interest in spelling out the mysteries of heaven than there is in showing how the heavens disrupt the worldly order of Rome. The first cosmos is sinful and impure to its depths because it is the cosmos over which Rome has reign and rule. It is the world that Roman cultic and economic discourse has constructed, and it is rotten to the core. Therefore, John does not seek to explicate its deep structures. He seeks to portray its end through the work of the Lamb and the participation of the saints in that work is envisioned as their endurance and resistance.

The second approach to cosmology in the apocalypse is to understand it primarily as a reference to the dissolution of the cosmos. Edward Adams gives

---

Archaeology in Memory of G. Ernest Wright, ed. Frank Moore Cross, *et al.* (Garden City: Doubleday, 1976), 414–452.

8. Bruce J. Malina, *On the Genre and Message of Revelation: Star Visions and Sky Journeys* (Peabody: Hendrickson, 1995), 30.

9. Franz Boll, *Aus der Offenbarung Johannis: Hellenistische Studien zum Weltbild der Apockalypse*, ΣΤΟΙΧΕΙΑ 1 (Leipzig: Druck und Verlag B. G. Teubner, 1914); Joseph Freundorfer, "Die Apokalypse des Apostels Johannes und die Hellensitische Kosmologie und Astrologie: Eine Auseinandersetzung mit den Hauptergebnissen der Untersuchung Franz Bolls: 'Aus Der Offenbarung Johannis'," *Biblische Studien* 23.1 (1929).

10. Malina, *Revelation*, 37.

11. Malina, *Revelation*, 26.

12. Malina, *Revelation*, 45.

the most thorough and careful treatment of this approach to the cosmological thought of the Apocalypse. Adams' work is a response to suggestions by N. T. Wright and others that the language of cosmic upheaval is conventional, first-century language for imagining socio-political change. Adams surveys Old Testament and Jewish literature, as well as sources from Greco-Roman natural philosophy, and concludes that, though it remains on the level of imaginative imagery, language of cosmic upheaval refers to a real cosmic catastrophe. He writes, "these writers use language and imagery of universal catastrophe for envisioning precisely that. Since a full-blown cosmic catastrophe (in which the whole solar system is shaken or totally destroyed) is outside human experience, there is no other way of envisioning it than by figure, analogy and imaginative construal."[13] Though he resists the label of "literal" for his understanding of cosmic catastrophe, he maintains that the idea of the material dissolution of the cosmos was widespread. Adams argues that the passing of the cosmos is a real event that John envisions, but that it is followed "by the appearance of a new creation, which is understood, albeit symbolically, in quite materialist terms."[14]

It is not self-evident why the new creation would only be symbolically material while the dissolution of the first creation is literally material, and Adams never supports this claim. The problems with Adams' argument are not with his assessment of the literature outside of the New Testament, it is rather his assumption that the same things need to be happening within the thought of the New Testament as well.[15] John does not seem to envision a cosmic catastrophe in which everyone is killed, as happens in 4 Ezra 7:29-30, where every person on earth dies and the earth is turned to primeval silence. Even as the cosmic catastrophe is in full force, John sees the idolaters still alive, cursing God, and dwelling amidst the very cosmos that has supposedly been done away with completely (as in Rev. 16:20-21).

The third approach, and by far the most common among recent approaches, is to perceive John's cosmological thought as constructing a "symbolic universe" or "worldview." This is the approach Elisabeth Schüssler Fiorenza takes when she argues that Revelation "seeks to persuade and motivate

---

13. Edward Adams, *The Stars Will Fall from Heaven: Cosmic Catastrophe in the New Testament and its World*, Library of New Testament Studies 347 (London & New York: T & T Clark, 2007), 17.

14. Adams, *The Stars Will Fall from Heaven*, 251.

15. See Adams, *The Stars Will Fall from Heaven*, 253: "In light of the comparative evidence [Old Testament, Jewish Apocalyptic and related writings, Greek natural philosophy, Stoic thought], language of cosmic catastrophe such as we find in the New Testament simply cannot be regarded as conventional, first-century language for referring to socio-political change . . . a catastrophe of cosmic dimensions (within an ancient cosmological framework) is genuinely in view."

by constructing a symbolic universe that invites imaginative participation."[16] David deSilva also takes this approach. Following Clifford Geertz's definition of religion as a set of symbols that functions to formulate a conception of order and existence, deSilva argues that John presents his Apocalypse as "a symbolic religious communication that engages directly in the construction and maintenance of one worldview over against competing worldviews."[17] In this view, John's cosmological language functions to legitimate his own worldview amidst a host of other competing worldviews.

This approach has its merits, especially given its grounding in rhetorical interpretation. Scholars who see John's cosmology function in this way do so because they are seeking to understand John's persuasive purposes. Nevertheless, the symbolic universe solution cannot account for the sense in John's text that he does seem to want to say something true about material reality. His language strains against its limit, but there is a sense in which the cosmic catastrophe on display is more than symbolic, as is the material reality of the new creation. The cosmos John evokes is not solely a construction; it also seems to be a participation in something that is there already. John does expect the world order of Rome to end, not simply as a subjective experience in the minds of his audience, but in a way that those inside and outside his community will experience somehow objectively. Likewise, he does expect himself and his audience to experience the new creation materially. Paul Minear, whose work is difficult to classify within these three categories, argues that John is underappreciated as a "metaphysical theologian."[18] That is, John was attempting to say something genuine about the reality of space and time, not simply one's subjective experience of it.[19]

---

16. Elisabeth Schüssler Fiorenza, *The Book of Revelation: Justice and Judgment*, 2nd ed. (Minneapolis: Fortress Press, 1998), 187. See also David L. Barr, "The Apocalypse as a Symbolic Transformation of the World: A Literary Analysis," *Interpretation* 38 (1984): 3950.

17. David A. deSilva, *Seeing Things John's Way: The Rhetoric of the Book of Revelation* (Louisville: Westminster John Knox, 2009), 96.

18. Paul Minear, "The Cosmology of the Apocalypse," in *Current Issues in New Testament Interpretation: Essays in Honor of Otto A. Piper*, ed. William Klassen and Graydon F. Snyder (New York: Harper, 1962), 33.

19. On the other hand, see Adela Yarbro Collins, basing her analysis on Jungian depth psychology, proposes that cosmic death and destruction may be implied in John's use of the number seven. According to her, the number seven represents an irreducible number and an unsolvable problem (at least in this life and world). She argues this fits well with "the theme of irreconcilable conflict between the kingdom of God and the kingdom of Caesar. The expected persecution cannot be ignored, evaded or overcome in any way except by individual death and cosmic destruction," Adela Yarbro Collins, *Cosmology and*

Indeed, John's cosmological language above all seeks to say something real and meaningful about the world, materially, physically, and symbolically. What is required, it seems, is a conception that can account for both a construction of a symbolic world and a participation in something that is already "out there."[20] When John talks about the destruction of the cosmos he is not talking about some other cosmos besides the one in which the Philadelphians and Laodiceans live. When John presents his vision of the new creation he is not talking about a reality completely severed from the real world of the people of Smyrna and Pergamum. There is both continuity and discontinuity. And yet, his presentation of the world seeks to construct the space in which they live in a certain way in order to move his audience to action. The way he presents his picture of the cosmos is intended to persuade. This requires a conception that allows interpreters to hold these two necessities together.

This, in short, led me to posit and articulate the concept of rhetorical cosmology. By rhetorical cosmology I mean that an individual's or a group's experience of the world is constructed discursively. How one understands the world and how one understands one's function within the world is a matter of discourse. A modern-day example of this idea is how a coal mining company a farming community might view the same mountain in Kentucky. Both groups have a discourse that shapes their understanding. One might argue that this difference in discourse does not alter the world that is under investigation, but it does have real implications, such as how each group conceives of and makes use of natural resources. For one group, resources can be conceived flatly as raw materials that can be extracted for profit; for the other group, the same resources may be understood as an ecology, a watershed, that supports human life and community only as humans interact with it in ways that limit damage and promote the health of the land. The mining company may talk of the land in terms of capital and industrial progress, and the farming community may talk

---

Eschatology in Jewish and Christian Apocalypticism, Supplements to the Journal for the Study of Judaism 50 (Leiden, New York, and Köln: Brill, 1996), 138.

20. Though developed independently, this study has subsequently benefited to a great degree from Walter Brueggemann's discussion of the world of praise in *Israel's Praise: Doxology against Idolatry and Ideology* (Philadelphia: Fortress Press, 1988). While not cited here frequently, readers familiar with that work will see many points of agreement between it and the argument I am presenting here. For example, Brueggemann articulates a need for conceptions that move beyond objectivist and subjectivist modes if our analysis is to successfully understand Israel's praise, 9. He continues later, "It is the act of praise, the corporate, regularized, intentional, verbalized, and enacted act of praise, through which the community of faith creates, orders, shapes, imagines, and patterns the world of God, the world of faith, the world of life, in which we are to act in joy and obedience," 25–26.

of the same land in terms of a heritage and place that can sustain long term local life.[21]

This modern analogy, however, only takes us so far. For the ancient world the relation between discourse and the form and future of the world was even stronger. For the ancients, the way one talked about the world had significance for every facet of life and existence: politics, economy, piety, interpersonal relationships, and so on. More than this, discourse gave shape to the world—it determined center and margin, ruler and dominated, permanent and temporary. Cosmological discourse gave voice to the question of what sustained and shaped the universe. In Asia Minor under Roman rule in the first century, the discourse that sustained and shaped the world was centered around the gods, Caesar, and Imperial Rome. This discourse originated and was maintained by the imperial cult. Cultic ritual, sacrifice, and the related economic exchange were integral for sustaining the order of the cosmos, an order administrated by the gods and Caesar. The relationship between the people and the gods was maintained and nurtured in order to give the cosmos stability and wholeness. The sacrificial and economic system functioned like a social contract: the gods sustained the world and the people sacrificed. The continuity of this arrangement functioned to keep the world in this stable condition. Any disturbance of this balance would introduce a sense of anomie or disorientation. Cosmic disturbances meant that something had gone awry with the arrangement between the people and the gods.[22] This situation would require diagnosis and repair so that the anger of the gods would not continue to burn and cause further damage to the cosmic fabric.

It is here that John's deployment of rhetorical cosmology comes into focus. I argue that John's discourse about the world is not intended to reveal the secret and mysterious inner workings of the cosmos, but rather that John intends to pit his own cosmological discourse in opposition to this cultic discourse concerning the world. John does this to intentionally disrupt the Roman world order and bring it to an end. In portraying the dismantling of the Roman cosmos, John clears the way to bear witness to God's creative work in making "all things new" (21:5). The end of Roman cosmological discourse and the entrance of John's Christological cosmic discourse is intended to bring about repentance—he hopes that the nations will turn from idolatry and the practices

---

21. See Wendell Berry, "Compromise Hell!" in *The Way of Ignorance* (Berkeley: Shoemaker & Hoard, 2005), 23; Wendell Berry, "The Landscaping of Hell: Strip-Mine Morality in East Kentucky," in *The Long-Legged House* (New York: Harcourt, Brace, and World, 1965), 17–36.

22. This is the logic of prodigies in the ancient world, about which much more will be said later in this study, see David E. Aune, *Revelation 6–16*, WBC 52B (Nashville: Thomas Nelson, 1998), 416419.

that sustain wicked Rome, and turn to worship of the true God whose coming reign is conceived of as beneficial and healing for the nations (22:2).

Chapter 1 begins the work of explicating this rhetorical cosmology by investigating how apocalyptic literature and discourse makes meaning. Here I investigate the rhetoric of apocalypse, in conversation with a host of scholars, but with ears particularly attuned to the work of socio-rhetorical interpretation (SRI). SRI provides the tools to discuss the way apocalyptic rhetoric functions to persuade as well as how it participates in, constructs, and talks about the world of space and time. In this chapter, I develop an account of apocalyptic discourse as rhetorical cosmology.

John's ultimate purpose in presenting his apocalypse to his audience is to encourage them to abandon practices that cooperate with and participate in the idolatry of Rome. His rhetorical cosmology is geared to shake them out of the world sustained by false worship and place them in the world of the coming God. The introduction of the entrance of God and, along with God, the new creation brings an end to the Roman cosmic system. John envisions this happening through a series of cosmic catastrophes brought about by divine wrath. God's entrance effects the dismantling of the cosmos as Rome construes it. The breakdown of the world meant that the gods were no longer maintaining good care of the world, and with the failure to maintain the world on the part of the gods, the people were no longer obligated to sacrifice to them. The breakdown of the Roman governed and sustained cosmos means a breakdown of the reign of Rome itself and its hold on the world. John's imagery of the dismantling of the cosmos is intended for exactly this purpose, to warn of God's impending judgment on the world system of Rome and to instill hope for God's new creation. This is the subject of chapter 2 of this study and sets up the exegetical work that follows.

The next four chapters set out to interpret the climactic seventh element of each of the three cycles in the Apocalypse. The cycles depict God's judgment upon the cosmological reality and discourse of Rome and the entrance of the new creation. The climactic seventh element perceives the final end of the Roman cosmic schema and the ultimate arrival of God's new creative work. This vision is rhetorical in that it presents its imagery to call hearers to action—John envisions that his audience can participate in some way in the divine work of unmaking and making new. John's call is for the continuing endurance and witness of the saints, a vocation that he envisions as having two dimensions. First, the saints are called to non-participation and non-cooperation with the idolatry of mainstream culture in Asia Minor. This includes not only non-participation in the various imperial cults devoted to worship of the emperor and other Roman gods, but also self-extraction from the economy which served to buttress the cosmological discourse of the cult. For John, participation in the cult or in the cultic economy was to live in a world system that stood under the judgment of God and the Lamb, because it already had been conquered by the Lamb's crucifixion. If the saints heed John's call to extricate themselves from the cosmological discourse of the cultic economy, they will participate in bringing it to its end by helping introducing a sense of anomie into the culture. The saints' endurance is given to participate in the divine work of dismantling the cosmos, thus breaking the sacrificial contract between the Roman people and their gods, and making repentance possible.

The saints can also participate in God's work of new creation. Just as their non-participation functioned negatively to bring the Roman cosmological reality to an end, so their worship of the one who sits on the throne and the Lamb can participate in ushering in the reign of God. The saints' praise narrates the coming new-creative work of God, offering the positive content in the midst of their endurance-as-negation. Praise is also an act of witness in the Apocalypse because it holds out the possibility of another world, another way of constructing and participating in the cosmic order. This alternative cosmos, held out in the midst of a quickly deteriorating cosmic reality, makes repentance possible. Thus John's rhetorical strategy is to convince his audience to take up, or to continue to take up, this two-fold vocation of non-participation and true worship. I have designated these two concepts as silence and praise for reasons that will become obvious over the course of the work.

The conclusion sets out the results of the work and spells out some of the implications of my argument. I will briefly suggest some ways this understanding of John's Apocalypse can intersect with the concepts of worship and political theology in the book. I will also lay out some future trajectories for putting my conception of rhetorical cosmology into conversation with recent treatments of "apocalyptic" political theology. Though the "parousia" of a full investigation of the political aspect of John's worship must be delayed, the topic remains a secondary interest in this study. It is my conviction that any account of an apocalyptic theological politics must not be content to settle for a reduction to a particular program or platform among a variety of options within the political marketplace. John does not offer his apocalypse as "the best way forward," nor is he interested in pragmatic compromise in order to solve the problems facing the present. Rather, what he is after in his political vision is no less than a redescription of the entire created order. Any account of a politics related to the vision found in the Apocalypse must begin and end with the Christological unmaking and making new of the cosmos. Therefore, this study might be conceived of as an exercise in addressing the political thought of the Apocalypse while, as Flannery O'Connor puts it, "paying attention to the sky." With John as our example we must seek to hold the political and cosmic together in a single vision.

1

"The Apocalyptic Technique": How John's Apocalypse Makes Meaning

> The Lamb that was slain had actually defeated the Beast who seemed omnipotent. Wherever the two creations had met, there the Beast had readily deceived his worshipers by appealing to their reliance on the observable continuities of space and time. But there also the Lamb had revealed to his servants the purpose of God in the present *kairos*, the nearness of the heavenly Jerusalem to the streets of Smyrna, the dawning of the light at the moment of great darkness.
> —Paul Minear, "The Cosmology of the Apocalypse"[1]

My goal in this study is to explore the way John presents his political theology within an overall vision of rhetorical cosmology. How is the political related to the cosmological? Or more specifically, what is the relation between the activity of God and the Lamb to unmake and make new the cosmic order and the activity that John urges upon his audience? The apocalypse of Jesus Christ effects a turbulent regime change not just on the political level, but within the entire created order. Indeed, it will be my argument that a thorough regime change politically cannot but include this cosmological upheaval as well. In light of this it is perhaps surprising, then, that John envisions his own testimony, set forth in his prophetic apocalyptic letter, to contribute in some way to this transition when it is read aloud in the midst of his addressees' gathered worship. My task is to investigate how John envisions this to take place. I will address this question fully in chapters 3 to 6, but here I wish to ask how John's Apocalypse

---

1. Paul Minear, "The Cosmology of the Apocalypse," in *Current Issues in New Testament Interpretation: Essays in Honor of Otto F. Piper*, ed. William Klassen and Graydon F. Snyder (New York: Harper, 1962), 34.

does its work. What I am after is something that we might identify as an "apocalyptic technique," or more specifically, John's apocalyptic technique.[2]

This question brings us into the territory of literary genre and rhetoric. Looking at the genre of apocalypse helps interpreters to know what to look for in a text—both what to anticipate and what might be surprising by its presence or absence. But the genre question, for reasons explicated below, can only take interpreters so far because it remains a conversation on the level of form, identification, and categorization.[3] To understand the power of a text we must understand how form and content are molded in persuasive ways to cause an effect on its audience. Rhetorical inquiry then will help interpreters understand how John's apocalyptic discourse seeks to move its audience and place them within this vision of worship as political and cosmic regime change. Therefore, I first seek to engage the genre conversation before turning to examine John's apocalyptic rhetoric.

THE GENRE DISCUSSION

To speak of genre is to seek to classify for the sake of interpretation.[4] Attention to genre helps to "orient and guide the reader's encounter with the text."[5] Once a reader can identify something familiar about how the text is constructed, she will have a pretty good idea of how to find her way through that text. Genre definition, however, requires more than just listing similar traits among pieces of literature. As David Barr has shown, no comprehensive list can contain all the similarities of a group of texts while at the same time attending to the specificities and peculiarities of particular texts within the group.[6] The upshot of all of this is that genre is a complex phenomenon, but also limited in scope.

---

2. I borrow this terminology, but not necessarily all of its content from John J. Collins, *The Apocalyptic Imagination: An Introduction to Jewish Apocalyptic Literature*, 2nd ed. (Grand Rapids and Livonia: Eerdmans and Dove Booksellers, 1998), 41.

3. This point is made from a different angle by Rowland who argues that there is very little common content to apocalypses, and that genre considerations should be limited to form. See Christopher Rowland, *The Open Heaven: A Study of Apocalyptic in Judaism and Early Christianity* (New York: Crossroad, 1982), 49, 70–71.

4. Gregory L. Linton, "Reading the Apocalypse as Apocalypse: The Limits of Genre," in *The Reality of Apocalypse: Rhetoric and Politics in the Book of Revelation*, ed. David L. Barr, SBL Symposium Series 39 (Atlanta: Society of Biblical Literature, 2006), 9, 12–14.

5. Linton, "Reading the Apocalypse as Apocalypse," 12.

6. David L. Barr, "Beyond Genre: The Expectation of Apocalypse," in *The Reality of Apocalypse*, 75–77.

The best starting point when turning to apocalypse as a genre is the work done by the Society of Biblical Literature Genres Project, led by John Collins.[7] The group's definition is well worn by now and has become the standard for those working with apocalyptic literature. They define "apocalypse" as

> a genre of revelatory literature with a narrative framework in which a revelation is mediated by an otherworldly being to a human recipient, disclosing a transcendent reality which is both temporal, insofar as it envisages eschatological salvation, and spatial insofar as it involves another, supernatural world.[8]

This definition concentrates on form and content and is helpful in a variety of ways, but there are reasons to be critical of it. First, as David Hellholm has articulated, the definition does not address function of the apocalyptic genre. Hellholm argues that it is literature intended to comfort a "group in crisis."[9] Collins himself has taken Hellholm's criticism into account and sees great promise in examining the illocution of apocalyptic literature, while pushing back on the narrowness of Hellholm's proposal.[10] Collins ultimately concludes that apocalypse functions in a broad sense to "shape one's imaginative perception of a situation and so lay the basis for whatever course of action it exhorts."[11] This is perhaps overly broad, but it may be the case that the range of effects that any genre may produce is too large in scope to take into account in one overarching definition.

Second, as David Barr points out, both the genre "apocalypse" and its definition are modern constructs.[12] The definition's function is taxonomic rather than inner-descriptive. Understanding this is not to discount the merit of the definition, but rather simply to draw attention to the fact that it stands

---

7. John J. Collins, ed., *Apocalypse: The Morphology of a Genre*, Semeia 14 (Missoula: Scholars, 1979).

8. Collins, *Apocalypse*, 9.

9. David Hellholm, "The Problem of Apocalyptic: Genre and the Apocalypse of John," in *SBL 1982 Seminar Papers* (Atlanta: Scholar's, 1982), 167. This specification of apocalypse's function is probably too narrow to fit the wide range of intended uses within the literature.

10. Collins, *The Apocalyptic Imagination*, 41. Collins argues that, "the nature of exhortations may vary…the literary function must be seen to be integrally related to form and content in what may be called the 'apocalyptic technique.'"

11. Collins, *The Apocalyptic Imagination*, 42.

12. Barr, "Beyond Genre," 78. See also Linton, "Reading the Apocalypse as Apocalypse," 28: "The term functions as a genre designation for modern readers because the genre apocalypse now exists in critical discourse, but to claim that it served as a genre designation for the original readers is not accurate since this was the first time the word was used to refer to a complete written work."

apart from its subject and evaluates it according to Enlightenment and modern standards. An apocalyptist's definition of apocalypse would look and feel quite different and would attend to matters in another way. Barr argues that ancients would in fact have a category for the apocalyptic phenomenon, but that it would not refer to a category of literature so much as a "claim to a certain kind of experience: they have had an apocalypse/revelation."[13] Likewise, we would hardly expect an ancient near-eastern apocalyptist to characterize the images and events in his or her work as having to do with "supernatural" phenomena.[14]

L. Gregory Bloomquist suggests that new ways of getting at apocalypse may be necessary to understand it more fully: "Further reflection on apocalyptic rhetoric may, then, necessitate an apocalyptic approach itself."[15] This is an important consideration, and will guide the following discussion of the genre and rhetoric of apocalypse.[16] Though modern readers can never claim to be inner-descriptive from our vantage point, we can as interpreters do our very best to take the apocalyptist at his or her word. Interpreters must give their best effort to hear the Apocalypse with John's churches' ears.[17] Approaching apocalypse from an audience perspective may be the best way to go beyond genre as merely a categorical phenomenon and understand it as a text whose constituent parts signal things to hearers.[18] To do this necessitates, at the very

---

13. Barr, "Beyond Genre," 78 n. 21. See also David E. Aune, *The New Testament in its Literary Environment*, Library of Early Christianity (Philadelphia: Westminster, 1987), 226; Elisabeth Schüssler Fiorenza, *The Book of Revelation: Justice and Judgment* (Philadelphia: Fortress Press, 1985), 150: "[I]t is doubtful that the author chose this title ["apocalypse"] to qualify his prophecy as an apocalyptic document."

14. Rather than "supernatural," a term foreign to the ancient world, having its origin in the 15th century, perhaps the word "heavenly" or "other-worldly" would be appropriate. See Malina, *Revelation*, 21; "Supernatural," in *The Oxford English Dictionary*.

15. L. G. Bloomquist, "Methodological Criteria for Apocalyptic Rhetoric: A Suggestion for the Expanded Use of Sociorhetorical Analysis," in *Vision and Persuasion: Rhetorical Dimensions of Apocalyptic Discourse*, ed. Greg Carey and L. Gregory Bloomquist (St. Louis: Chalice, 1999), 181–203, 200.

16. Great strides have been made in the scholarship of the last forty years on the imperial cult, as we will see in the next chapter. The ritual and honor in worship of the emperor and his family and of the imperial regime is no longer considered mere flattery or disposable decorum, but has lately been seen for what it was in that culture: the fabric of social relationality. See Holland Hendrix, "Thessalonicans Honor Romans," Th.D. diss., Harvard University (Cambridge: Harvard, 1894), 327; S. R. F. Price, "Rituals and Power," in *Paul and Empire: Religion and Power in Roman Imperial Society*, ed. Richard A. Horsley (Harrisburg: Trinity Press International, 1997), 71

17. See J. Louis Martyn's attempt to exegete Paul's letter to the Galatians by "hearing with Galatian ears" in *Galatians: A New Translation with Introduction and Commentary*, AB 33A (New Haven & London: Yale University Press, 1997), 40-41.

18. Barr, "Beyond Genre," 77.

least, a suspension of the hermeneutic of suspicion, if not its outright dismissal, and also draws attention to the importance of a text's effective history, that is, how the text has actually affected readers at various times.[19]

Very early in a reading or hearing of the Apocalypse it is evident that the work is a multi-faceted book. Linton refers to it as a hybrid genre, which leads him to question whether the book can be read as an apocalypse at all.[20] John himself calls the work an ἀποκάλυψις (1:1) and a προφητείας (1:3) and it is clear from the epistolary opening that John intends it to be circulated as an open letter to seven (or more) churches (1:4-6).[21] It is therefore appropriate to look at each of these genres in turn, paying special attention to the facets of each that contribute to the way they make meaning and setting each of these next to the specificities of John's Apocalypse in order to examine how John employs them.

APOCALYPSE

Scholars have traditionally differentiated the categories of apocalypse as a genre, apocalyptic eschatology as an ideology, and apocalypticism as a social movement, but it is nearly impossible, and indeed quite counterproductive, to speak of them in isolation.[22] I will proceed by speaking of these phenomena together, with the realization that they are nuanced concepts and that one should not be too optimistic about what can be said regarding the social reality of apocalypticism.[23] First, apocalypses are "revelatory literature…disclosing a transcendent reality." Apocalypses reveal transcendent realities in both temporal and spatial terms. Often scholars propose eschatology as a primary feature of the literary genre.[24] This is true regarding both time and space. Another way of

---

19. See Markus A. Bockmuehl, *Seeing the Word: Refocusing New Testament Studies*, Studies in Theological Interpretation (Grand Rapids: Baker Academic, 2006), 6499; David Armstrong-Reiner, *"You Opened the Book": An Instrumental Understanding of the Patristic Use of the Revelation to John* (Saarbrücken: VDM Verlag Dr. Müller, 2009).

20. Linton, "Reading the Apocalypse as Apocalypse," 18–26. We should not miss the irony here: a genre of literature that receives its title from the one work many consider not to belong fully to the genre!

21. See Richard Bauckham, *The Theology of the Book of Revelation*, New Testament Theology (Cambridge: Cambridge University Press, 1993), 1–17.

22. Klaus Koch, *The Rediscovery of Apocalyptic*, SBT 2/22 (London: SCM, 1972); Paul D. Hanson, "Apocalypses and Apocalypticism: The Genre," in *The Anchor Bible Dictionary*, vol. 1, ed. David Noel Freedman (New York: Doubleday, 1992), 279–282.

23. Paul D. Hanson, "Apocalypses and Apocalypticism: Introductory Overview," in *The Anchor Bible Dictionary*, vol. 1, 281; John J. Collins, "Apocalypse and Apocalypticism: Early Jewish Apocalypticism," in *The Anchor Bible Dictionary*, vol. 1, 284, 287.

stating this is that apocalypses are concerned with limits—the end of history as well as the far reaches of visible and accessible physical reality.[25]

Apocalypses are often, though not exclusively, interested in eschatology and the end of history. This interest in history and its end is specifically oriented toward divine judgment. As apocalyptic literature and thinking began to develop out of the Israelite post-exilic prophetic tradition there began to be a kind of pessimism regarding the direction of history.[26] Whereas the prophetic tradition expressed an optimistic eschatology where the divine plan and direction for the creation would be realized in history through historical forces, apocalyptic eschatology increasingly emphasized that this divine fulfillment would take place outside of the historical realm of politics and human instrumentality.[27] However, this does not necessarily entail a historical dualism. According to Richard Bauckham, neither does this entail an abandonment of the promises of God for creation. Rather, as apocalyptic thought developed within its context in the post-exilic experience of history as under the domination and rule of foreign regimes, the transcendence of history is a refusal to accommodate the prophetic promises for history to Gentile rule. The apocalyptists seemed to be saying that God would indeed accomplish God's promises, but not within the processes and dictates of the current establishment. Bauckham is instructive here:

> [T]he apocalyptists did not begin with a dogma about the nature of history: that God cannot act in the history of this world. They began with an empirical observation of God's relative absence from history *since the fall of Jerusalem*. It did not appear to them that [God] had been active on behalf of [God's] people during this period . . .

---

24. Martin Rist, "Apocalypticism," in *The Interpreter's Dictionary of the Bible*, vol 1, ed. David A. Buttrick (Nashville: Abingdon, 1962), 158.

25. See Bloomquist, "Methodological Criteria for Apocalyptic Rhetoric," 197–198: "[P]resent analysis of the earliest tendencies within discursive cultures of early Christianity [*sic*] literature suggests that there is value in analyzing the social practice and function of early Christians as nomads, that is, a group with *no fixed address* . . . It is in this way that apocalyptic rhetoric appears to share characteristics of the social and cultural location of sophistic, and even cynic, rhetoric, for each of these function within a despotic system but 'at the periphery, where they can decodify existing social and institutional codes, and where they themselves cannot be overcodified by the despotic apparatus.' "

26. See Christopher Rowland, "Apocalypticism," in *The New Interpreter's Dictionary of the Bible*, vol. 1, ed. Katherine Doob Sakenfeld (Nashville: Abingdon, 2006), 191: "In prophetic eschatology the future arises out of the present, whereas in the apocalyptic literature the future is said to break into the present."

27. See Paul D. Hanson, *The Dawn of Apocalyptic* (Philadelphia: Fortress Press, 1975), 11; Richard Bauckham, *The Jewish World Around the New Testament* (Grand Rapids: Baker Academic, 2010), 41.

This was not a retreat from history but precisely an expectation that God would vindicate [God's] people and [God's] justice on the stage of history, though in such a way as to transcend ordinary political possibility.[28]

Bauckham demonstrates that the terminology of two ages did not arise until the late first century CE (see 4 Ezra 7:50), and therefore apocalypticism did not begin with the abstract dualistic philosophy of history, but emerged out of a particular experience of history by a particular social stratum. The result of this is that, in most cases, apocalypticism is not an escapist, disembodied philosophy of history, but rather a grounded, particular, and historical practice of history.[29]

In addition to its concerns with the limits of time, apocalypticism is also an exploration of the limits of physical space. Apocalypses may contain revealed knowledge about "astronomy, or the creation, or celestial worlds, or matters concerning the heavenly Jerusalem."[30] The material world is often regarded as a wonder, working in harmony and obedience with God's purposes.[31] Its steadiness and consistency is set in contradistinction with the rebelliousness and lawlessness of humanity (1 Enoch 5:12, 4-6; 36:4; 72:1). When the cosmos is portrayed as out of joint or standing under divine judgment it is "understood as a part of the punishment of human sin, not as a necessary destruction of a hopelessly corrupted cosmos."[32] In the same way the eschatological apocalypse refuses to concede history to imperfect governance, cosmological apocalypse transcends the physical reach and scope of those in power. Again, this is not in order to escape material reality, but to critique and relativize the power of the foreign empires were exercising over that reality.[33]

---

28. Bauckham, *The Jewish World Around the New Testament*, 58.

29. Bauckham, *The Jewish World Around the New Testament*, 60–61.

30. Larry J. Kreitzer, "Apocalyptic, Apocalypticism," in *Dictionary of the Later New Testament and Its Developments*, ed. Ralph P. Martin and Peter H. Davids (Downers Grove: InterVarsity, 1997), 57. See also Stone, "Lists of Revealed Things."

31. Hanson, "Biblical Apocalypticism: The Theological Dimension," *Horizons in Biblical Theology*, 7.2 (1985), 6–7: "[O]ne finds especially in the apocalyptic writings of the Hellenistic and Roman periods a *search for cosmic harmony* expressed in highly imaginative descriptions of the heavenly bodies, the winds, the topography of heaven and of the far reaches of the earth, coupled with attempts to relate such far ranging data to the institutions and concepts regulating human life like temple sacrifice and the calendar."

32. Donald E. Gowan, "The Fall and Redemption of the Material World in Apocalyptic Literature," *Horizons in Biblical Theology* 7 (1985), 99–100.

33. Apocalypses are often delivered by otherworldly beings such as angels or human seers who have attained a kind of heavenly or special status. This mediator lends the message an air of authority that the

The transcendent in apocalypses is not only a category of content but also form. In addition to speaking about "heavenly" or "other-worldly" phenomena, they also employ expressive language and mytho-poetic imagery designed to articulate "feelings and attitudes rather than [describe] reality in an objective way."[34] The language of apocalypse is intentionally symbolic and evocative and is not intended to be literal, logical, or universal.[35] Adela Yarbro Collins argues that this evocative language is employed in order to persuade the reader to adopt a position on a particular issue. Apocalyptic language is a "call for *commitment* to the actions, attitudes, and feelings uttered . . . It makes no attempt to report events or to describe people in a way that everyone would accept. Rather, it provides a highly selective and perspectival view."[36]

The evocative language serves a second related function. As David Barr has pointed out, following David Aune, an apocalypse uses language in such a way that "the audience does not just learn about the experience of the seerer [sic], they also experience that original revelation as it is 're-presented' and 're-actualized' for them."[37] Apocalypses therefore do not seek to merely convey information, but to make present an experience of revelation for an audience. The message is conveyed through the medium of the revelatory experience. Barr suggests this phenomenon is akin to what happens in the transformative power of religious ritual.[38]

Prophecy

The Apocalypse also bears characteristics of prophetic genre, specifically early Christian prophecy. It is probably best not to hold too distinctly the category of prophecy from that of apocalypse. Apocalyptic thought developed from, among many other streams of influence, post-exilic Israelite prophecy—some of which Hanson refers to as "early apocalyptic" (Isa 24–27; 56–66; Zech 9–14).[39] Nevertheless, there is a gulf between the thought of the biblical prophets of

---

seer might not have on her own. If the message is delivered by a figure outside of the purview of the merely human stratum, an audience will be more willing to listen and accept the message.

34. Collins, *The Apocalyptic Imagination*, 17.

35. Contra Hanson, "Biblical Apocalypticism," 6.

36. Adela Yarbro Collins, *Crisis and Catharsis: The Power of the Apocalypse* (Philadelphia: Westminster, 1984), 144.

37. Barr, "Beyond Genre," 85. See also David E. Aune, "The Apocalypse of John and the Problem of Genre," *Semeia* 36 (1986), 89: An apocalypse functions to "mediate a new actualization of the original revelatory experience."

38. Barr, "Beyond Genre," 86.

39. Hanson, "Apocalypses and Apocalypticism: Introductory Overview," 281. See also J. Collins, "Apocalypses and Apocalypticism: Early Jewish Apocalypticism," 284.

the late fifth century BCE and the apocalyptists of the second century BCE, both chronological and philosophical. In that gap emerges the practice of pseudonymity and historical surveys via prophecy *ex eventu*, as well as highly developed angelologies and cosmologies.[40] Perhaps the biggest distinction between late prophecy and early apocalyptic thought is the transcendence of death in the form of resurrection. As John Collins indicates, late prophecy's eschatology was a vision of old age that included death, but apocalyptic thought proposed that a human can "pass over to the world of the angels or become a companion to the host of heaven."[41] Thus Collins makes the appeal that scholars consider post-exilic prophecy to be "late prophecy" rather than "early apocalyptic."

Bauckham proposes bridging this gap, in part, by considering much apocalyptic thought as interpretation of prophecy. Apocalyptists lived after the end of the prophetic spirit (1 Macc 4:46) and thus took up and developed the prophetic tradition for their own era. In Bauckham's view they viewed their vocation as "inspired interpreters of prophecy."[42] For Bauckham this difference in self-understanding produces a different sense of authority as well, one that does not stand on its own but is derives its authority from that of the prophets.[43] This explains for him the phenomenon of pseudonymity:

> Pseudonymity is therefore a device expressing the apocalyptist's consciousness that the age of prophecy has passed: not in the sense that he fraudulently wishes to pass off his work as belonging to the age of prophecy, but in the sense that he thereby acknowledges his work to be mere interpretation of the revelation given in the prophetic age. Similarly, the *vaticinia ex eventu* are not a fraudulent device to give spurious legitimation to the apocalyptist's work; they are his interpretation of the prophecies of the past, rewritten in the light of their fulfilment in order to show how they have been fulfilled and what still remains to be fulfilled.[44]

Here it is important to advance Collins' suggestion that to relate apocalyptic thought too closely with its prophetic antecedents can lead to making value judgments about the inferiority of apocalypse compared to prophecy.[45]

---

40. Bauckham, *The Jewish World Around the New Testament*, 43–44.
41. Collins, "Apocalypses and Apocalypticism: Early Jewish Apocalypticism," 284.
42. Bauckham, *The Jewish World Around the New Testament*, 53.
43. Bauckham, *The Jewish World Around the New Testament*, 53.
44. Bauckham, *The Jewish World Around the New Testament*, 54–55.

Bauckham makes this interpretive move regarding the derivative authority of apocalyptic, which implies a lack of independent productivity. Notwithstanding this, his point is well taken that apocalyptic often makes present and develops for a new era the late Israelite prophetic imagination.[46]

Christian prophecy stands inside this tradition of interpreting messages from God, especially messages of promises fulfilled or being fulfilled, in light of contemporary events. Christian prophecy interpreted the fulfillment of God's purposes for history and the cosmos in light of the concrete events surrounding the advent, life, death, resurrection, and *parousia* of Jesus of Nazareth.[47] The characteristic setting for Christian prophecy was the worship gathering, where the one who received a revelation by the Spirit would speak by the Spirit (1 Cor. 14:26-33; Hermas, *Mand.* 11:9). These messages were understood as oracles to the church from God or Christ where the prophetic speaker's voice was taken up into the divine speech (Odes Sol. 42:6). Prophecy also took the form of visions that were later reported to the church (Acts 10:9—11:18; 2 Cor. 12:1-4; Hermas, *Vis.* 1–4).

John certainly conceives his own vocation to be in the stream of biblical and Christian prophecy. He calls his work prophecy, intends it to be read aloud in a gathered worship setting (Rev 1:3), and expects it to be received as prophecy (22:18-19). Allusions to the biblical prophets abound in John's vision, and he has picked up many of the major biblical themes, though no direct quotations exist.[48] John is clearly reinterpreting the ancient prophecies and promises for his own context and era in light of the events surrounding the slain Lamb, the Messiah Jesus. His own voice is taken up into the divine speech and intended to present the fulfillment of God's vision and intention for creation. As Bauckham argues, John perceives his own work as "the climax of prophetic revelation, which gathered up the prophetic meaning of the Old Testament scriptures and disclosed the way in which it was being and was to be fulfilled in the last days."[49] This is reflected when John hears that when the seventh angel blows his trumpet, "the mystery of God will be completed, as God proclaimed to God's slaves the prophets" (10:7).

---

45. Collins, *The Apocalyptic Imagination*, 20.

46. Bauckham, *The Jewish World Around the New Testament*, 64: "Their transcendent eschatology, which is apocalyptic's theological centre, is already developed in post-exilic prophecy, and the apocalyptist's role is to intensify it and enable their own generation to live by it."

47. Bauckham, *The Theology of the Book of Revelation*, 5.

48. deSilva, *Seeing Things John's Way*, 158–174.

49. Richard Bauckham, *The Climax of Prophecy: Studies on the Book of Revelation* (London & New York: T & T Clark, 1993), xi. Cf. Bauckham, *The Theology of the Book of Revelation*, 5.

Ultimately for John, prophecy is witness to Jesus in worship. In 19:10 along with the angel's command to worship God, we hear that "the witness to Jesus is the spirit of prophecy." Witness here is the Greek μαρτυρία [*martyria*]. Central to the concept of prophecy in the Apocalypse is "martyring" for Jesus.[50] John's work of prophecy is to bear witness to Jesus in the context of the seven cities in Asia, to indicate the places and times in the lives of the audience where God is active. This work of bearing witness is exactly how John is interpreting and developing the promises from God given to the prophets as he sees them fulfilled and being fulfilled.[51] The testimony of Jesus makes the prophetic promises present in the lives of John's audience. It causes the past to rush into the present even as it draws the promised fulfillment of the future. John's prophetic vision invites his hearers into an eschatological constellation comprised of divine faithfulness and promise in the past, the indeterminate present, and the future of creation made whole.

LETTER

The third genre consideration to take into account is that Revelation presents itself as a letter. This is evident given its epistolary frame (1:4-6; 22:16-21) and the letters to seven churches in Asia Minor at the beginning (1:11; 2-3). At the outset we may ask how important these epistolary features are to the work as a whole? Also, what relation does the epistolary frame have to the rest of the Apocalypse? Answering these questions will go a long way in determining the significance of how the letter features of the Apocalypse contribute to the way the work makes meaning.

One suggestion is that the epistolary features are incidental to the work because of John's absence due to exile on Patmos.[52] This doesn't account for the fact that the letters and hence the overall message are from Christ—who is certainly not exiled on Patmos—and not from John (despite the epistolary introduction being in John's name it is a "revelation of/from Jesus Christ which God gave"). In the text, Christ specifically commands John to write letters to

---

50. "Martyring" is here a more appropriate term than martyrdom. The technical sense of martyrdom did not arise until after the time of the Apocalypse. Also, martyring has a more active sense and captures the activity better than martyrdom which denotes a status.

51. Bauckham argues that John is working with a very particular set of Old Testament texts, *The Climax of Prophecy*, x–xi.

52. Frederick David Mazzaferri, *The Genre of the Book of Revelation from a Source-Critical Perspective*, BZNW 54 (Berlin: de Gruyter, 1989), 231–233. See also Adela Yarbro Collins, "The Early Christian Apocalypses," *Semeia* 14 (1979), 70–71; David E. Aune, *Revelation 1–5*, WBC 52a (Dallas: Word, 1997), lxxxiii; Collins, *The Apocalyptic Imagination*, 270.

seven churches (1:11), and the content of those letters are tied very closely to moments in the visionary section.[53] In addition, there seems to be a very deliberate and purposive aspect of the work as a written and literary entity, an aspect that suggests the writing is meant to do something rather than just serving as something dictated by circumstances of absence.[54] Therefore, it seems safe to say that the letter form is a very integral part of the Apocalypse as a whole and therefore has some bearing on how the Apocalypse functions to make meaning.[55]

Letters in the ancient world were sent to stand in for the sender in the sender's absence.[56] However, the letter was not just an incidental accommodation to an inconvenience in availability. In other words, it is not just what is said in the letter that is important, but the fact that it is said in a letter. J. Louis Martyn has attended to the way that Christian letters function, especially letters with an apocalyptic message.[57] Martyn argues that an investigation of the argument of a letter needs to include the "letter's work."[58] Since the letter is a stand in for presence, it would be expected to do what the one normally present would do. In this case, the letters to the seven churches are addressed from Christ, while the overall letter, which comprises the Apocalypse, is addressed from John. Therefore, the letter would seek to create the same effect or event that would be created when Christ and John are present with the hearing communities. From our discussions of apocalypse and prophecy above, the letter would have its setting in the gathered worship of the seven churches and be expected to reveal and interpret God's activity and intent for the current situation or exigency of the audience. It would be expected to draw the mysteries of heaven into the midst of the congregation, or vice versa. Martyn states that a letter's work is to create an "aural event" when the messenger read the letter aloud.[59] Martyn's point is Pauline in reference, but the

---

53. See for instance how the gifts promised to the one who conquers in the letters are fulfilled in the eschatological new creation.

54. Cf. Bauckham, *The Theology of the Book of Revelation*, 3–5.

55. Bauckham, *The Theology of the Book of Revelation*, 12.

56. See Robert W. Funk, "The Apostolic *Parousia*: Form and Significance," in *Christian History and Interpretation: Studies Presented to John Knox*, ed. W. R. Farmer, *et al.* (Cambridge: Cambridge University Press, 1967), 249–268.

57. J. Louis Martyn, "Events in Galatia: Modified Covenantal Nomism versus God's Invasion of the Cosmos in the Singular Gospel: A Response to J. D. G. Dunn and B. R. Gaventa," in *Pauline Theology*, vol. 1 (Minneapolis: Fortress Press, 1991), 160–179.

58. Martyn, "Events in Galatia," 161.

59. Martyn, "Events in Galatia," 161.

same could be said for the Apocalypse, as John expects and demands the letter to be read aloud (1:3).

We can begin to see this aspect of epistolary work when we examine how it is employed in the Apocalypse. In the letter addressed to Ephesus, Jesus designates himself as the one who "walks around in the midst of the seven golden lampstands" (2:1) which are said to be the seven churches (1:20). Thus, when the letter is read aloud it becomes a reminder and even a making-present of the one who addresses the congregations—the revelation of this Apocalypse is "of Jesus Christ" and the letter presents him as the one who is present.[60] Similarly, all of the letters begin with Christ's words "I know" (οἶδα). This knowledge of the various situations of the church again creates an event where their various strengths and weaknesses, successes and failings, have not gone unnoticed. As they hear the Apocalypse in the midst of whatever they are facing, they can be confident that Christ is neither absent nor ignorant of them.

The letters also anticipate events to occur when the letter is read aloud. John does not intend the letters to simply describe something to be the case, but is expecting something to happen when the lector reads the letter. In the letter to the church in Laodicea Christ says, "Listen! I am standing at the door knocking; if anyone hears my voice and opens the door, I will enter to that one, and feast with that one and that one with me" (3:20). When the messenger reads the letter aloud, the community hears Christ's words of approach, and, as there would usually be a meal during this gathered worship, they are encouraged to consider their common meal the feast that Christ wants to eat with them.[61] This feasting with Christ is meant to point ahead in the text to the marriage feast of the Lamb, thus making the feasting with Christ a proleptic participation in the eschatological feast.[62] This feasting, understood as a participation in the marriage feast, is the event the letter anticipates as the outcome of its reading. In this way and others, the letters make clear at the outset that the Lamb depicted here as the cosmic and supra-historical divine being is present with the seven churches as they hear and perform the letter.

---

60. See David L. Barr, "The Apocalypse of John as Oral Enactment," *Interpretation* 40 (1986), 252.

61. Barr, "The Apocalypse of John as Oral Enactment," 253. See also Stanley P. Saunders, "Between Blessing and Curse: Reading, Hearing, and Performing the Apocalypse in a World of Terror," in *Shaking Heaven and Earth: Essays in Honor of Walter Brueggemann and Charles B. Cousar.* ed. Christine R. Yoder, *et al.* (Louisville: Westminster John Knox, 2005), 143, 145.

62. Eugene Peterson suggests the same method is at work when the open door and throne are mentioned in the letter to Laodicea and then in the next chapter John sees an open door and a throne in heaven, *Reversed Thunder: The Revelation of John and the Praying Imagination* (New York: HarperCollins, 1988), 59.

Finally, the letter contains the exclamation "amen" four times in its opening and closing (1:6, 7; 22:20, 21).[63] "Amen" is a word that calls for participation when read aloud, a word "by which listeners join in an oath, a blessing, a curse, a prayer, or a doxology they have [just] heard and affirm their readiness to bear the consequences of this acknowledgement."[64] By using this word at both the beginning and the end of the letter, John is bringing his hearers into the presence of Jesus and Almighty God and compelling them to understand themselves not as observers of the unfolding apocalyptic drama, but as participants.[65] When the letter's hearers say "amen" along with the reader, they are already implicated. They agree to the way things are said to be in the letter, anticipating and calling forth the coming of Christ portrayed in John's vision.

Apocalyptic Rhetoric as Rhetorolect

While the foregoing discussion of genre is helpful with formal and categorical matters, if one wants to investigate the politics of worship in the Apocalypse—what the text is intended to do and how it works to accomplish it—one must turn to rhetoric. Genre may be able to tell us that apocalypse discloses "a transcendent reality . . . that involves another . . . world" but only rhetoric can show us the dynamic interplay between this world and the next. Only rhetoric can display and enact the power (*dynamis*/dynamite) of the clash of worlds.

Since the groundbreaking work of Elisabeth Schüssler Fiorenza, rhetoric and power have been inextricably linked—therefore rhetoric is political and politics are rhetorical.[66] Rhetorical investigation seeks to identify the kinds of effects produced by discourse and to understand how that discourse produces such effects.[67] A text has power and effects in the world, and a rhetorical interaction with the text is not solely scientific, as if one could unearth the text's

---

63. This is not to mention the numerous occurrences in the visionary section itself.

64. J. Hempel quoted by Martyn, *Galatians*, 92.

65. See Martyn, *Galatians*, 106: "Paul brings the Galatians climactically into God's presence by inviting them to utter the word 'Amen!' It is a signal of his conviction that his own words can and will become the active word of God, because God will be present as the letter is read to the Galatians in their services of worship. One might even say that by using the word 'amen,' Paul intends to rob the Galatians of the lethal luxury of considering themselves observers. With him, they stand in God's presence."

66. See especially, Elisabeth Schüssler Fiorenza, *The Book of Revelation: Justice and Judgment*, 2nd ed. (Minneapolis: Fortress Press, 1998), 205–236.

67. Wilhelm Wuellner, "Hermeneutics and Rhetorics: From 'Truth and Method' to 'Truth and Power'," *Scriptura* S 3 (1989), 35.

one intention. To approach a text rhetorically is to produce new meanings and effects as one interacts with the words and symbols of a text and with one's audience.[68] Rhetorical inquiry thus understands reading as an active production rather than passive reception—it seeks to understand the power and effects of a text even as it participates in some way in its power and effects.[69]

Vernon Robbins' work in developing socio-rhetorical interpretation (SRI) as an interpretive approach to the biblical text is exemplary in this respect. SRI was first introduced to the field of New Testament studies by Vernon K. Robbins in 1984.[70] Robbins describes his work not as a method but as an interpretive analytic that seeks to bring different fields of specialization into contact with one another in order to "create a context for generating new insights, new areas of research and new specialties that lead to an account of first-century Christianity."[71] Ultimately Robbins seeks to be neither exclusionary (which presupposes that what is excluded is inferior), nor inclusionary (which tends to draw different viewpoints into the singular interpreter's horizon), but invitational where strategies drawn into the conversation "will contribute significantly new insights as a result of their particular experiences, identities, and concerns."[72] Robbins intends the work of SRI to function as a kind of "prolegomenon to a constructive [political] theology,"[73] and so works well for our purposes of examining the rhetoric of John's politics of worship.

Prior to and concurrent with Robbins' work, which has developed over the course of more than thirty years, rhetorical criticism of the New Testament

---

68. Schüssler Fiorenza, *The Book of Revelation*, 209.

69. One need not participate affirmatively in a text's power and effects, one can resist or disagree with the argumentative effects of a text, but one is still participating in the scenario that text has set up in advance.

70. Vernon K. Robbins, *Jesus the Teacher: A Socio-Rhetorical Interpretation of Mark* (Philadelphia: Fortress Press, 1984).

71. Vernon K. Robbins, *The Tapestry of Early Christian Discourse: Rhetoric, Society and Ideology* (London & New York: Routledge, 1996), 11–12. The major difference between the two is that a method employs a limited number of reading strategies to arrive at a conclusion that is superior to conclusions that use different analytical strategies. A method employs its strategies to the exclusion of other methods' strategies. An interpretive analytic, in Robbins' usage, applies a multiplicity of strategies in order to solicit additional methods and strategies that may shed light on a text at a point or issue not attended to by one particular method or strategy. Vernon K. Robbins, *The Invention of Christian Discourse*, vol. 1, Rhetoric of Religious Antiquity (Blandford Forum, Dorset: Deo Publishing, 2009), 4–5.

72. Robbins, *The Invention of Christian Discourse* 1, 5.

73. Robbins, *The Tapestry of Early Christian Discourse*, 11. The specific type of "political theology" Robbins pursues is "guided by discourses of emancipatory transformation" which is a narrow focus, but certainly inclines toward a political horizon.

primarily concerned itself with the classical rhetoric of antiquity.[74] Amos Wilder was an important proponent of rhetorical criticism within the field of New Testament studies, and a re-emergence of the importance of rhetorical issues occurred with the work of classicist George Kennedy.[75] These classical rhetorical approaches include "a concern for the social nature of reality, the interrelationship between language and human actions, and how language attempts to create effects on an audience."[76] Robbins, inspired by Wilhelm Wuellner's approach to rhetorics[77] and by proponents of the "new rhetoric,"[78] introduced into this approach a host of literary and social-scientific interests and insights, which produced his quest to discover and analyze various textures within a text.[79]

Perhaps Robbins' most important contribution to the field of SRI came in his magnum opus *The Invention of Christian Discourse*.[80] In that work, he appreciatively criticized the practitioners of classical rhetorical criticism for assuming the wrong underlying situations of New Testament argumentation. Classical rhetoric understands the basic social reality of persons as based in the Graeco-Roman urban environment.[81] In this context the three most important social locations are the law court, the political assembly, and the civil ceremony, which underlie the rhetorical practices of judicial (or forensic), deliberative (or symbouletic), and epideictic (or demonstrative) rhetorics, respectively.[82] However, Christian rhetoric does not assume these same underlying social situations for its argumentation. Rather, as Robbins argues,

> These conventional social institutions in cities throughout the Roman empire regularly created problems, suffering, conflicts,

---

74. For a concise and helpful introduction to the development of SRI, see David B. Gowler, "Socio-Rhetorical Interpretation: Textures of a Text and its Reception," *JSNT* 33.2 (2010), 192–195.

75. George A. Kennedy, *New Testament Interpretation through Rhetorical Criticism* (Chapel Hill: University of North Carolina Press, 1984).

76. Gowler, "Socio-Rhetorical Interpretation," 194.

77. Wuellner, "Hermeneutics and Rhetorics."

78. Chaïm Perelman and Lucie Olbrechts-Tyteca, *The New Rhetoric: A Treatise on Argumentation* (Notre Dame: Notre Dame University Press, 1969).

79. Robbins, *The Tapestry of Early Christian Discourse*.

80. Robbins, *The Invention of Christian Discourse* 1. This multi-volume work is still in the process of being published.

81. Robbins, *The Invention of Christian Discourse* 1, 2.

82. Robbins, *The Invention of Christian Discourse* 1, 2. See also George A. Kennedy, *Classical Rhetoric and its Christian and Secular Tradition from Ancient to Modern Times*, 2nd ed. (Chapel Hill & London: The University of North Carolina Press, 1999), 86–87.

persecution, imprisonment, and even death for early Christians. To counter these institutions, early Christians developed argumentation that used picturing based on social interaction related to households, political kingdoms, imperial armies, imperial households, temples, and individual bodies of people. This picturing of multiple social situations created Christian rhetorical discourse in the form of wisdom, prophetic, apocalyptic, precreation, priestly, and miracle argumentation during the first century CE.[83]

Thus to base an understanding of Christian argumentation on the social situations of classical rhetoric is to misunderstand the basis and direction of a particular discourse. First century Christians found it necessary to "invent" their own discourse because they could not make the traditional forms of discourse work for them. Again, Robbins' point is salient:

> A major reason early Christians created distinctive rhetorolects was that they could not depend on civil courtrooms, political assemblies, and ceremonies to "hear their cases" equitably, exhort the people to make decisions that would protect environments in which they could live safely and happily, and celebrate values that would affirm, nurture, and inspire people to think and act in ways that would build positive relationships and actions in the contexts in which they lived. All too often, the civil locations of courtroom, political assembly, and civil ceremony brought punishment, defeat, and celebration of values that threatened rather than nurtured their lives and their households. In this context, early Christians created discourses that "thought beyond and outside" the local contexts of the courtroom, political assembly, and civil ceremony to the location of the inhabited world in God's cosmos.[84]

Robbins contends that early Christians developed new modes of discourse from familiar aspects of their world in order to carve out an argumentative niche from which to communicate with each other in various ways. These new modes of discourse he calls "rhetorolects," a portmanteau of rhetoric and

---

83. Robbins, *The Invention of Christian Discourse* 1, 3.

84. Robbins, *The Invention of Christian Discourse* 1, 15. Robbins points to Martyn's observation of the epistolary rhetoric of Galatians: "The oral communication for which the letter is a substitute would have been an argumentative sermon preached in the context of worship—and thus in the acknowledged presence of God—not a speech by a rhetorician in a courtroom," Martyn, *Galatians*, 21.

dialect.[85] A rhetorolect is "a form of language variety or discourse identifiable on the basis of a distinctive configuration of themes, topics, reasonings, and argumentations."[86] The rhetorolect is the basic unit through which one may analyze any number of argumentative devices and strategies used in a communicative discourse. Robbins alternatively refers to rhetorolects as "belief systems" or "forms of life."[87] This study will investigate apocalyptic rhetorolect as John employs it in the book of Revelation.

Rhetorolects are invented not by creating argumentations out of thin air, but rather by working with familiar themes and final topics (*topoi*), recontextualizing and reconfiguring them.[88] *Topoi* are not simply common ideas or themes within a discourse, but are the bases or gathering points where various kinds of argumentation happen.[89] The early Christians took up, rearranged, and recontextualized these familiar topics and focal points so that they could communicate with each other in ways congruent to their convictions and confession.[90] Robbins refers to the mixing of familiar *topoi* with new settings and contexts as "conceptual blending," borrowing an insight from the cognitive sciences.[91] In apocalyptic rhetorolect, the entire cosmos is blended with the familiar *topoi* relating to a vast territory under the rule of an emperor.

These *topoi* are of two kinds, what Robbins calls the "pictorial descriptive" and "the enthymematic argumentative."[92] Robbins term for rational enthymematic argumentation is rhetology. Rhetology concerns rational argumentation, and looks to the way an author builds a case by reasoning with an audience. Inquiry into how an author reasons about God is called theology, or how she deals with Christ is called Christology, and so forth. Most rhetorical criticism tends to be done by attending to logical reasoning and enthymemes rather than pictorial or imagistic reasoning. This state of affairs has changed with the increasing employment of SRI. Now more than ever, image, or what Robbins calls the visual texture of a text, has been taken to be an integral part of argumentation.[93] In order to attend to pictorial and

85. Robbins, *The Invention of Christian Discourse* 1, 7.
86. Robbins, *The Invention of Christian Discourse* 1, 7.
87. Robbins, *The Invention of Christian Discourse* 1, xxvii.
88. Robbins, *The Invention of Christian Discourse* 1, 83. See Robbins' discussion of intertexture in *The Tapestry of Early Christian Discourse*, 96–143.
89. Robbins, *The Invention of Christian Discourse* 1, 83.
90. See Robert G. Hall, "Arguing Like an Apocalypse: Galatians and an Ancient *Topos* Outside the Greco-Roman Rhetorical Tradition," *NTS* 42 (1996): 434–453.
91. Robbins, *The Invention of Christian Discourse* 1, 8.
92. Robbins, *The Invention of Christian Discourse* 1, 85.

graphic argumentation, interpreters must work with rhetography. Rhetography refers to the "the graphic images people create in their minds as a result of the visual texture of a text."[94] These images call to mind certain constellations of significance that are catalyst for persuading the audience to be for or against certain attitudes or actions.[95] These argumentative images are often as important as logical reasoning in a rhetorolect. It is clear, therefore, that rhetography must work together with rhetology.[96] Rhetography investigates visual argumentation that creates images in people's minds and evokes familiar contexts that provide a platform on which argumentation can take place.[97]

Once interpreters begin to pay attention to rhetography, many elements of a text not traditionally considered argumentative emerge as crucial for how a text persuades an audience. Rhetography opens the door to considering the rhetorical force of things like space, the body, and orality. SRI finds insights from the field of critical spatiality to be particularly illuminating on the conceptions and practices of space in a text. Argumentation has to do with ideas as situated in specific places, like the household, city, synagogue, temple, kingdom, or empire. Understanding materialized within "lived experiences" people had in particular spaces in the first century Mediterranean world.[98] Critical spatiality holds that all facets of spatial understanding are "human constructs that are socially contested."[99] Berquist argues that the work of Henri Lefebvre is the foundational and most important work in critical spatiality because it explores the idea that constructions of space are creations of political practice and social system, and how certain dominant ideologies of space work to conceal their constructedness.[100]

---

93. Robbins, *The Invention of Christian Discourse* 1, 86–87. See also Edith M. Humphrey, "In Search of a Voice: Rhetoric through Sight and Sound in Revelation 11:15—12:17," in *Vision and Persuasion*, 141–160; deSilva, *Seeing Things John's Way*, 193–228.

94. Vernon K. Robbins, "Rhetography: A New Way of Seeing the Familiar Text," in *Words Well Spoken: George Kennedy's Rhetoric of the New Testament*, Ed. C. Clifton Black & Duane F. Watson (Waco: Baylor University Press, 2008), 81.

95. Robbins, *The Invention of Christian Discourse* 1, 17.

96. Robbins, *The Invention of Christian Discourse* 1, 17.

97. Robbins, "Rhetography," 81.

98. Robbins, *The Invention of Christian Discourse* 1, 88–90.

99. Jon L. Berquist, "Critical Spatiality and the Construction of the Ancient World," in *'Imagining' Biblical Worlds: Studies in Spatial, Social, and Historical Constructs in Honor of James W. Flanagan*, ed. David M. Gunn and Paula M. McNutt, JSOTSup 359 (London: Sheffield Academic, 2002), 15.

100. Berquist, "Critical Spatiality," 19. This aspect of the spatial ideology will be an important facet of our examination of Roman imperial cult rhetoric.

Because space is constructed, this means it is not a static category, but inherently social, conceived as a practice rather than bare representation.[101] Space is always "according to" some person or persons, it always appears attached to one or more identities, as Berquist argues, "any talk of space is talk of meaning—the meaning that interpreters attach to space."[102] This means that at any given time there could be two or more competing co-existing spatialities.[103] This insight is important in approaching the Apocalypse, because John, as I will argue in chapter 2 and following, sets to work to convince his audience to take up a different ritual practice of space which exists simultaneous to the ritual spatiality practiced by the Roman imperial cult.

Fractal space is another important notion brought to the front by critical spatiality. Fractal geometry does not deal in merely straight lines or curves, but rather with complex curves that repeat at varying intervals, angles, and scales.[104] Berquist provides a vivid example of how fractal spatial thinking works:

> [Consider] how one measures a coastline. One can draw a straight line from one point of coast to another (perhaps from one state border to the next) and measure the straight line. Such a measurement greatly underestimates the distance that it takes to drive along a coastal road with its many curves. A still longer path would be that of the beach walker, and if it is a rocky coast with many rocks, one has to decide whether to step over the rock or to trace its contours. For humans, we can step over the rocks, but smaller creatures, such as ants, must circumnavigate the rock, thus taking a longer path to traverse the "same" distance. That decision replicates itself with every grain of sand. The sand appears small on one scale, but if one wants a finer measurement, then the difference between the sand particle's diameter and circumference becomes highly significant . . . There is not a homogeneity within space.[105]

This point should not be dismissed as splitting hairs. This indeed can illuminate how John conceives the work of the church as she moves through space that is dominated by Caesar and his propagandizing imperial cult. Indeed, fractal space may be the best way to understand the logic of a statement uttered in the

---

101. Berquist, "Critical Spatiality," 20, 25–26.
102. Berquist, "Critical Spatiality," 22.
103. Berquist, "Critical Spatiality," 24.
104. Berquist, "Critical Spatiality," 16.
105. Berquist, "Critical Spatiality," 16.

midst of the dramatic tension of the Apocalypse: "The kingdom of the world has become the kingdom of our Lord and of our Lord's Messiah" (11:15). The apocalyptic rhetorolect that John employs may be saying something quite like "there's more than a few ways to navigate the same cosmos."[106] Even while John's churches exist in the empire, they navigate the cosmos differently than most of the empire's subjects.

Spatial concerns are not limited to geographical matters, but include "micro-spaces" such as the body.[107] The body may be conceived spatially too, because "the body is a site with positions, situation and orientations; activities are written upon the body, for the body is a surface that is virtually cartographic; and the practices of the body are performances that map bodily concerns into social spheres."[108] This focus on bodies in critical spatiality has inspired increased attention to bodies within rhetorical discourse. Just as the printed word and historical referents worked together to make arguments, so do people's bodies contribute to meaning making as they create sounds with their mouths, make utterances, and move their bodies through space and time to communicate.[109] Robbins argues that early Christians lived in a rhetorical rather than oral culture, because they knew writings existed and referred to them, even if they couldn't always read them.[110] The audience of the Apocalypse certainly understood that the words they heard had the efficacy of blessing when read aloud from a scroll (1:3). This means that argumentative image and word (both rhetography and rhetology) come alive in a setting of the oral/aural exchange—the text does its

---

106. Another way to understand this phenomenon is to say that space is narratival. This means for this study an approach different from many historical-critical studies that would seek to understand in any mention of space and place the historical reference in space and time. The approach of this study is much closer to the vision of narrative that Hans W. Frei builds in his *The Eclipse of Biblical Narrative: A Study in Eighteenth and Nineteenth Century Hermeneutics* (New Haven & London: Yale University Press, 1974). Space in the narrative of the Apocalypse is not meant to conform or refer to anything distinct from itself, rather the interpreter is meant to conform her interpretation to the spatial world of the text, 130, 307, 318.

107. Berquist, "Critical Spatiality," 28. Berquist distinguishes between large-sized spaces (empire, kingdom, world), medium-sized spaces (city, synagogue, household), and small-sized spaces (body), Jon L. Berquist, "Theories of Space and Construction of the Ancient World," AAR/SBL Constructs of Social and Cultural Worlds of Antiquity Group, November 20, 1999: http://cwru.edu/affil/GAIR/papers/99papers/jberquist.html.

108. Berquist, "Critical Spatiality," 28. Berquist continues: "Just as it is hardly possible to imagine a social practice that does not take place in space, one cannot conceive of social activities that take place without bodies."

109. Robbins, *The Invention of Christian Discourse* 1, 9.

110. Robbins, *The Invention of Christian Discourse* 1, 10–11.

work not as text alone, but as text in the presence of gathered bodies, as a text working on bodies.

This point has led some scholars to begin to search texts for their oral and aural significance. Bernard Brandon Scott and Margaret E. Dean have set out to make a comprehensive "sound map" of the Sermon on the Mount in Matthew.[111] In their view, the reading aloud of a text in the presence of an audience creates its own public and conceptual space for reception. This space is created through sound, and therefore, sound organizes and structures a reading of a text in addition to conceptual and textual clues.[112] This aspect of performed texts is a significant factor in understanding how John's Apocalypse functions. Repetition of soundalike words and phrases, as well as words that convey auditory phenomena, are an important part of the text's work.[113] One cogent example is the contrast between the woe (οὐαί) and the hallelujah (ἀλληλουϊά) that would be heard as Revelation 18 would be read aloud in Greek.

Thus far, I have described SRI and its approach to rhetorical criticism through exploring rhetorolects. I will now turn to the task of constructing an account of apocalyptic discourse as rhetorolect. Throughout I will be indebted to insights from SRI, but my main purpose will be to argue that apocalyptic discourse in John's vision is supremely interested in cosmology. Thus, an account of worship and the political in John must be determined on a cosmic scale. This will pave the way for discussing the contest between John's cosmic political vision and what he perceives to be the major threat to his communities: the encroachment of Rome's cosmic political vision.

Apocalyptic Discourse in John's Apocalypse

Apocalyptic discourse employs and configures apocalyptic *topoi* in a variety of ways to achieve a range of persuasive purposes.[114] As a rhetorolect, or form of life, apocalyptic discourse maps the audience and their local situation onto a cosmic canvas where God is perceived as a heavenly emperor who (often through angelic beings, holy persons, and other representatives) unmakes all evil in the cosmos and creates an environment where God's holiness flourishes and fills all.[115] Apocalyptic discourse is "an 'all-consuming' mode of writing

---

111. Bernard Brandon Scott and Margaret E. Dean, "A Sound Map of the Sermon on the Mount," in *Treasures Old and New: Recent Contributions to Matthean Studies*, ed. David R. Bauer and Mark Alan Powell, SBL Symposium Series 1 (Atlanta: Scholars, 1996): 311–378.

112. Scott and Dean, "A Sound Map of the Sermon on the Mount," 314.

113. See Robbins, *The Invention of Christian Discourse* 1, 11.

114. Carey, "Introduction," 10.

115. Robbins, *The Invention of Christian Discourse* 1, 336.

and conceptualization . . . a 'totalistic' way of viewing all the actions of God in every time and space in the universe."[116] In the apocalyptic mindset, evil is the result of a resistance to divine rule and order, and a transgressing of divinely instituted boundaries throughout the cosmos. Evil is, therefore, not a problem strewn randomly through God's cosmos, but exists as an alternative order, corrupting the goodness of God's entire creation.[117] Evil is not merely a historico-political problem, but a cosmic one, the rectification of which lies outside the boundaries of mundane causality and instrumentalities.[118]

Apocalyptic is thus concerned with cosmology—the space and time of the created order—in a particular way.[119] The apocalyptist's cosmos is a world order in flux and in dispute. Her cosmic vision is simultaneously that of two edges butting up against one another (the known and unknown, the "worldly"[120] and the heavenly) and of two stases co-inhering—the way things really stand within the way things appear to stand.[121] The Apocalyptic word is spoken at the edge of the known (that which is opposed to God) in order to make known what is unknown or mysterious (the holy character and activity of God).[122] This word testifies to the event of the unknown encroaching on, unmaking, and remaking the known. Amos Wilder characterizes all true apocalyptic as conveying a sense of "anomie" or loss of structure that calls everything into question for an audience.[123] The language appropriate to the revealed vision can

---

116. Robbins, *The Invention of Christian Discourse* 1, 333.

117. Robbins, *The Invention of Christian Discourse* 1, 329.

118. Robbins, *The Invention of Christian Discourse* 1, 329–330.

119. I regret that at publication time I had not been able to engage in a deep way with the groundbreaking study of Sean Michael Ryan, *Hearing at the Boundaries of Vision: Education Informing Cosmology in Revelation 9*, Library of New Testament Studies 448 (London: T & T Clark, 2012). I do look forward to exploring how his work in hypothetical audience reception and cosmology can inform, interact, and improve my work.

120. "World" should be understood here in the broadly Johannine theological sense of an order oriented against the divine reign and rule rather than in a geological or sociological sense.

121. On this nuanced sense of duality see N. T. Wright, *The New Testament and the People of God*, Christian Origins and the Question of God, vol. 1 (Minneapolis: Fortress Press, 1992), 297–299. See also Jacques Ellul, *Apocalypse: The Book of Revelation* (New York: Seabury, 1977), 24: Revelation "seeks to disclose the 'mysterious riches' of the present, the hidden dimension of this world in which he finds himself . . . a more profound, more essential reality than that which we see immediately, and this reality can be comprehended only starting form a consideration of the end time."

122. Amos N. Wilder, "The Rhetoric of Ancient and Modern Apocalyptic," *Interpretation* 25.4 (1971), 445.

123. Wilder, "The Rhetoric of Ancient and Modern Apocalyptic," 440. See N. T. Wright's discussion of the similarity between this phenomenon and our metaphor of something being "earth shattering," *The New Testament and the People of God*, 282–283.

no longer rely on familiar assumptions or categories, but must express a reality based on portent and symbol, its language functioning as "non-language" and its rhetoric working by "enormity or paradox."[124]

The word witnesses in such a way to the event, exists so closely within its situation of rupture and indeterminacy, that it becomes itself a partaker in the event, not just an observer and indicator of it. It, in some way, becomes the voice of the event itself.[125] The enunciation of this word makes the apocalyptic event present among its hearers, and the time and space of the event becomes the time and space of the audience.[126] The language of apocalypse is not so much referential and representational as it is participatory and poetic. That is, it does not so much indicate an event or set of events as it makes those things present.

The space of the audience is reconfigured by the apocalyptic performance. It is important to understand at the outset that the "rupture" and "reconfiguration" of the audience's sense of spatiality is not dualistic. It does not imagine a contest between God and the created order. The apocalyptic stance toward the created order is not as negative as some popular construals would have it. What is more often the case is that the cosmic space shares the curse on account of the fall of humanity, rather than falling under the curse itself.[127] In 1 Enoch 2–5 humanity is utterly corrupted but the cosmic bodies continue to function as they were intended.[128] Later, 1 Enoch 6–9 details how the giant offspring of fallen angels and human women commit "sin" by consuming all the crops that could be grown, and then turning to eat birds, wild beasts, reptiles, fish, and people. Finally the earth brings "an accusation against the oppressors" (1 Enoch 7:6).[129] The book of Jubilees portrays the cosmos in a divinely ordered state. Despite this fact, three types of sin affect the natural world: the fall, ongoing human sin, and the sins of angels.[130] Prior to the fall, animals and humans shared a common language, but after the fall animals lost

---

124. Wilder, "The Rhetoric of Ancient and Modern Apocalyptic," 444.

125. Wilder, "The Rhetoric of Ancient and Modern Apocalyptic," 445.

126. See Michael Leff, "Rhetorical Timing in Lincoln's House Divided Speech": "Time as experienced in the text becomes the vehicle for transforming time as experienced in the world to which the text refers." Quoted in Stephen D. O'Leary, *Arguing the Apocalypse: A Theory of Millennial Rhetoric* (New York: Oxford University Press, 1994), 13.

127. See Gowan, "The Fall and Redemption of the Material World in Apocalyptic Literature," 99–101.

128. See Harry Alan Hahne, *The Corruption and Redemption of Creation: Nature in Romans 8.19-22 and Jewish Apocalyptic Literature*, Library of New Testament Studies 336 (London and New York: T & T Clark, 2006), 38–39.

129. James H. Charlesworth tr., *OTP* 1: 16; cf. Hahne, *The Corruption and Redemption of Creation*, 41.

130. Hahne, *The Corruption and Redemption of Creation*, 69–70.

the ability to speak (Jubilees 3:28). In the last days, a flood of rampant evil (as opposed to the Enochian/Noachic flood) will cause the deterioration of creation (compare with Lev. 18:26-28; Num. 35:33-34), but a return to the law will aid in effecting its restoration (Jubilees 28:16-31).[131] In 2 Baruch, the Seer is told to proclaim judgment upon the gentiles for using creation in unrighteous ways (2 Baruch 13:11-12). There are additional examples that make it clear that the evidence is far from unanimous about duality and the destruction of the cosmos in Apocalyptic thought. It is fair to say that the spatial rupture of apocalyptic is not necessarily dualistic and doesn't necessarily mean the catastrophic end of the material world.[132]

John shares this general understanding when he refers to judgment coming not upon the earth itself but upon its "inhabitants" τῶν κατοικούντων (Rev. 6:10) and "destroyers" τοὺς διαφθείροντας (11:18). Thus the problem with space is not so much its corruption *in se*, rather cosmic space is corrupted and compromised because of what has been done to it, because of the reign to which it has been subjected. Therefore, the climactic spatial rupture comes not in chapter 21 where the new heavens and new earth are created, but rather in the announcement that "the reign of the world has become the reign of our Lord and our Lord's Messiah" (11:15). Or rather, the announcement of regime change is the meaning of the passing of the old and arrival of the new. Indeed, the cosmos, while not necessarily tame in John's vision, seems to ultimately be

---

131. See Hahne, *The Corruption and Redemption of Creation*, 71–72, and especially 75, where the world inherited by the righteous is not a completely other creation, but the renewed cosmos.

132. This is not to ignore the fine work by Edward Adams on the subject of the dissolution of the cosmos in *The Stars Will Fall from Heaven*. Adams demonstrates that the dissolution of the cosmos was a widely shared belief across the Greco-Roman world, and that this view found its way into parts of the New Testament. At the same time Edwards argues that this dissolution does not necessarily mean annihilation of the material world and a consequent dualism between material reality and non-material reality, or the present world and the world to come. Often conflagration or dissolution led to rebirth and a new beginning. This second part of Adams argument is less convincing than the first, at least in the case of the Apocalypse. John's eschatological vision is less indebted to Stoicism than, say, Paul's or the author of 2 Peter. Indeed, though the sky vanishes and the mountains are removed from their place "ἐκ τῶν τόπων" (Rev. 6:14), and though heaven and earth flee before the presence of the coming God and "no place" is found for them "τόπος οὐχ" (20:11), there does seem to remain a sense of location to this "no place." Where else do the rulers and powerful hide than in caves and among the rocks of the mountains (6:15)? And are we to believe that the ones facing judgment are suspended in the void (20:12-13)? It must be, instead, that the dissolution of the cosmos is rhetorically and politically constructed. Indeed, this is my argument in this study, especially in chapters 3 to 6. This is not to make it a less real or material phenomenon—the real world of the hearers and indeed all the inhabitants of the earth is drastically altered and affected, but the space of God's action remains the whole time "the all" (4:11; 21:5).

at the beck and call of God for the purpose of judgment (12:6, 14-16). It is not the cosmos as such that stands under judgment, but the cosmos as governed by unrighteous rulers that stands in need of reformation.

The cosmos, rather than being the object of destruction, is often conceived as the stage of the dramatic acts of God. It might be more appropriate to say that the cosmos is envisioned as the site rather than the object of deconstruction. All space in apocalyptic discourse therefore becomes the theater of God's judging, redeeming, transforming, and sanctifying activity. Discourse about the cosmic activity of God functions "as an 'all consuming' mode of writing and conceptualization . . . [creating] a 'totalistic' way of viewing all the actions of God in every time and space in the universe."[133] All space is conceptualized and configured from within the narrative in a visual-aural manner. In vortex-like fashion, the performative reading makes all the space in the cosmos present to the audience and orders it around the center of the universe, the throne of Almighty God and the slain Lamb.

The spaces that comprise John's spatial configuration are Patmos, the seven cities, earth[134], heaven, under the earth, the wilderness, Mount Zion, Babylon, the Sea, and the New Jerusalem.[135] There are also middle spaces that serve as the site of traversals across boundaries. These middle spaces in the Apocalypse are midheaven (μεσουράνημα; 8:13; 14:6, 8-9; 19:17) and the clouds (νεφέλη; 1:7; 10:1; 11:12; 14:14-16)).[136] It may even be possible to also talk about unclassifiable spaces which exist beyond the bounds of observable and livable space such as the lake of fire (20:10, 15), and "no place" (τόπος οὐχ) which is heaven and earth as they stand before the presence of the judging God (20:11). This schema shows that the narrative thrust of the Apocalypse construes space as theological; it exists to reveal Christ as God's active presence in the cosmos.[137] This argumentative strategy functions spatially similar to the way the periodization of history does temporally, relating the space of the audience to the divinely ordered spatial whole.

---

133. Robbins, *The Invention of Christian Discourse* 1, 333.

134. There are many spaces that together comprise earth, such as mountains, kingdoms, etc.

135. See Steven J. Friesen, *Imperial Cults and the Apocalypse of John: Reading Revelation in the Ruins* (Oxford: Oxford University Press, 2001), 157–161: heaven, earth, underworld, with the wilderness and the lake of fire as unclassifiable spaces; Michael Gilbertson, *God and History in the Book of Revelation: New Testament Studies in Dialogue with Pannenberg and Moltmann*, Society for New Testament Studies Monograph Series 124 (Cambridge: Cambridge University Press, 2003), 82: heaven, earth, region under the earth, and sea.

136. Gilbertson, *God and History in the Book of Revelation*, 83 n. 6.

137. See Gilbertson, *God and History in the Book of Revelation*, 85, 96.

The pronouncement of the Apocalypse in the midst of the gathered church effects John's reconfiguration of space. This begins with the micro-space of the body. The performative announcement of the apocalypse is "a rhetorical ritual that recreates all regions of time and space in the body and in the world on the basis on their relation to the sacred or the profane."[138] When the ritual is completed the body has been acted upon, and the body as a micro-space has been transformed by divine activity and pronouncement, judgment, and salvation.[139] The ears and eyes of the audience have beheld various sounds and sights of the imagination (for example, Rev. 10:1-11), they have been placed and positioned in various spaces in heaven and earth (7:9; 14:1-4; 21:1-22:5), and their bodies have been ritually marked as belonging to God (7:3).

The church gathers bodily in the setting of the household to hear the apocalyptic word uttered. The household is not configured like the civic space of a temple where sacrifices to the gods, along with prayers for protection and preservation of the current spatial order, would be offered. The household is not the cosmos in miniature like many temples,[140] and thus the performative apocalyptic utterance makes "strange requests" of the space given to John.[141] And yet the word transforms the household space, making it the site of the heavenly throne room, the battleground where the beast makes war on the Lamb and his followers, and the location of the descent of the new Jerusalem.[142]

After the household, the next space reconfigured is that of the city. Robbins notes how the earth-material[143] tradition of apocalyptic discourse is particularly interested in the urban environment. It demonstrates

> [A] focus on "urban" worlds which rulers use as bases for local power and far-reaching destruction of others, and where people accumulate wealth in a manner that causes large numbers of people to live in poverty and starvation. The "answer" from the heavens is the creation of an "alternative city" with everlasting protection, eternal

---

138. Vernon K. Robbins, "Rhetorical Ritual: Apocalyptic Discourse in Mark 13," in *Vision and Persuasion*, 97.

139. Robbins, "Rhetorical Ritual," 97; Robbins, *The Invention of Christian Discourse* 1, 345.

140. Friesen, *Imperial Cults and the Apocalypse of John*, 130.

141. Friesen, *Imperial Cults and the Apocalypse of John*, 179.

142. See Peterson, *Reversed Thunder*, 63: "The throne, the sea, and the altar are the glorious originals of the pulpit, font, and table in the house churches where St. John's congregations gathered week by week in their Lord's Day worship."

143. See Robbins' discussion of the two traditions of apocalyptic discourse: "earth-material" and "angel-spirit," Robbins, *The Invention of Christian Discourse* 1, 406–478.

health and food, and wealth characterized by "refined" and "precious" earth materials which are pure and holy.[144]

The spatial arrangement of the unjust urban environment bends and wraps around its architectural contours—statues and monuments "warp space to create the effects of a city."[145] The Roman imperial cult cosmology positions all space around Rome as permanent and non-contingent center.[146] John's apocalyptic re-construal of space undoes this, calling into question the spatial certainties of imperial center and satellite cities with the descent of the heavenly city as the final signifier of the victory of a slain Lamb.[147] The space in John's vision is thus a space rendered unfamiliar and slightly askew: "walls with gates that are never closed, day without night, land without sea, habitation without temples, splendor without poverty, kings who offer their glory to the Creator, and nations that walk in the light of God's glory."[148]

Ultimately, apocalyptic discourse conceives the world as dependent upon the judgments of God. The spatial reality of the cosmos may be mysterious or hidden from the audience's understanding unless made open and clear. The revealed word makes sense of the space of the audience and indeed creates its own space for its own hearing.[149] The public space created by the reading of

---

144. Robbins, *The Invention of Christian Discourse* 1, 331.

145. Berquist, "Critical Spatiality," 25–26

146. See the discussion of Phlegon's *Book of Marvels* as a literary example of grounding imperial Rome as center of the world with the monstrous frontier at the margins, Christopher A. Frilingos, *Spectacles of Empire: Monsters, Martyrs, and the Book of Revelation*, Divinations (Philadelphia: University of Pennsylvania Press, 2004), 43–46.

147. Frilingos, discussing the way John makes Rome into the monstrous spectacle it usually associated with the outskirts of empire, writes, "Phlegon locates the display of the hippocentaur in Rome, but Revelation makes Rome into a display. The careful presentation of the Roman Empire, layered with exotic and monstrous details, is only part of John's labors. To make this depiction of Rome into 'fact,' to turn Rome into Babylon, it must also be made into an exhibition." Frilingos, *Spectacles of Empire*, 61.

148. Friesen, *Imperial Cults and the Apocalypse of John*, 164.

149. See Hall, "Arguing Like an Apocalypse," 436: "Apocalyptists assume a world that depends on God's decrees. In such a world arguments based on the balanced probabilities and judicious distinctions of Greek philosophy and rhetoric are irrelevant, for the world is mysterious—irreducible by human reason. Human beings can understand the world and their place in it only if God reveals the inscrutable heavenly judgments that constitute their situation. Apocalypses frequently address specific questions by revealing the judgments of God and their effects in the world: they reveal how God orders the cosmos, how God orders history, or how God orders angelic and human society to urge human beings to identify with what God is doing and therefore to act or think as the author prescribes. Argumentative force depends not primarily on a chain of deductive or inductive reasoning but on the explanatory power of the world view disclosed when God reveals his judgments."

the Apocalypse is not only the listening space, but also the acting space, where the audience can take the time to live into the world created by the enunciated text. Thus the space of the Apocalypse is not only or primarily schematic, but is operational.[150] This operational space for John has a liturgical character, it is not space conceived in the abstract, but space that exists to be traversed over, to be worked upon, and ultimately it is space within which to be killed and resurrected. The saints' existence is irreducibly spatial as they are characterized and identified specifically as ones who "follow the Lamb wherever he goes" (14:4).

Since space is operational rather than static, to inhabit space is to dwell in time and thus John's discourse also reconfigures time. One way of configuring time is to divide it into eras and set forth an account of history. This periodization of history, where the climax of history is portrayed as the author's and audience's own time, was a popular feature in much apocalyptic discourse and in the culture preceding and surrounding it.[151] Argumentatively, periodization seeks to redefine all history and situate its audience within this holistic temporal vision, or more precisely seeks to place its audience at the end of the historical span, at the climactic moment of the historical drama.[152] Partitioned time informs the audience where they are within the historical whole.[153] Some may mistakenly think that they have a lot of time, but the division of time makes clear that "the time is short" (1 Cor. 7:29) or "there will be no more interval" (Rev. 10:6, my translation). Or alternatively, some may make the mistake that the delay is shorter than it is when there may be more waiting required (see 6:10; 13:10; 14:12). The division of time makes clear the time in which one is living. Knowing this can help a person know how to use time wisely.[154]

Time, like space, is discursive, and thus is not experienced by all in every place in the same manner.[155] The declaration of the apocalypse marks time

---

150. On this see the differentiation between maps and itineraries in Michel de Certeau, *The Practice of Everyday Life*, tr. Steven Rendall (Berkeley: University of California Press, 1984), 118–122.

151. See John J. Collins, "Temporality and Politics in Jewish Apocalyptic Literature," in *Apocalyptic in History and Tradition*, ed. Christopher Rowland and John Barton, Journal for the Study of the Pseudepigrapha Supplement Series 43 (London: Sheffield Academic, 2002), 29–33. Usually an imperial propagandist would list out a succession of kingdoms with the final kingdom in the series being the speaker's own kingdom. This was done by Persians, Greeks, and Romans. Collins notes how radical Daniel's appropriation of this tactic is when Daniel's vision suggests the overthrow by the kingdom of God of all earthly kingdoms in the succession, 30.

152. O'Leary, *Arguing the Apocalypse*, 15.

153. Robbins, *The Invention of Christian Discourse* 1, 338–339.

154. Robbins, *The Invention of Christian Discourse* 1, 339.

and effects a rhetorical epoch. Stephen D. O'Leary, following John Angus Campbell, identifies a rhetorical epoch as "an era so marked by a strategic, stylized symbolism that it divides history into a 'before' and 'after.' . . . Rhetorical epochs and their representative symbols reflect such a major shift in human self-understanding that their advent constitutes a revolution."[156] By partitioning time the author seeks to place the audience on the cusp of the divinely ordained moment of action—they are people, as Paul says of the Corinthians, "upon whom the ends of the ages have fallen" (1 Cor. 10:11).

There is certainly some aspect of periodization in the Apocalypse, especially keeping in mind the cycles of seven, which function to define a certain historical span of history for its audience. However, John's primary argumentative emphases lie elsewhere. John's concern with temporality is less concerned with an account of all history, but seeks to build a vision of lived temporality, or an apocalyptic practice of time itself.[157] John's concern with time is much more performative and recitative so he spells out durations of meaningful time that permeate the temporal experience of the audience of the Apocalypse.[158] This sense of time may be called "calendrical"[159] or "ethical"[160] or even "narrative"[161] but it may most aptly be called "liturgical" after its setting in the gathered worship of the church and the narrated time of worship within the visions themselves (for example, "the Lord's Day," Rev. 1:10).

Following Steven J. Friesen's five kinds of calendrical time, I understand the Apocalypse to contain worship time, vision time, present time, vindication time, and new time.[162] Friesen's model is adequate because it focuses on operational and performative time. This model works more as a set of

155. O'Leary, *Arguing the Apocalypse*, 44.

156. O'Leary, *Arguing the Apocalypse*, 45.

157. See Gilbertson, *God and History in the Book of Revelation*, 109: "[T]he text offers a view of reality which is irreducibly temporal, without giving a chronological account of history." See also Bruce J. Malina, "Christ and Time: Swiss or Mediterranean?" *The Catholic Biblical Quarterly* 51 (1989), 5–6, where he argues that the primary time orientation preference of ancient Mediterranean people was present oriented rather than past or future oriented. That is, they were less concerned with the overall sweep of history than they were with their present circumstances.

158. See Gilbertson, *God and History in the Book of Revelation*, 114–115: "[T]he development of the temporal horizons of the text expands backwards from the present through the historical and primordial past, and forwards from the present into the penultimate and ultimate future . . . with this expansion comes a renewed and sharpened focus on the present."

159. Friesen, *Imperial Cults and the Apocalypse of John*, 157–161.

160. O'Leary, *Arguing the Apocalypse*, 220.

161. Harry O. Maier, *Apocalypse Recalled: The Book of Revelation after Christendom* (Minneapolis: Fortress Press, 2002), 135–148.

temporalities rather than as a periodization schema. This does not discount historical schemas, but understands that those schemas carry little meaning without the practices of lived time. Thus, worship time is the foundational sense of time because it is the practice of time through which other senses of time are experienced.[163] Worship time spans heaven and earth, connecting two realms and marking differences between those inside and outside the community.[164] The enactment of the Apocalypse in worship time approximates the visionary experience (vision time), and allows the church to live in vindication time in its present. New time is the time after time, which is not a grand synthesis of time, nor a universalization of worship time, but brings time and language to its breaking point.[165] New time remains outside of the control and purview of the apocalyptist, audience, and the surrounding culture—it is mystery yet to be revealed and can only be experienced within worship time as longing (μαρανα θα / ἔρχου; 1 Cor. 16:22; Didache 10:6; Rev. 22:20).

Just as space in the Apocalypse is narratival, so is time. Time is narrated in the Apocalypse not so much to indicate something about time, but to produce an experience of time, a temporality.[166] The Apocalypse tells time to move its audience along a stream or several streams of time rather than to inform them about properties or moments in time. The Apocalypse *makes* time. John's rhetorical mixture of time causes various temporalities to whirl around and through its audience, closing the gap between the time of recalled narration and the audience's present through varied narrative tenses.[167] Present

162. Friesen, *Imperial Cults and the Apocalypse of John*, 157–161. See also Gilbertson, *God and History in the Book of Revelation*, 110 where the temporality of Revelation is delineated as "present, primordial past, historical past, penultimate future, and ultimate future."

163. Friesen, *Imperial Cults and the Apocalypse of John*, 158–159.

164. Friesen, *Imperial Cults and the Apocalypse of John*, 158.

165. Friesen, *Imperial Cults and the Apocalypse of John*, 161.

166. See Certeau, *The Practice of Everyday Life*, 79: "[N]arrated history creates a fictional space. It moves away from the 'real'—or rather it pretends to escape present circumstances . . . In precisely that way, it *makes* a hit ('*coup*') far more than it describes one…Its discourse is characterized more by a way of *exercising itself* than by the thing it indicates . . . It produces effects, not objects."; See also Collins, *The Apocalyptic Imagination*, 17: "Biblical scholarship in general has suffered from a preoccupation with the referential aspects of language and with the factual information that can be extracted from a text. Such an attitude is especially detrimental to the study of poetic and mythological material, which is expressive language, articulating feelings and attitudes rather than describing reality in an objective way. The apocalyptic literature provides a rather clear example of language that is expressive rather than referential, symbolic rather than factual."; Collins, *Crisis and Catharsis*, 144.

167. Maier, *Apocalypse Recalled*, 134–139 especially, 138: "In various ways John both overcomes and insists on the temporal gap between his actual time of recalled narration and the fictional time of the events as they happened. In doing so he wrests from what was (the heard and seen of 22:8) an abiding

tense declarations in the midst of recalled vision narration create temporal and eschatological constellations between past, present, and future.[168] Harry Maier notes how this phenomenon works in several places in the Apocalypse to create the space and time within which to act. In Revelation 14:13, a voice from heaven announces in the present tense, "Blessed are those who die in the Lord, *from now on*." This brings the past and present together with the future creating a "dynamic relationship."[169] Just before this, two angelic interjections are heard the first announcing a time for repentance and judgment and the second proclaiming the fall of Babylon as a completed event. Maier notes how the diverse and achronous temporalities swirl around which "open, even demand, a time for repentance, endurance, and costly testimony."[170] The present of the audience, which before had seemed either ordinary or even threatened, is now "alive with possibilities [and] alternatives."[171]

A similar temporal logic is at work in the announcement of 11:15. The audience hears the sound of a loud voice proclaiming the completed fact of the regime change from the kingdom of the world to the kingdom of the Lord and of his Messiah (ἐγένετο). This is followed by the future-tense announcement of his reign extending into eternity (βασιλεύσει). The transfer of kingdom authority is announced in the present as a completed fact that will continue into the future of the audience's present and beyond. When they hear the announcement, the audience knows that they exist in the time of the reign of the Lord and not the reign of the world. The future reign of God and the Lamb is brought into the audience's troubled present.

Bringing divergent temporalities together is not the only way the Apocalypse plays with time. Time is also experienced in various ways by different groups of people in the narrative. Once again, Maier's analysis is penetrating:

> [T]he earthbound nations, or their pagan representatives, [are] tangled up in idolatry and the forward thrust of visionary cycles. Contrasting these are John's heavenly or heaven-blessed characters, the worshipers of God, who break into and disrupt the narrative

---

sense of imminence ('what must soon take place'—1:1), and even immanence ('what is'—1:19). The traversal of this interval opens the present to new possibility."

168. Maier, *Apocalypse Recalled*, 139.
169. Maier, *Apocalypse Recalled*, 141.
170. Maier, *Apocalypse Recalled*, 144.
171. Maier, *Apocalypse Recalled*, 147.

sequences with varying apocalyptic prospects, at once slowing earthbound clocks and making them beat ever faster.[172]

Time seems to rush ahead horizontally for those who worship the beast, with the cycles of seven increasing in speed like a runaway train. In the meantime, worship time, both in heaven and on earth, seems to interrupt or at least slow down the relentless pace of time's forward progression.[173] Maier utilizes the musical term *ritardando* to describe this phenomenon, but a more apt term might be *fermata* because the temporal delay seems to be at the discretion of heaven—holding for an indeterminate interval, as long as necessary for carrying out the divine plan.[174] This means that these two temporalities exist in the moment face to face, opposed to each other as two divergent practices of time within the same space. This serves to "open the present up in a startlingly fresh way" making each moment one of decision, of witness, of choice between true worship or false.[175]

These insights about the rhetorical construction and transformation of time and space are crucial to understanding the way John's Apocalypse works—not only the persuasiveness of its arguments, but how it produces effects before and within the audience, transforming their own space (including bodies) and time (including their present moment of comfort or affliction). John intends the Apocalypse to transform the space and time of his audience. Qualitative duration[176] ("How Long O Lord?" 6:10) thus seems to be the focus, rather than periodization of large sweeping sections of salvation history. The announcement of the transfer of power from the kingdom of the world to the kingdom of God is not considered a rehearsal of a future event, but rather the takeover from the outside of the audience's present reality.[177] As Barr makes clear, "The liturgical recital of the Apocalypse becomes a real experience of the Kingdom of God. The liturgy is the manifestation of God's rule. . . . The eschatological world is realized in the cultic event."[178]

And yet the change goes deeper than mere "symbolic transformation." The Apocalypse does not simply create a new subjective approach to the world.[179]

---

172. Maier, *Apocalypse Recalled*, 148.

173. Maier, *Apocalypse Recalled*, 152–153.

174. We might recall, by analogy, the way the rhythm of the Mass is interrupted and delayed for as long as it takes for everyone to receive the Eucharist. If people continue to come up to receive the next step in the liturgy must continue to be deferred.

175. Maier, *Apocalypse Recalled*, 153.

176. Malina, "Christ and Time," 13.

177. Certeau, *The Practice of Everyday Life*, 85.

178. Barr, "The Apocalypse as a Symbolic Transformation of the World," 47.

Rather, the established order has been overthrown; the space is inhabited now in such a way that the person and reign of Christ really is present.[180] This is the case because the apocalyptic word does not construct a world *ex nihilo*, but takes advantage of the space it inhabits. It uses the place given to it, reconfiguring and transforming it.[181] The proclamation of the reign of God has "illocutionary force." Liturgical time is an operational time that is a paradoxical remembering of a future. The space inhabited by the hearing community during the liturgical time of the performance of the Apocalypse is transformed—it becomes part of the realm of God's sovereignty, like a territorial outpost claimed and ordered by a foreign and future imperial center.[182] Traditionally this state of things has been referred to as "already and not yet." However, it becomes clear that within liturgical time, no part of the transformed space is left outside of the apocalyptic claim, the place where Apocalypse reveals God and Christ as reigning—where it is enunciated—is really under their authority; nothing is left for the "not yet."[183]

Thus it again becomes beneficial to rethink the idea of apocalyptic periodization and temporality, at least as it occurs in John's vision. We might say, using Malina's categories, that periodization has to do with historical time, which is the author's construction of an *order* of time, is "marked by epochs" or "qualitative periods," and orders the past and future in ways that are significant to the present.[184] Temporalization has to do with operational time. Operational time is experienced as *duration*, is based on social practice and processes, and focuses on the present time not measurable by definable units

---

179. Barr, "The Apocalypse as Symbolic Transformation of the World," 49: "[T]he believing community which encountered the Apocalypse as a living performance would be transformed, and so would the world they live in, for they would understand that world differently."

180. Barr, "The Apocalypse of John as Oral Enactment," 252: "[T]he oral performance of the Apocalypse served to make Jesus present. There is a kind of secondary—or rather tertiary—incarnationalism in the reading of the Apocalypse."

181. Certeau, *The Practice of Everyday Life*, 86: "How does it effect its 'breakthrough' in the occasional mode? In short, what constitutes the *implantation of memory in a place* that already forms an ensemble? That implantation is the moment which calls for a tightrope-walker's talent and sense of tactics; it is the instant of art. Now it is clear that this implantation is neither localized nor determined by memory-knowledge. The occasion is taken advantage of, not created. . . . It inserts itself into something encountered by chance on the other's ground."

182. Certeau, *The Practice of Everyday Life*, 85: "Memory mediates spatial transformations. In the mode of the 'right point in time' (*kairos*), it produces a founding rupture or break. Its foreignness makes possible a transgression of the law of the place. Coming out of its bottomless and mobile secrets, a '*coup*' modifies the local order. The goal of the series is thus an operation that transforms the visible organization. But this change requires invisible resources of a time which obeys other laws and which, taking it by surprise, steals something from the distribution owning the space."

183. Malina, "Christ and Time," 29.

but as something which must "run its course."[185] John's use of what I have named liturgical time is a special blending of historical time and operational time. The historical order is not abstract and separate from lived temporality; rather the *order* finds its existence in the *duration*. Time exists in the Apocalypse as operational rather than strictly chronological. This means that events are not measured in increments but as events that have the quality of duration. They happen not by a measured time, but at "the right time" and once they occur they travel to their end. This is not the same as saying the process has already begun, for that could be said just as easily with a periodization scheme. Instead, what this signifies is that the conditions necessary for time and space to be brought to its purpose have been brought about; the acting space in which the time will be fulfilled has been opened up.

Conclusion

Just how this is the case will be the work of chapters 4 to 7. For now it is enough to synthesize the foregoing discussion. Apocalyptic discourse is concerned to a great extent with cosmology. Through conceptual blending, the earliest Christians communicated apocalyptically by envisioning the entire cosmos as God's vast empire. John is less concerned with an examination of the nature and properties of the cosmos than he is with the dynamic encounter between the creator God and the Lamb with the cosmos. John's eschatological communities exist within this dynamic vision; the times and spaces of the history of the universe swirl around them as they are gathered into the vortex of the one who sits on the throne. This is not to say that reality exists in a state of flux, but that the cosmos—all time and space—shakes, pushes against, or dances in the presence of the coming God.

This is, in short, John's apocalyptic vision of worship as politics: life lived in the cosmos as visited and inhabited by God. The grotesque sights, the vivid colors, the deafening sounds, and the unstable foundations pictured and presented in John's Apocalypse are immersive images. They create a world into which John invites his hearers so they can experience the activity of God and the Lamb in their midst. The imagistic and aural phenomena John brings before his audience provides the stage on which he can present his vision of how God is at work to judge and renew the cosmos.[186] Once this

---

184. Malina, "Christ and Time," 27–28. The distinction between order and duration is derived from the discussion of time in narrative texts in Shlomith Rimmon-Kenan, *Narrative Fiction: Contemporary Poetics*, 2nd ed. (London & New York: Routledge, 2002), 46–56.

185. Malina, "Christ and Time," 26–28.

cosmic stage is constructed by John's apocalyptic rhetoric it remains for his audience to grapple with the implications of the divine activity in the face of their own everyday situations and activities. As I will argue in the next chapter, the apocalyptic presentation of a cosmic reality will inevitably clash with a cosmological discourse that does not share the same assumptions. John, in presenting his argumentation on an apocalyptic and cosmic stage, sets his audience on a collision course with Roman imperial cosmological discourse.

---

186. See Robbins, "Rhetography," 99: "The argumentative texture of each rhetorolect is a result of the interaction of its particular rhetography with its particular rhetology. This means that an early Christian rhetorolect is a network of significations and meanings associated with social-cultural-ideological places and spaces familiar to people in a certain geophysical region."

2

The War of Worldcraft: John's Cosmic Rhetoric Against Roman Imperial Cult Discourse

> Proclaiming a near end confronts people with a decision that cannot wait . . . it can rudely unmask the sins of the status quo, thus bringing to dramatic and needed expression the divine discontent with the world as it is, a world bad enough that it needs to be improved out of existence.
> —Dale C. Allison Jr., *The Historical Christ and the Theological Jesus*[1]

> Then they'll raise their hands, sayin' we'll meet all your demands
> But we'll shout from the bow your days are numbered.
> —Bob Dylan, "When the Ship Comes In"[2]

Worship of Caesar is an extremely complex historical phenomenon, and in the space given I will not be able to parse out its full intricacies. Only a monograph devoted to the subject could do it justice, and fortunately there are more than a few excellent examples. What I set out to do in this chapter is set the cosmological aspect of cultic activity in focus. This cosmological aspect may have been more or less subconscious to the everyday Greco-Roman person, but nevertheless it still functioned to structure the world in which he or she lived. In this chapter, I first establish that Roman imperial cult worship employed a discourse that constructed a cosmos. This cosmological

---

1. Dale C. Allison Jr., *The Historical Christ and the Theological Jesus* (Grand Rapids: Eerdmans, 2009), 98.
2. Bob Dylan, "When the Ship Comes In," Ó 1963, 1964 by Warner Bros. Inc.; renewed 1991, 1992 by Special Rider Music.

cultic discourse—or rhetorical cosmology—established the world of Roman dominance and sustained Roman rule through ritual and image. I then will look at how this rhetorical cosmology functioned not just at the cultic level, but also in the economic realm. Trade through Roman coinage was a key way in which Rome extended its own cosmological discourse. If not in the larger culture, then at least in John's view, to participate and flourish in the Roman economy through trade meant to participate in the cosmology crafted by the cult. Finally, I will look at John's strategy of countering this rhetorical cosmology. If the Roman world was constructed through cult ritual, image, and exchange, John sought to cancel out the whole system by non-participation. His strategy of non-participation upsets the system and introduces an unsettling anomie. The world in flux that John envisions in the cosmic catastrophes is a way of breaking the cosmic bond between Roman gods, Caesar, and the world constructed through the Roman system of sacrifice. In short, if John's communities refuse sacrifice, they will be seen as introducing anomie into the Roman social and cosmic order. Then John reports the breaking apart of the world through divine judgment, thus confirming this pagan suspicion. Once the world begins to come undone, the contract that the inhabitants of the earth have with the gods and with Caesar will have been understood to be broken as well, and true worship may occur throughout the world. This insight will guide the study into the next section of investigating the cycles of seven and their rhetorical and cosmological politics.

Imperial Cult Rhetoric as World Building: Cosmic Renewal and Sustenance

Worship in the ancient world differs in significant ways from its modern counterpart. The ancient world knew nothing of a separation of religion and politics. In the world of John's Apocalypse, piety was intimately related to power. Worship or honor given to the gods or to semi-divine beings (like a human Caesar understood to be equal to the gods) was a way of expressing their power and status relative to others with less power and status.[3] Ittai Gradel argues that there was no distinction between secular honors and worship in the Roman Empire. Worship of humans as divine "differed in degree, not in kind, from 'political' or 'secular' honours. Massive differences in social status—as that between gods and humans—found expression in weighty honours."[4] The key to

---

3. Ittai Gradel, *Emperor Worship and Roman Religion*, Oxford Classical Monographs (Oxford: Clarendon, 2002), 25–26.
4. Gradel, *Emperor Worship and Roman Religion*, 52.

any honors, whether secular or divine, was power. Therefore, because Caesar's power was absolute and unquestioned—just as was Jupiter's—his status was that of a divine being.[5]

Understanding this phenomenon requires a recalibration of our late-modern approach to worship and power. Divinity in the ancient world was not a dogmatic question of absolute status, but was more a matter of relative status. We should not understand power as a possession wielded over others and buttressed by force. Instead, power formed the fabric of all social relations—hence relative power leads to relative divinity or honors.[6] Thus the question of whether Caesar was *divine* in any absolute sense was not ruled out, but neither was it relevant. Caesar's *power* vis-à-vis the Roman world was absolute therefore his divine status was unquestioned.[7]

A similar recalibration of the modern approach to ritual is in order. In the ancient world ritual wasn't denigrated to the status of symbol, a mere reflection of the true beliefs and thoughts people held. Rather it was seen as a constructive activity rather than a reflective activity. Ritual was the way to navigate through the social web of power. It therefore structured the world, giving it its shape—such activity provided the social order's acting space, rather than necessitating it beforehand.[8] Price argues that the imperial cult "created a relationship of power between subject and ruler . . . [it] was a major part of the web of power that formed the fabric of society."[9] Ritual within the cult shaped society, not merely defining the emperor, but providing a way of conceptualizing the world as a system whose structure defines the position of the emperor within that system.[10] It is also important to note that as a system of power, ritual is not shaped by the "cognitive beliefs" of any individual Roman citizen, but rather by the social practices of the society.[11] Ritual crafted a social world, a symbolic totality, into which people were positioned in relation to other people, groups of people, other cities, the emperor himself, and the

---

5. Gradel, *Emperor Worship and Roman Religion*, 72.

6. S. R. F. Price, *Rituals and Power: The Roman Imperial Cult in Asia Minor* (Cambridge: Cambridge University Press, 1984), 242. Also see Danker's study on the ubiquity of honorary language in the Greco-Roman culture, Frederick W. Danker, *Benefactor: Epigraphic Study of a Greco-Roman and New Testament Semantic Field* (St. Louis: Clayton Publishing House, 1982).

7. Gradel argues that to worship the emperor's *numen*—equivalent to worshiping his power—was to worship the emperor himself as divine, *Emperor Worship and Roman Religion*, 234–245, passim.

8. Price, "Rituals and Power," 71; Gradel, *Emperor Worship and Roman Religion*, 3–4.

9. Price, "Rituals and Power", 71.

10. Price, *Rituals and Power*, 7–8.

11. Price, *Rituals and Power*, 9–11.

Roman institution, the "Roman imperial order."[12] Ritual didn't *express* a belief about the world—it *was* that belief.

This ritual was the rhetoric or discourse through which Roman imperialism perpetuated and extended its vision of the world.[13] The rhetoric of the imperial cult functioned to define society, history, and indeed the whole cosmos in a way that made Roman power inevitable and unquestionably beneficial—the best of all possible outcomes.[14] For at least the wealthy elite connected to the provincial cults,[15] the prolongation of the world order was the focus of the cult mythology. As Friesen argues, "The logic of imperial cults allowed for no termination of the world."[16] This was because the imperial cult's primary function was the building of a cosmology. The discourse of the cult defined the experience of space and time for the everyday Roman citizen, creating a "meaningful geography in which Rome was central" and a sense in which time was shaped through festivals and holidays.[17]

The cult's main purpose was to build the world within which its citizenry existed. The cult constructed a world where Rome would always reign because Rome had brought the world into existence. The provincial proconsul of Asia honored Augustus' victory at Actium by heralding it as the "beginning of all things."[18] The world was brought into existence by Augustus' (and his successors') conquest, and therefore required the permanence and repetition of Roman victory to continue in existence. As Friesen writes, "The discourse of imperial cults was committed to preventing the imagination from imagining the end of this world."[19] The rhetoric of the imperial cult constructed a world in which inhabitants of Rome and the provinces lived, moved, and had their being.

---

12. A helpful collection of essays engaging Price's work on ritual and politics in relation to Pauline thought is found in Richard A. Horsley, ed. *Paul and the Roman Imperial Order* (Harrisburg: Trinity Press International, 2004). Horsley's group's work on Paul within the Roman Empire is a very useful set of tools to understand the socio-political and theological world of the New Testament. Many of the insights from Paul's context can be translated for John's seven churches as well.

13. See Steven J. Friesen, *Imperial Cults and the Apocalypse of John: Reading Revelation in the Ruins* (Oxford: Oxford University Press, 2001), 17–19.

14. Friesen, *Imperial Cults and the Apocalypse of John*, 19.

15. Friesen makes a distinction between the less accessible provincial cults and the more local and mundane municipal cults, which were less concerned with mythology positioning Rome at the cosmic center, and more concerned with local myth-making, *Imperial Cults and the Apocalypse of John*, 94–95.

16. Friesen, *Imperial Cults and the Apocalypse of John*, 130.

17. Friesen, *Imperial Cults and the Apocalypse of John*, 124–126.

18. Friesen, *Imperial Cults and the Apocalypse of John*, 32–33.

19. Friesen, *Imperial Cults and the Apocalypse of John*, 130.

Around 29 BCE the Asian provincial council held a competition for ascribing the highest honors to Augustus. The Roman proconsul, Paullus Fabius Maximus won the prize in 9 BCE with this offering:

> (It is hard to tell) whether the birthday of the most divine Caesar is a matter of greater pleasure or benefit. We could justly hold it to be equivalent to the beginning of all things, and he has restored . . . every form that had become imperfect and fallen into misfortune; and he has given a different aspect to the whole world, which blithely would have embraced its own destruction if Caesar had not been born for the common benefit of all. Therefore people would be right to consider this to have been the beginning of the life of breath for them.[20]

The province of Asia, in response to Maximus' entry, declared the highest honors for Augustus:

> Whereas the providence which divinely ordered our lives created with zeal and munificence the most perfect good for our lives by producing Augustus and filling him with virtue for the benefaction of mankind, sending us and those after us a saviour who put an end to war and established all things; and whereas Caesar [*sc.* Augustus] when he appeared exceeded the hopes of all who had anticipated good tidings, not only surpassing the benefactors born before him, but not even leaving those to come any hope of surpassing him; and whereas the birthday of the god marked for the world the beginning of good tidings through his coming. . . .[21]

Cultic rhetoric like this built a cosmos for Rome, setting out its eternal existence and its newness through Augustan rule and conquest. Though the provincial cult was the occupation of the elite,[22] there were other venues to practice cult for both rich and poor, privileged and humble. There is less archaeological evidence for poorer cult practice such as the *cultores*, but not because the cults were rare, rather "their members were humble people, slaves and freedmen of low social standing and limited economic means."[23] The wealthy were able

---

20. Quoted in Price, *Rituals and Power*, 55.
21. Quoted in Price, *Rituals and Power*, 54.
22. Friesen, *Imperial Cults and the Apocalypse of John*, 94–95.
23. Gradel, *Emperor Worship and Roman Religion*, 224.

to establish more lasting monuments of cultic activity[24], but this by no means excludes the ubiquity of cultic activity throughout all classes of Greco-Roman society.[25] John's Apocalypse may give us a glimpse into this ubiquity in the description of those receiving the beast's economic mark as "all, the small and the great, the rich and the poor, free people and slaves" (Rev. 13:16).[26]

The ubiquity of the discourse of the imperial cult is also attested by the proliferation of images, which were the political mythmakers and storytellers in the ancient world.[27] Images, Paul Zanker argues, were the primary mode of constructing a social world and producing the culture of the empire. Through images—on statues, walls, inscriptions, coins, and elsewhere—the emperor told his own story in order to shape the story the empire's inhabitants told about themselves. Whether or not a political project or activity undertaken by Augustus was a success or not was a secondary concern. Instead, "the imagery of lasting happiness transcended any reality and eventually came to shape the common perception of reality."[28] Zanker observes that, in order to give permanent expression to the mood of optimism that Augustus had garnered, he used an already extant myth about a new "Saturninan" age of happiness. A comet was expected in 17 BCE, so he seized the opportunity to announce that the long awaited *saeculum* had arrived. From May 30 through June 3 the great Secular Games took place, "heralding the beginning of a new age."[29] Coins minted in the year of the festival showed imagery of a young Caesar below the image of a comet streaking overhead.[30] The promise contained within the Secular Games and established on various monuments for years afterward was that of abundance and fertility in nature and in men and women too.[31]

---

24. See the inscription in Ephesus circa 81 CE: "On behalf of the health of our Lord Emperor Titus Caesar and (on behalf of) the permanence of the rule of the Romans, the damaged wall surrounding the Augusteion was repaired," in Friesen, *Imperial Cults and the Apocalypse of John*, 130.

25. Gradel, *Emperor Worship and Roman Religion*, 16: "The sacrificial rites were meant to be appreciated and learnt from watching them in progress. They were, in fact, so common and ubiquitous in the Graeco-Roman world that there was hardly ever any point in describing them more closely."

26. Contra David E. Aune, "The Influence of Imperial Court Ceremonial on the Apocalypse of John," *Biblical Research* 28 (1983), 20, who connects John's use of "small and great" to the *consensus omnium*. There is little evidence that John is picking up Ciceronian political theory. It is more likely that this usage is idiomatic for John and is a poetic and imagistic rendering of "all of society."

27. Paul Zanker, *The Power of Images in the Age of Augustus*, trans. Alan Shapiro (Ann Arbor: University of Michigan Press, 1988).

28. Zanker, *The Power of Images*, 172.

29. Zanker, *The Power of Images*, 167.

30. Zanker, *The Power of Images*, 168.

31. Zanker, *The Power of Images*, 172.

Not only did images function throughout the empire to propagate the "official narrative" of Imperial Rome, it also constructed the entire cosmos in which Roman citizens lived. Zanker's masterful interpretation of statuary and relief is instructive here. One cogent example of the cosmic and political intermingling in Roman Imperial identity is the use of the vine motif. According to Zanker, "Jagged leaves, flowers of all sorts, and fruits and plants both realistic and fantastic, even crawling little creatures, all suggest nature's growth, so alive that it seems to be real. But when one steps back again and takes in all the vines at once, one has the strong impression of a strictly observed order governing every detail."[32] No matter how wild and "free" the growth, every bud and leaf has its prescribed place and position. Additionally, the fact that some of the plants are new and fantastical could serve to signify that the world has truly been made new under Augustus' reign.[33]

The Prima Porta statue, commissioned to honor Augustus' victory over the Parthians, is another interesting intermingling of politco-military power and cosmic representations of heaven and earth. The statue depicts Caesar victorious, but it is the reliefs of the breastplate that bring the ideology of Roman victory into focus. In the center, the Parthian king extends the legionary eagle (recovered by Rome in the victory) to a breastplated figure in military pose (representing Rome or Mars Ultor himself). However, this central piece is couched in a much larger cosmic picture containing not only elements of Roman politics, but also visions of a golden age for the nature order. Two women on either side represent conquered provinces and client states. There are other figures representing the borderlands and those places not yet conquered by Rome. Zanker indicates that, "on the cuirass relief the victory over the Parthians is celebrated as the culmination of a perfect world order."[34] Mother earth is found reclining underneath the central focus and the image is meant to invoke the *Ara Pacis*. The figures of Apollo and Diana appear nearby to strengthen this vision of victory as the fullness of the new age. Above the central image of victory are found the sun and moon god.[35] Zanker concludes that this imagery suggests that, "The victory in Parthia is thus celebrated as both the prerequisite and the consequence of the *saeculum aurem*. The unique historical

---

32. Zanker, *The Power of Images*, 179–180.

33. Zanker, *The Power of Images*, 181: "Another innovation was the combining of real and imaginary plant species. Grapes, figs, and palmettes all growing out of acanthus branches; ivy and laurel spiraling between heavy volutes; garlands bearing all manner of fruit; all this was meant to characterize the new age as a paradise on earth."

34. Zanker, *The Power of Images*, 189.

35. Zanker, *The Power of Images*, 189–192.

event is turned into a paradigm of salvation in which the gods and the heavens act as guarantors but need not intervene directly."[36] Zanker's study of images is very instructive for looking at how images tell the story not only about the emperor, but also about the world over which he rules.

Participants in this cultic activity helped to construct and reinforce this vision of the cosmos. The rhetoric of the imperial cult shaped meaningful space and time throughout the Greco-Roman world. Rome and her victor Caesar stood at the center of the renewed and redeemed world, with the provinces receiving benefits for their status as loyal clients.[37] Cultic discourse also negotiated spatial relationships within the provinces, as the various cities competed for the honor of being called *neokoros* or "a caretaker of a temple of the Sebastoi."[38] The experience of time was molded by imperial cult discourse as well. Festivals provided rhythm of rest and remembrance, and, as with the synchronization of the provincial and Roman calendar, time derived its meaning from the actions of the Roman emperors.[39]

Economy and the Social Order

Modern minds may be tempted to understand the cult as only functioning through religious ceremonial set apart from the mundane and socio-political realities of the everyday inhabitant of the empire. This would be to mistake the religious reality of the Greco-Roman world as having the same assumptions about religion as the post-Enlightenment West. As demonstrated above, religion and worship was no private affair in the Roman world, it formed the fabric of social relation. But neither was it cordoned off from the experience of everyday life—set apart as some interior experience to be recalled only at designated time. The rhetoric that formed the cosmological reality of the Roman Empire wasn't reserved for cult ceremonial alone, but functioned in and through all relations and strata of the social order as well—from household to province.

Nowhere is this more evident than in the economic structures and practices throughout the empire. The economies of the cities within Asia Minor flourished during the period when Revelation was written. J. Nelson Kraybill points out an increase in shipwrecks from 200 BCE to 200 CE, which suggests that there was more seaborne trade in the Mediterranean in that era than at

---

36. Zanker, *The Power of Images*, 192.
37. Friesen, *Imperial Cults and the Apocalypse of John*, 54.
38. Friesen, *Imperial Cults and the Apocalypse of John*, 55; see also 124.
39. Friesen, *Imperial Cults and the Apocalypse of John*, 54; see also 126.

any other time until roughly one thousand years afterward.[40] Pliny the Elder counted Ephesus, Smyrna, Pergamum, Sardis, and Laodicea among the ten wealthiest cities in the province.[41] Within that context of economic growth there were more opportunities for advancement, even for those with little means to begin with, than ever before. Trade allowed even people who were not from wealthy lineage to advance up the social pyramid, as demonstrated by the inscription at Ephesus honoring a certain T. Flavius Montanus, whose election to the office of κυαίστωρ, a financial office, allowed him to eventually achieve a senatorial position.[42] Commerce provided the means for people of low means and esteem to advance up the social stratum, but "people of modest means who wanted to operate a major commercial venture needed the support of a wealthy financier."[43]

Of course, commerce was only one of the options for people of low status to climb the social ladder. The military provided another means of obtaining honor and prestige in society. However, Jews and Christians preferred commerce because the violence (for Christians) and the idolatry (for both Jews and Christians) was repellant to them.[44] John, however, problematizes this solution for upward mobility by indicting the economic practices in the province. For John, the economy was just as idolatrous an option for making one's way in the world as the military.[45] This is because he thought the everyday life of an inhabitant of the empire was immersed in the cult. Is there evidence that this was the case? Was the cultural air filled with the influence of Roman imperial rhetoric? I have argued that the imperial cultic discourse was world building—it established its own cosmos—therefore it is not surprising that this rhetoric would filter into every aspect of a culture.[46]

---

40. J. Nelson Kraybill, *Imperial Cult and Commerce in John's Apocalypse*, JSNTSup 132 (Sheffield: Sheffield Academic, 1996), 81.

41. Kraybill, *Imperial Cult and Commerce in John's Apocalypse*, 82.

42. Kraybill, *Imperial Cult and Commerce in John's Apocalypse*, 82. See also Monumenta Asiae Minoris Antiqua XI: MAMA XI 104 (Akomenia), http://mama.csad.ox.ac.uk/monuments/MAMA-XI-104.html.

43. Kraybill, *Imperial Cult and Commerce in John's Apocalypse*, 86.

44. Kraybill, *Imperial Cult and Commerce in John's Apocalypse*, 86-90.

45. Kraybill, *Imperial Cult and Commerce in John's Apocalypse*, 100.

46. Aune, "Influence of Imperial Court Ceremonial," 6–7, who points to the ready availability of the ceremonial activity from the public character of the traveling court which accompanied Caesar, as well as literature and rhetoric, and also in Roman coinage which expressed imperial propaganda popular at the time. "In all these ways, residents of Asia Minor (the most important center for rhetoric and one of the areas in which the imperial cult was strongly entrenched) could have absorbed a combination of real and ideal images and conceptions of the character and function of the ceremonial of the imperial court."

It certainly seems that the mythology of the cult found its way into the everyday lives of Roman imperial subjects. Though the ritual of some of the cults would have been inaccessible to many poorer populations, and our evidence for cult liturgy is scarce, Gradel argues that much of cultic ritual activity was so commonplace that people were expected to learn it by seeing it. This eliminated the need for written instruction describing them in great detail.[47] This coupled with the fact that poorer associations, such as the *cultores*, would have had less ability to make lasting monuments of dedication to the objects of their worship, means it would be a mistake to rule out the probability that cultic activity was at least appreciated, if not participated in, by those across all social strata.[48]

Nevertheless, there is quite substantial evidence that the cultic discourse found its way into the ordinary lives of non-elites. Because they traveled easily across great distances of the empire, coins were perhaps the closest thing to the modern world's newspaper. Coins depicted a story about the world that was easily recognizable across cultures and languages. The story was often cultic and therefore cosmological. Roman coins in Pergamum and Ephesus depicted deities in temples and cultic activity honoring gods like Jupiter, Roma, and Diana. Another common theme portrayed on coins was Roman conquest and victory. Some coins depicted architecture like the statue of the divine Caesar Augustus inside the temple of Augustus. A sestertius shows the emperor Caligula sacrificing a bull to Divus Augustus in the temple of Augustus. Trafficking in coins like these spread the imperial cosmological message of a divine Caesar as the cause and sustainer of the world. Prospering by using the coins would likely be linked to an acceptance of the implicit message proclaimed by the imagery of the coins. The ancient world spoke about the production of coins both in terms of εἰκόν (image) and χάραγμα (mark).[49] Participating and thriving in an economy through the use of these coins was a tacit acceptance of the cosmological vision delineated by the rhetoric of the imperial discourse.

But it was not solely the means of economic transaction that told Rome's story of the cosmos. It was also the context of that economic exchange. Describing an image of a sestertius issued by Nero, Kraybill argues that the cult saturated the harbors where economic exchange was so prominent:

---

47. Gradel, *Emperor Worship and Roman Religion*, 16.
48. Gradel, *Emperor Worship and Roman Religion*, 223–224.
49. Kraybill, *Imperial Cult and Commerce in John's Apocalypse*, 138.

Religious and Imperial symbols abounded at these [Italian] harbors, as illustrated by a remarkably detailed coin issued by Nero in 64 CE. The coin is a sestertius portraying the harbor at Ostia . . . On this one coin appear the Emperor, merchant ships, a war galley, an individual making sacrifice, a temple and the god Neptune. The numismatic image of Ostia, pressed into the hand of countless Roman subjects, combined the very elements that John of Patmos considered an unholy configuration: commerce, pagan gods, the Roman military—and the imperial cult.[50]

The confluence of cult and economy created, in John's opinion, a beastly alliance between everyday activity and idolatry. Economic activity was nearly synonymous with the cultic ritual.[51] Kraybill points to the saturation of many guilds with cultic ritual to reinforce this point.[52] One must be careful when relying on the evidence Kraybill amasses, because it is primarily from the second century rather than the first. Kraybill contends, however, that this second century evidence represents the "full flowering of institutions already well-established at the time John was on Patmos."[53] Whether or not this is the case, it is at least possible to say this is the way John viewed the economic activity of Rome. According to John one could not participate in economic exchange without receiving the beast's mark and worshiping his image (13:14-17)—both terms that were used about the minting of coins.[54] In John's view to take part in imperial economic activity was to sacrifice in the cult.[55] To succeed within that culture meant to betray the Creator of the cosmos—in effect it was to step out of the cosmos constructed by John's vision and into a cosmos governed by a different set of undergirding structures.[56]

If it is the case that economic activity is so problematized in the Apocalypse, then relating to outsiders seems to be the key crisis for John and his

---

50. Kraybill, *Imperial Cult and Commerce in John's Apocalypse*, 127.

51. Jörg Frey, "The Relevance of the Roman Imperial Cult for the Book of Revelation: Exegetical and Hermeneutical Reflections on the Relation between the Seven Letters and the Visionary Main Part of the Book," in *The New Testament and Early Christian Literature in Greco-Roman Context: Studies in Honor of David E. Aune*, Supplements to Novum Testamentum 122, ed. John Fotopoulos (Leiden & Boston: Brill, 2006), 253.

52. Kraybill, *Imperial Cult and Commerce in John's Apocalypse*, 127–131.

53. Kraybill, *Imperial Cult and Commerce in John's Apocalypse*, 131.

54. Kraybill, *Imperial Cult and Commerce in John's Apocalypse*, 138.

55. The *Testament of Judah* also makes this close connection between economic prosperity (and the desire for it) and idolatry: "My children, love of money leads to idolatry, because once they are led astray by money, they designate as gods those who are not gods" (19:1).

communities. Steven Friesen argues that John and the churches held a shared disdain for the cult, but differed on how to approach a multiplicity of issues regarding their neighbors and colleagues within mainstream Roman society.[57] I think it is less clear that John and his audiences held the same views on participation in the cult, or at the very least the cultic activities required in economic exchange (see 13:11-18; 18:4-5, 11-19).[58] Nevertheless, when such a basic thing as buying and selling goods becomes anathema, the question becomes how to proceed with everyday life—how does one interact with his or her neighbors when one is being persuaded that participation in their economy is sinful? John's rejection of the rhetorical cosmology of the Roman imperial cult, and his call for the same stance from his audiences, seems to be the concrete way John intends for followers of the Lamb to interact with their fellow subjects of Rome. In other words, non-participation is not just a call out from society, but is the means of interacting with others within society and the economy. Non-participation is John's strategy for participation in society, and his rejection of Rome's cosmology is his way of living in the cosmos. The logic of this stance is the subject of the next section.

John and the Breaking of the Contract

John's position of non-participation within the wider society and the economy was a harsh one. Indeed it seems like the way of life John commended was a source of trouble for the churches in Asia. If a church lived comfortably they were not walking in the way of Christ (Rev. 3:17), and if they were facing persecution and trouble this was a sign they were doing something right (2:9). Not everyone addressed by John shared his vision, as it seems at times like he is refuting dissenting opinions (13:11-18; 18:4-5). This is probably because the lifestyle advocated by John made it very difficult to operate in society—John refused to be pragmatic.[59] The very public abstention from cult and economy was a very visible and risky enterprise for John's communities.

---

56. See Frey, "The Relevance of the Roman Imperial Cult," 254. Frey argues that John's commendation, through Christ, of those who are poor but are really rich (2:9) "seems to advocate distancing oneself from the successful economy."

57. Steven Friesen, "Satan's Throne, Imperial Cults, and the Social Settings of Revelation," *JSNT* 27.3 (2005), 352.

58. Kraybill argues that while most scholars tend to view the mourning merchants of Rev 18:11-19 as non-Christians, it is very likely that John is painting a picture of *Christian* merchants mourning the loss of their livelihood when God's judgment comes upon the pagan system, *Imperial Cult and Commerce in John's Apocalypse*, 100.

59. Kraybill, *Imperial Cult and Commerce in John's Apocalypse*, 139.

There would almost certainly be a loss of social status and financial stability for those refusing to participate in economic exchange or those opting out of festivals and civic ceremonies. Henk Jan de Jonge, discussing the public character of cultic activity, writes,

> [C]ities, in prescribing rules for the celebration of festivals of the imperial cult, often expected the involvement of the whole community. For instance, the arrangements for the Caesarea at Chios instructed all inhabitants to wear bright clothes. What were Christians to do in that situation? For the celebration of festivals connected with the imperial cult, several cities passed decrees instructing all citizens whose houses were situated along the route of the procession, to sacrifice on altars outside their houses and even to provide their own altars. What were Christians to do if their houses happened to be located along the route of the procession? About the middle of the second century, Antoninus Pius' birthday was celebrated at Ephesus with a distribution of money to each citizen from public funds to enable everybody to make sacrifices. What was a citizen to do who happened to be a Christian?"[60]

Christians who refused to participate in this civic activity could be singled out as disturbing the social order. They could also face charges of disloyalty to Rome and be killed, as evidenced by the case of Antipas and later by Pliny's letter to Trajan.[61]

Does John's logic here run deeper than a seeking after suffering, persecution, and discomfort? John is neither a sadistic hardliner nor a pragmatist. He is not a sadist because he understands the state of affairs that necessitates this costly witness as awry, out of joint—suffering is not a good in itself but a necessity given the situation. The martyrs' cry of "how long" from beneath the altar demonstrates a longing for justice that implies all is not as it should be. But, as Kraybill indicates, neither is he a pragmatist, looking for a sensible compromise between the empire and the church. So while he doesn't expect followers of the Lamb to live bereft of home or possessions, nor expect the dissolution of human society, he does expect his audience to live in stark contrast to their neighbors. Ultimately he looks for the healing of the nations

---

60. Henk Jan de Jonge, "The Apocalypse of John and the Imperial Cult," in *Kykeon: Studies in Honour of H. S. Versnel*, Religions in the Graeco-Roman World 142, ed. H. F. J. Horstmanshoff, *et al.* (Leiden, Boston, MA, and Köln: Brill, 2002), 136–137.

61. Kraybill, *Imperial Cult and Commerce in John's Apocalypse*, 140.

and the time when the kings of the earth will carry their glory into the city of God (Rev. 22:2; 21:24).[62] This signals that John's political vision aims for a telos beyond suffering resistance.

Richard Bauckham characterizes John's work as "political resistance literature."[63] By this he means that John's vision stands as a critique against and relativizes "all worldly power."[64] What John is after is a vision of divine sovereignty and transcendence.[65] Transcendence purges the political imagination from the necessity of conforming human interaction with the divine with horizontal human interaction. Bauckham cautions against this impulse to draw immediate parallels between what happens in the divine-human encounter and what happens in relations between humans.[66] This point is well taken as this approach can have the unintended consequence of devolving into pure critique, pure negativism on the political stage. It is clear that John is not just against power. As Oliver O'Donovan suggests in conversation with Bauckham, John's work is not anti-political, but rather purges *and* expands the boundaries of political imagination.[67] John's vision does not negate all worldly power. In his perspective, there is a kingdom and a sovereignty to be established in the material world and within history (if not through historical processes).[68]

And yet it is not clear that John goes about setting up an alternative kingdom in direct confrontation with Rome.[69] Revelation is not the outline of a political program. This may seem counterintuitive at first blush, but when one realizes that John encourages economic and political activity as non-participation one sees that John is not setting up a counter-kingdom. In fact, as literature standing within the apocalyptic tradition, it is striking that John does not lay out a vision of political succession or the restoration of a restored,

---

62. Kraybill, *Imperial Cult and Commerce in John's Apocalypse*, 194–196.

63. Richard Bauckham, *The Theology of the Book of Revelation*, New Testament Theology (Cambridge: Cambridge University Press, 1993), 38.

64. Bauckham, *The Theology of the Book of Revelation*, 39.

65. Bauckham, *The Theology of the Book of Revelation*, 43–47.

66. Bauckham, *The Theology of the Book of Revelation*, 44.

67. Oliver O'Donovan, "History and Politics in the Book of Revelation," in *Bonds of Imperfection: Christian Politics, Past and Present*, Oliver O'Donovan and Joan Lockwood O'Donovan (Grand Rapids: Eerdmans, 2004), 25–30.

68. As Oliver O'Donovan says elsewhere, "The kingdom of God is not a mere kingdom, but it is a real kingdom," Oliver O'Donovan, *Desire of the Nations: Rediscovering the Roots of Political Theology* (Cambridge: Cambridge University Press, 1996), 2.

69. Contra Friesen, *Imperial Cults and the Apocalypse of John*, 181: "John considered the churches to be an alternative sovereignty, a polity resisting the imperialism of his time."

sovereign Israel.[70] Instead we are given a weak politics, or a politics of weakness. And in a context of politics as cosmological discourse, a weak politics amounts to a weak cosmology. John's vision for countering Rome is not to set up an alternative society or sovereignty; it is to diminish its hold on the world through "resolute weakness."[71] But this weakness is mighty in the sense that Caesar's hold on the world diminishes with every refusal to participate in the world he established. John believed as much as Paul did that "the form of this world is passing away" (1 Cor. 7:31). So an apocalyptic counter-politics was not large enough in scope for John, rather what was necessary was a counter cosmology. And to participate in Caesar's cosmological discursive politics made living in the new cosmology impossible. So we might say for John: new cosmology, yes—coup, no.[72]

The result is that, in a world governed by a discursive political cosmology, a refusal to participate effects instability within that cosmology. The world gets turned upside down and disorients the way things are with the way things are not. This was perhaps John's purpose in opposing cosmologies—less a destruction of the world and more a deconstruction of the world. The Roman world, discursively sustained through cult and economy, relied on the gods and the divinized Caesars to order and govern well. Perhaps John knew, along with other likeminded Christians at the time, that "to refuse sacrifice was to refuse the gods."[73] Therefore, we might say that when Caesar receives divine honors in cult and market, a refusal to sacrifice is a refusal not only of his divine honors but also a refusal of Caesar, and therefore a refusal of Caesar's world—his system.

There is certainly evidence that ecclesial outsiders considered this to be the case with the early Christians in Asia Minor. In the eyes of their neighbors, Christians who refused to sacrifice were reaping the benefits of the *pax Romana*—social stability, and economic prosperity—without returning their reciprocal responsibility to the gods of Rome for the provision of these things. This withholding of thanks, according to de Jonge, was seen as a possible catalyst of deprivation of these benefits. Without the sacrifice required by the logic of reciprocity, the social contract could be broken and the protections

---

70. There are numerous examples of apocalyptic literature written as propaganda to prop up a movement or regime or to refute a movement or regime's legitimacy (see for example, Daniel 11:32-34 where Judas Maccabeus is referred to as giving "a little help"; The "Animal Apocalypse"). See also Friesen, *Imperial Cults and the Apocalypse of John*, 213.

71. Friesen, *Imperial Cults and the Apocalypse of John*, 216.

72. This is an adaptation from C. Kavin Rowe's discussion of Luke's political vision in Acts in *World Upside Down: Reading Acts in the Greco-Roman Age* (Oxford: Oxford University Press, 2009), 5, 50, 91.

73. Gradel, *Emperor Worship and Roman Religion*, 15.

provided by the gods and the emperor might be revoked.[74] Even more, the Christians' attitudes about and stance toward cultic sacrifice brought to mind an ancient, even primeval lawlessness. This non-participation conjured in the pagan mythic imagination images of "a reversed world," a state of anomie and instability.[75] The cultic and economic imagination of Rome constructed a world sustained by Rome, Rome's gods, and the divinized Caesar, therefore Christians' non-participation was seen as a danger to this world order, a threat to the ongoing nature and stability of the world.[76]

The worship of the emperor and the Roman gods, through cult ritual and economic activity created a social contract based on mutuality and reciprocity. By bestowing on Caesar all manner of honors, the people were placing a moral obligation on the emperor to bestow benefaction by ruling well—to sustain and order the *Pax Romana*. If he did this he would receive the highest honor of divinity after death. However, as Gradel argues, "if he broke the contract, his honours would be withdrawn and his memory condemned. This, and not an attempt to falsify history, was the main point behind damnation of his memory."[77] This arrangement went for the relation between the people and the gods as well. Again, Gradel writes, "when national disasters, such as imperial deaths, occurred, the temples of the immortals were closed, by which measure they were deprived of worship."[78] The gods were constantly allured with promise of worship for keeping the world in good order, and conversely were threatened with lack of worship and honor when that world order was itself threatened. Sacrifices were promised to the gods if the emperor and his family were kept in good health. Gradel cites the example of an oath taken by the Arval Brothers on January 3, 81 CE:

> The chairman [of the Arval college] C. Junius Tadius Mefitanus performed the vows for the welfare of the emperor Titus . . . and of Domitian Caesar . . . and of Julia Augusta and of their children, and after having sacrificed the animals promised by the chairman of the preceding year, he sacrificed to Jupiter Optimus Maximus two steers, to Juno Regina two cows, to Minerva two cows, to the

---

74. de Jonge, "The Apocalypse of John and the Imperial Cult," 137.
75. de Jonge, "The Apocalypse of John and the Imperial Cult," 138.
76. de Jonge, "The Apocalypse of John and the Imperial Cult," 140: "Pagans felt that the Christian ideology undermined and subverted their world in a way that reminded them of the lawlessness and rebellion of primeval ages."
77. Gradel, *Emperor Worship and Roman Religion*, 369.
78. Gradel, *Emperor Worship and Roman Religion*, 369.

public Welfare [*Salus*] two cows, promising [them the same] next year in the following words which were recited by L. Pompeius Celer: 'Jupiter Optimus Maximus, if emperor Titus . . . and Domitian Caesar . . . , of which two we hereby specifically make mention, will be alive and their family safe when the Roman people the next time shall arrive at the date of the 2nd January, and you till the date have preserved them safely from danger and they at that time will be in the same condition as that in which they are presently—if you grant us this good outcome of which we hereby specifically make mention, and you preserve them in the same or better condition than the one in which they are presently in; in return for your doing this, we promise that you will in the name of the college of the Arval Brothers receive [further] two steers with gilded horns.' [Followed by the same formula to Juno Regina, Minerva, and Salus Publica individually.][79]

Gradel continues, "In this case the stick-and-carrot system failed: Titus died on 13 September. The gods did not keep their part of the bargain; and so they did not receive their victims—with gilded horns—the next 3 January."[80]

If the Roman cultic world was sustained by a logic of mutuality and reciprocity, then John's hardline stance against the cultic economy and his vision report of a world in flux, chaos, and decay was essentially an intentional breaking down of this logic. As mentioned previously, John envisions not so much a destruction of the world as a deconstruction of the world. John's cosmological apocalyptic rhetoric functioned to introduce this apocalyptic anomie into the world of Rome's cult and economy.[81] John saw the incursion of divine judgment and disaster upon the world as a sort of breach of contract with Rome's gods. The logic goes something like this: if John's communities refuse sacrifice, they will be seen as introducing anomie into the Roman social and cosmic order. Then John reports the breaking apart of the world through divine judgment, thus confirming this pagan suspicion. Once the world begins to break apart, the contract with the gods and with Caesar will have been understood to be broken as well.

This approach seems to get at what John is doing in the scenes of plagues, judgments, and natural disasters in a way that has been previously overlooked.

---

79. Gradel, *Emperor Worship and Roman Religion*, 370–371.

80. Gradel, *Emperor Worship and Roman Religion*, 371.

81. Amos N. Wilder, "The Rhetoric of Ancient and Modern Apocalyptic," Interpretation 25.4 (1971), 440.

John is canceling out the pact the Roman public has with their gods, he is breaking the deal between them and demonstrating their powerlessness and fraud in the face of the soon-to-be-and-already-enthroned God and his Messiah. It is from within this framework of "rhetorical cosmology" that I wish to approach the climaxes of the cycles of seven in the Apocalypse. That will be the work of chapters 4 to 7 of this study. However, it will be helpful to unpack this insight before moving on to the text.

First, the terminology of "symbolic universe" does not seem to be strong enough for what John is working with here. Both the Roman cultic discourse and John's apocalyptic discourse are not simply ways of *conceiving* of the world, they are, as has been said previously, ways of *constructing and participating in* the world. This is not merely a matter of interpretation. The language of worship in cultic discourse is not flattery that can be discarded for the real kernel of political "fact."[82] The worshiped emperor was not a different entity than the emperor in the "real world."[83] And if the world constructed by the discourse was real, then we should expect the judgment John envisions to be real. There will be some sort of material judgment, but it does not seem as though material reality is completely dissolved and done away with. I prefer the term deconstruction rather than destruction or dissolution.[84] Thus, I stake out a position somewhere between those taken by N. T. Wright[85] and Edward Adams.[86]

Second, John once again seems to be confounding the conventions of the Apocalyptic genre. The cycles of seven have often been understood as taking up the apocalyptic mainstay of periodization of history (see 1 Enoch 83–85; 4 Ezra 14; 2 Baruch 56–74). However, approached from within the framework of rhetorical cosmology, John does not seem to be setting up a timeline of history. He is after something altogether different. For John, history does not march ever forward to its inevitable conclusion—something even in the midst of chaos one might be tempted to call "progress." Instead, history is understood to be constructed when the world of Caesar meets the judgments of the apocalyptically constructed world of God. Therefore, we would be prudent to understand the cycles not as John's layout of the course of history, but as John's understanding of Caesar's world deconstructed and God's world emergent.

---

82. Price, *Rituals and Power*, 241.

83. Price, *Rituals and Power*, 243.

84. See Allan J. McNicol, "All Things New," *Christian Studies* 21 (2005–2006), 39–45. McNicol prefers the idea of radical renovation of the material world rather than complete dissolution and re-creation.

85. See N. T. Wright, *The New Testament and the People of God*.

86. See Edward Adams, *The Stars Will Fall from Heaven: Cosmic Catastrophe in the New Testament and its World*, Library of New Testament Studies 347 (London and New York: T & T Clark, 2007).

Finally, the encounter envisioned here between Rome's rhetorical cosmology and John's—this war of worldcraft—is not primarily about God overpowering Caesar. It does not even seem to be God "putting Caesar in his place" (as in Tertullian's "look behind you, remember you are but a man"[87]). This is no divine takeover or coup. Instead, as I will argue in chapters 4 to 7, the clash of worlds here has a missionary objective. God's new creation does not emerge in judgment alone, but in justification—it puts the world back right.[88] What I mean by this is, by envisioning the deconstruction of Caesar's world through judgment, John is breaking the contract between the Roman people and their gods. John understands that the breaking apart of the world literally stops sacrifice. Therefore, much of John's message is a call for repentance to those lulled and allured by the temptations of economic prosperity within Caesar's world. But another aspect exists in John's vision as well: the judgments of God that begin to erode Caesar's constructed world will also break off the oaths and honors given to Caesar and the other gods of Rome. If the status quo is broken, sacrifice to Caesar ceases. And John knows the first step to worshiping in truth is to stop worshiping falsely. John's standards were difficult for his audiences to measure up to. As Friesen notes, "They were so high that to keep them would make it almost impossible to survive under Roman authority in imperial society. That was precisely John's point."[89] John makes it impossible to live under Roman rule so that his audiences can live under the rule of God and the Lamb. How John's visions accomplish this task is the subject of the following chapters.

---

87. Tertullian, *Apologeticus* XXXIII.4, Tertullian, *Apology, De Spectaculus,* Minucius Felix, Loeb Classical Library translated T. R. Glover and Gerald H. Rendall (Cambridge: Harvard University Press, 1931), amended.

88. It is important to understand that this is not God's world pitted dualistically against Caesar's world as a response to Caesar's reign and rule. John's vision of God's good creation is prior (see Rev. 5). K. K. Yeo aptly writes, "it was the vision of Christ that drove this book, not Roman persecution . . . the Christian vision of a consummated future of 'the way things ought to be' makes apparent the evil nature of 'the way things are' in the Roman world, which leads Christians to oppose the way things are and thereby to be persecuted for it," K. K. Yeo, "Hope for the Persecuted, Cooperation with the State, and Meaning for the Dissatisfied: Three Readings of *Revelation* from a Chinese Context," in *From Every People and Nation: The Book of Revelation in Intercultural Perspective*, ed. David Rhoads (Minneapolis: Fortress Press, 2005), 215.

89. Friesen, *Imperial Cults and the Apocalypse of John*, 209.

3

The Three Cycles of Seven as Object of Interpretation

In the preceding chapters of this study I examined and distilled a specific apocalyptic rhetorical "technique" of world building (*weltkonstruktion*). This aspect of apocalyptic discourse was then set in conversation with the cosmological rhetoric of the Roman imperial cult, where I argued that cultic discourse was also world building. This set up a collision between two worlds, or rather two accounts of the world, existing in the same space and time. Two rhetorical cosmologies exist as alternatives. But there is no dualism envisioned here, for the battle is for the space and time of the one good creation of God. In John's understanding, the Roman world is created, renewed, and sustained by Caesar and the gods, and the cultic discourse that upholds this cosmology. The Beast maintains a hold on the world through worship and economy. Ultimately John attempts break this hold by breaking down the cosmological stability of this arrangement. Only then can God's good creation emerge as given. For John, God is creator and sustainer of the entire cosmos, while Caesar's claim to creation, renewal, and sustenance of the creation is a blasphemous counterfeit.

In chapters 4 to 7 I examine how this phenomenon plays out in the text of John's Apocalypse by looking at the three cycles of plagues visited upon the world. I will argue that the entrance of apocalypse into the space and time sets up a contest between two worlds. This apocalyptic contest/protest functions rhetorically to dismantle the rhetorical cosmological construction set up by the cult (which John regards as a demonic counterfeit of the world created by God). Only once this construction has been taken apart can John's vision of a new heaven and earth emerge as given. Therefore, the three cycles of plagues function rhetorically as this dismantling of Caesar's rhetorical cosmology, with the seventh element of each cycle representing the finality of judgment and the emergence of the new creation. As will become clear through analysis of the texts, the seventh elements are also participatory (whereas the other elements are not) so that within the emergence of the new creation, John and his hearers have a part to play in the drama. Before examining each text, however, I must first establish the three sets of seven as a single object of investigation.

Relating the Cycles to Each Other

The three cycles of seven in the Apocalypse have presented a conundrum throughout their history of interpretation both in terms of literary structure and historical significance. These cycles dominate the middle section of the book and propel most of the action forward, stopping every once in a while to notice a temple measurement here or a beastly confrontation there. But how is this section to be understood as a whole? There are really only a few options available to interpreters. Do the cycles run through a linear progression through time, one event happening upon the end of the other? Or is it rather like a Russian Matryoshka nesting doll, with each cycle narrowing its scope so that the final cycle has been folded up into the vision of the second and that folded into the first?[1] Or perhaps we might see the cycles as multiple takes on a single phenomenon, circling as it were like a vulture over a carcass, each time from a slightly different vantage point with a slightly different emphasis.

The recapitulation theory of interpretation has recently fallen out of fashion, with several scholars arguing in favor of a linear-progressive interpretation. First, proponents of the linear approach argue that the content and scope of the judgments varies from cycle to cycle, so that they do not line up as parallel judgments. The content is similar at times, but not enough that one could understand them to be mere repetition. For example, the trumpet cycle and the bowl cycle both have plagues relating to the sun, however, in the former the sun is darkened, while in the latter the sun's heat becomes so intense that it scorches the earth. Not only does the content refuse to line up perfectly, but the scope of the judgments, even for similar phenomena across the cycles seems to increase, first from a quarter of the earth in the seals, then to a third in the trumpets, then finally the totality of the world is envisioned in the cycle of bowls. It may also be significant that the bowls are called the last of the plagues.[2]

Another aspect pointing toward a successive view of the cycles is that certain plagues seem to presupposed events from previous cycles. For example, in the trumpets cycles the plague of demonic locusts affects all those who had

---

1. See Ben Witherington III, *Revelation*, The New Cambridge Bible Commentary (New York: Cambridge University Press, 2003), 129–130.

2. See James L. Resseguie, *The Revelation of John: A Narrative Commentary* (Grand Rapids: Baker Academic, 2009), 56–57.

not received the protective seal given by God's angels during the cycle of seals. Likewise, the first bowl plague of boils is said to strike all those who had received the beast's mark, which had happened previously in the narrative text. The giving of the beast's mark does not belong to any cycle itself, but it does suggest some sort of linearity to the progression.[3]

Third, Frederick David Mazzaferri argues for a linear, if not strictly chronological, interpretation based on the intensification of the theophanic phenomena that accompany the final element of each cycle.[4] Richard Bauckham likewise traces the addition of detail from the first appearance of meteorological and geological accompaniment of theophany in 4:5, through 8:5, 11:19, and finally in 16:21.[5] Mazzaferri is hesitant to link this to a chronological arrangement of the events in history but still understands the seventh bowl as the climactic event in a progressive series.[6] In this view, the cycles represent, at the very least a literary and narrative progression until the end is finally reached.[7]

The case for a linear-progressive interpretation of the three cycles has much to offer, but I intend to argue against it in favor of a (modified) recapitulation approach. First, the failure of every element in each cycle to match up perfectly with the other two does not necessarily disqualify them from functioning as parallel passages. This is the same work that testifies to turning to "see a voice" (1:12), hears the announcement of a lion, but sees a lamb instead (5:5-6), and finally hears a group's number as 144,000 but sees an uncountable multitude (7:4, 9). Precision is not John's ultimate concern even when he is clearly indicating the same thing in two different ways. It may even be said that John's imprecision is an intentional argumentative strategy to thwart the senses of his audience—another way of apocalyptically revealing the strange to be familiar and the familiar strange. The fact that the elements do not appear to be direct parallels does not necessarily rule out that each cycle recapitulates the previous cycle.

---

3. Dale Ralph Davis, "The Relationship Between the Seals, Trumpets, and Bowls in the Book of Revelation," *Journal of the Evangelical Theological Society* 16.3 (1973), 150.

4. Frederick David Mazzaferri, *The Genre of the Book of Revelation from a Source-Critical Perspective*, Beiheft zur Zeitschrift für die neutestamentliche Wissenschaft und die Kunde der ältern Kirche 54 (Berlin: de Gruyter, 1989), 341.

5. Richard Bauckham, *The Climax of Prophecy: Studies on the Book of Revelation* (London and New York: T & T Clark, 1993), 202–209.

6. Mazzaferri, *The Genre of the Book of Revelation*, 341.

7. Resseguie, *The Revelation of John*, 59.

Second, the fact that certain elements of later cycles presuppose elements from previous cycles does not necessitate a straight linear approach. For example, Revelation 14:8 depicts an angel announcing the fall of Babylon as a completed event (ἔπεσεν, aorist tense) before the actual fall of Babylon is depicted later in chapters 16 and 18. In Revelation 14:9-11, a torrent of tenses make one uncertain of any account of temporal location and progression. This passage also relies on the presupposed reception of the mark of the beast, but places that reception in the ongoing present. Then the future tense arrives when the angel announces that those receiving the mark *will drink* the wine of God's wrath. Finally, this future judgment is described once again in the present ongoing tense: "the smoke of their torment goes up forever and ever" (v. 11, NRSV). In addition to this, a voice from heaven declares blessed those who die in the Lord "henceforth." Is this henceforth from the time of the future punishment of those receiving the mark? Or is the henceforth referring to the time of the public reading to John's audience? Or henceforth from some other unspecified time in the future? All this is enough to conclude that John's linking of events littered throughout the rest of the vision do not necessarily indicate smooth linear progression from one location to the next. As Harry Maier puts it, John's vision plays "games with time."[8]

Third, while it is true that the theophanic elements multiply in each successive cycle, this does not necessarily lead to a progressive intention of John's part. In fact, this aspect may actually strengthen the recapitulation argument, because it indicates that each cycle has the same telos: each cycle ends in theophany. And though the theophanic elements intensify with each cycle, this could just indicate a clearer vision of the end with each cycle. It's akin to how multiple flyovers of a city yields one the opportunity to fill in more and more detail about the city because one can concentrate on different aspects of the city each time one flies over it. In the same way, John's vision of the divine visitation of creation is clarified and brought into crisper focus with each cycle's examination of the same events.

The analogy of flying over a city is strengthened by the fact that it has one object of observation. Multiple flyovers yield multiple views of *one* city. In the same way, the multiple cycles have one object in view: the *telos* of history in its visitation by God. David Barr identifies this as the primary obstacle to a linear-progressive reading of the cycles.[9] The end is suggested around the seventh seal

---

8. Harry O. Maier, *Apocalypse Recalled: The Book of Revelation after Christendom* (Minneapolis: Fortress Press, 2002), 123.

9. David L. Barr, "Apocalypse as Symbolic Transformation of the World: A Literary Analysis," *Interpretation* 38 (1984), 43.

(Rev. 7:9—8:5), announced at the seventh trumpet (11:15-19), and announced again at the seventh bowl (16:17-21; 19:1-8). Add to this the announcement of the end in and around 21:6, and that makes at least four announcements or suggestions of an ending. Clearly, John does not envision three or four ends of the world; history does not meet three or four successive goals. Nor are we to understand there to be three or four returns of God and Christ. Indeed, there is one visitation envisioned by John and that is the vision of the goal of history as "the home of God is among mortals. He will dwell with them; they will be his peoples, and God himself will be with them" (21:3 NRSV).

This was the interpretive approach of Valentinus, Revelation's earliest (extant) commentator. Earliest is not always better or best, but earliest is closest to the original author's and audience's language and setting. Valentinus argues for a recapitulative logic of the movement of the seven cycles:

> And although the same thing recurs in the phials [as in the trumpets], still it is not said as if it occurred twice, but because what is decreed by the Lord to happen shall be once for all . . . We must not regard the order of what is said, because frequently the Holy Spirit, when He has traversed even to the end of the last times, returns again to the same times, and fills up what he had *before* failed to say. Nor must we look for order in the Apocalypse; but we must follow the meaning of those things which are prophesied.[10]

Joseph Mangina echoes this sentiment, arguing that the one who is said to be both the alpha and the omega, the beginning and the end is Jesus Christ—therefore it is not improbable that the one who is the end and who is at the end would be present to the church by means of traversing back through history. Mangina writes, "In each successive vision the same apocalyptic reality is shown forth . . . We can thus see Revelation as a kind of 'apocalyptic haggadah,' a rehearsal, a narrative, a memory of an event in the past that is somehow *not* past, but our present reality, and that toward which all of reality is headed. Time is not annulled but transformed."[11]

My own approach is a modified recapitulation theory. Each cycle has the same basic subject in mind, which is the experience of the duration of time and history as the cosmos moves toward its goal of being the habitation of God. Each cycle is an experience of the one end envisioned by John as the goal of his

---

10. Valentinus, *Commentary on the Apocalypse* 7.2, quoted in Joesph L. Mangina, *Revelation*, Brazos Theological Commentary on the Bible (Grand Rapids: Brazos, 2010), 30–31.

11. Mangina, *Revelation*, 31.

prophecy and the goal of cosmic time. Rather than Valentinus' understanding of the Spirit's rushing forward and back to the beginning, I argue that John has three specific things to say about the experience of the end and the participation in that end. Rather than muddling up the three thrusts by placing them all in one progression, he sees three different aspects to the same ending. To accomplish this argumentation he must guard against the audience thinking the end of each cycle is a finish line. Therefore, the interludes and digressions tucked away in various places among the cycles function as protections against assuming the end has arrived until the end arrives in the text. The interludes function as a kind of hesitation in the progression from the sixth to the seventh elements in the cycles of seals and trumpets.[12] This element of pause does not occur between the sixth and seventh bowl. It may be as if John is placing these pauses in the text in order to alert the audience that there is yet more to say about the end they are seeing and experiencing.[13]

This phenomenon indicates another important aspect of the cycles: their liturgical and performative aspect. There is, by nature of its textuality, a literary and narrative progression to the cycles,[14] but perhaps the most important progression is a liturgical progression. The liturgical performance of the apocalypse necessitates an experienced linearity when simultaneity cannot be reproduced in lived time. Therefore, in the midst of worship, when the Apocalypse is liturgically performed within and by the congregation[15], the interludes reserve the end for the final cycle even while one experiences the end at the conclusion of each cycle. Each end then has a slightly different aspect while containing within its logic the same goal or telos, the same principle. This is why each end also carries within it a slightly different logic of action, a slightly different eschatological and liturgical and cosmological activity, while

---

12. For a deeper discussion of how interludes functioned rhetorically in the ancient world see Peter S. Perry, *The Rhetoric of Digressions: Revelation 7:1-17 and 10:1—11:13 and Ancient Communication*, Wissenschaftliche Untersuchungen zum Neuen Testament: 2, Reihe 268, (Tübingen: Mohr Siebeck, 2009).

13. This is somewhat akin to what Dale Ralph Davis argues for, but with a different purpose, in saying that the pauses attempt to ensure that the audience does not understand "that the events of the seventh seal and seventh trumpet do not occur in immediate succession to the events which precede them," in Davis, "The Relationship Between the Seals, Trumpets, and Bowls," 152-153.

14. See Resseguie, *The Revelation of John*, 59.

15. For a sense of the Apocalypse being performed in the context of gathered worship see Ugo Vanni, "Liturgical Dialogue as a Literary Form in the Book of Revelation," *New Testament Studies* 37 (1991): 348-372; Jean-Pierre Ruiz, "Betwixt and Between on the Lord's Day: Liturgy and the Apocalypse," in *The Reality of Apocalypse: Rhetoric and Politics in the Book of Revelation*, ed. David L. Barr, SBL Symposium Series 39 (Atlanta: Society of Biblical Literature, 2006), 221-241.

keeping the same goal in mind: to participate and hasten the theophanic end, to dwell in the cosmos created, newly created, and inhabited by God and Christ. At any rate, the closely related nature of the seals is clear at the surface level, and my basic interpretation of the logic of the cycles is not fatally harmed if one does not accept this logic of recapitulation.

Relating the Cycles to the Rest of the Apocalypse

Responding to a Recent Theory

Since the cycles dominate the middle portion of the Apocalypse, it is reasonable to assume they are a major architectonic feature of the book as a whole. Therefore, it is appropriate to set out at the beginning an understanding of how the cycles fit into the vision of the entire book. One interpretation advanced recently is that all or some of the sets of seven letters, seals, trumpets, and bowls are an example of the prophetic covenant lawsuit (*rîb*).[16] Gordon Campbell advances this argument finding that each cycle produces God's case against a people who have broken the covenant contract with God and points to God's (eschatological) activity to repair the broken covenant relationship.[17] This lawsuit is based on the suzerain vassal treaty form where two parties, one more powerful than the other, agree to terms with stipulations of either blessing or cursing for following or breaking the treaty. Other scholars have put forward similar interpretations regarding the letters and cycles.[18]

While the Apocalypse does have much in common with Israelite prophecy, the argument that the cycles are based on the covenant lawsuit form is unconvincing. For one, the definition of a covenant lawsuit is a lot more precise than scholars have tended to make it. A lawsuit can only be said to take place when one party appeals against the other party to a third and impartial mediator. A grievance alone is not enough to establish the covenant lawsuit form. Michael De Roche has shown that sometimes the divine grievance is taken up and

---

16. For a thorough treatment of the concept of the prophetic lawsuit in the Old Testament see James Limburg, "The Root [*RÎB*] and the Prophetic Lawsuit Speeches," in *JBL* 88.3 (1969): 291–304.

17. Gordon Campbell, "Findings, Seals, Trumpets, and Bowls: Variations Upon the Theme of Covenant Rupture and Restoration in the Book of Revelation," in *Westminster Theological Journal* 66 (2004): 71–96.

18. See David W. Graves, *The Seven Messages of Revelation and Vassal Treaties: Literary Genre, Structure, and Function*, Gorgias Dissertations (Piscataway: Gorgias, 2009); Alan S. Bandy, *The Prophetic Lawsuit in the Book of Revelation*, New Testament Monographs 29 (Sheffield: Sheffield Phoenix, 2010); Alan S. Bandy, "The Layers of the Apocalypse: An Integrative Approach to Revelation's Macrostructure," *JSNT* 31.4 (2009): 469–499.

remedied by direct divine intervention.[19] The *rib* does not entail a covenant lawsuit. De Roche makes the distinction by saying "a *Rib* is a contention, a lawsuit is a particular way of solving a contention."[20] In the Apocalypse, God is not appealing to an impartial third party to resolve a dispute, but is instead intervening directly. This does not mean, as De Roche and David Graves point out, that John's use of the metaphor of a law court is ruled out, but it does cast doubt that John means the cycles to be taken as covenant disputation before a third-party judge.[21]

Another critique of the lawsuit approach is that apocalyptic rhetorolect, as I demonstrated in chapter 2, does not focus on confrontation within a kingdom. That is rather the basis of prophetic rhetorolect, which confronts those within a kingdom who are not living according to the righteousness of the king.[22] An apocalyptic rhetorolect, on the other hand, blends the experience of the audience within empire with the space of God as emperor and God's cosmos as an empire. Apocalyptic discourse concentrates on transformation rather than confrontation.[23] Since God is acting in the cycles with the ultimate goal of de-creation and new creation, the emphasis falls squarely on transformation—regime change—rather than confrontation intended to bring subjects into obeisance.

Finally, the prophetic lawsuit approach does not account sufficiently for the liturgical aspect of the apocalypse as a whole. The place of the Apocalypse in the gathered worship setting is not solely condemnatory, functioning as a one-way street from divine accuser to guilty audience. Rather, the audience participates in the worship and praise imaged in the work, praising along with the creatures, elders, and all of creation.[24] If the audience is participating in the

---

19. Michael De Roche, "Yahweh's *Rib* Against Israel: A Reassessment of the So-called 'Prophetic Lawsuit' in the Preexilic Prophets," *JBL* 102.4 (1983): 563–574.

20. De Roche, "Yahweh's *Rib* Against Israel," 569.

21. De Roche, "Yahweh's *Rib* Against Israel," 571; Graves, *The Seven Messages of Revelation*, 40.

22. Vernon K. Robbins, *The Invention of Christian Discourse,* Vol.1, Rhetoric or Religious Antiquity (Blandford Forum, Dorset: Deo Publishing, 2009), xxvii.

23. Robbins, *The Invention of Christian Discourse* 1, 329, 336–337, 342–345. Note especially what Robbins says at 343, "God's activities of transformation are not limited to the abilities or efforts of humans to transform themselves through repentance and obedience, nor are they limited to the abilities or efforts of humans to transform themselves during their time of life on earth . . . The processes of transformation come from the realm of God and concern God's transformation of humans, the world, and time itself into 'heaven-like' personages and spaces, and into eternal 'non-time.' " Or again at 345: "apocalyptic discourse itself is a rhetorical ritual. Through its assertions and argumentation, it recreates all regions of time and space in the body and in the world on the basis of their relation to the sacred or the profane."

worship of God and the Lamb, it is not demonstrable that they are guilty of breaking covenant or contract. Rather the participatory nature of the work is not to condemn but to redirect—from false worship to true. If the audience is participating in worship by performing the Apocalypse, they are keeping covenant; they are holding the spirit of prophecy by worshiping God and keeping the testimony of Jesus.

THE ECHOES OF NOACHIC APOCALYPTIC TRADITIONS IN THE BOOK OF REVELATION: A NEW SOLUTION

The three cycles of seven function as the engine of drama in the Apocalypse. They bridge the beginning and the end with structure as well as movement. Therefore, my own proposal relates the structures in a narratival way with both the throne-room scene in chapters 4 and 5 and the climax of the vision in the new creation envisioned in chapters 21 and 22. John's vision begins with God enthroned in heaven surrounded and praised by all manner of creation "in its right place" around the throne. John reports that the one seated on the throne is surrounded by a rainbow.[25] The presence of a rainbow signals back to Ezekiel 1:28 with a focus on the glory and splendor of God. In addition to this, in both Ezekiel and John's use of this image, the Noachic covenant stands in the background. But the visual argumentation of the rainbow does not just remind audiences of the covenant with Noah, but the entire Noah narrative in Genesis 6–9. This story is fundamentally about the unmaking and remaking of the world and would go on to provide rich fodder for apocalyptic reflection.

Indeed, in some strains of apocalyptic thought Noah functions as a bridge figure between the old and new world divided by the deluge.[26] Noah is chosen

---

24. The liturgical character to the Apocalypse is well established; see, e.g. Vanni, "Liturgical Dialogue"; Ruiz, "Betwixt and Between on the Lord's Day"; Stanley P. Saunders, "Between Blessing and Curse: Reading, Hearing, and Performing the Apocalypse in a World of Terror," in *Shaking Heaven and Earth: Essays in Honor of Walter Brueggemann and Charles B. Cousar*, ed. Christine R. Yoder, et al. (Louisville: Westminster John Knox, 2005), 141–155; Paulo Augusto de Souza Nogueira, "Celestial Worship and Ecstatic-Visionary Experience," trans. Leslie Milton in *JSNT* 25.2 (2002): 165–184.

25. The LXX consistently translates *qeset* as τόξον, as do other Greco-Roman writers (See Josephus, *Ant.* 1:103). The word here, ἶρις, is according to Aune functionally equivalent, but represents a paganization so that John's audience does not miss its significance, David E. Aune, *Revelation 1–5*, Word Biblical Commentary (Dallas: Word, 1997), 285. See also Edmondo Lupieri, *A Commentary on the Apocalypse of John*, trans. Maria Poggi Johnson and Adam Kamesar (Grand Rapids: Eerdmans, 2006), 142.

26. See the discussion of Noah as bridge figure in Andrei Orlov, " 'Noah's Younger Brother': The Anti-Noachic Polemics in *2 Enoch*," in *Henoch* 22.2 (2000): 207–221; See also Michael E. Stone, "The Axis of History at Qumran," in *Pseudepigraphic Perspectives*, ed. E. G. Chazon, et al. (Boston and Leiden: Brill, 1999), 141, 143.

as a human who is privy to God's design for future creation (and passes this knowledge on to his son Shem). But Noah is also depicted as a kind of cosmic and angelic figure, whose face is glorious and whose eyes pour forth the brightness of the sun (1 Enoch 106:4-12). Enoch explains Noah's special qualities by referring to God's activity ("The Lord will surely make new things upon the earth," 106:13) and Noah's vocation within that divine activity ("for he will comfort the earth after all the destruction," 107:3). Noah exists as a figure through whom God will "make another world rise up from his seed" (2 Enoch 70:10). The image and symbol of Noah represents God's work of cleansing the world from evil and making it a place of righteousness.

However, that is not the only aspect of the Noachic apocalyptic traditions. For the traditions realize that the deluge did not expunge evil from the earth forever. Indeed, Enoch informs Methuselah that after the flood will occur "still greater oppression than that which was fulfilled upon the earth the first time" (1 Enoch 106:19). The divine promise to abstain from destruction of the world symbolized in the rainbow is given cryptic description in the Enochic tradition. It is said to last "so long as heaven is above the earth" (55:2).[27] This probably leaves room for future divine destructive activity. Andrei Orlov has argued that the Book of Noah (of which only fragments survive[28]) probably contains a tradition that the ongoing evil after the flood was due to Noah's actions.[29] Orlov argues that 3 Baruch 4 contains a tradition with roots in the Book of Noah which depicts Noah discovering and planting a vine after the flood.[30] This vine was the tree planted by Sataniel in the Garden of Eden—the same tree that caused the fall of Adam and Eve and their expulsion from the garden. Noah inquires of God whether or not he should replant the tree and receives an affirmative answer with the caveat that he should "alter its name, and change it for the better" (3 Baruch 4:15). But the vine still possesses its evil, and becomes a root cause for the ongoing presence of evil in the post-diluvian world: "The tree still possesses its evil. Those who drink wine in excess do all evil: Brother does not show mercy to brother, nor father to son, nor son to father. And from

---

27. It is highly possible that John is taking up this idea when he pictures a heavenly city "coming down" to earth after the first heavens and earth have passed away. In the work of the one on the throne and the Lamb, heaven is no longer above the earth in John's view and therefore the suspension of divine unmaking and making new is lifted.

28. See 1 Enoch 6:1-11:2; 54:7-55:2; 60:1-24; 65:1-69:25; 106:1-107:3; Jubilees 7:20-39; 10:1-15; 20:7; 21:10; Genesis Apocryphon and Syncellus; see also Andrei Orlov, "The Flooded Arboretums: The Garden Traditions in the Slavonic Version of *3 Baruch* and the *Book of Giants*," *CBQ* 65.2 (2003), 199.

29. Orlov, "The Flooded Arboretums," 197–199.

30. See the less detailed account of Noah planting a vine upon debarkation in Jubilees 7:1; 10:1-14.

the evil of wine comes forth murder and adultery, fornication and cursing, as much evil as exists because of wine" (3 Baruch 4:16-17).

It is possible that John's throne room vision of the sea contains this understanding of the Noachic covenant coexisting with the ongoing presence of evil in the world. Scholars have debated the meaning of the various appearances of the sea in the Apocalypse, but especially the significance of "something like a sea of glass, like crystal" in front of the throne (Rev. 4:6). The sea makes several other appearances throughout the work as it is the source of the Beast in chapter 13. It seems to be an element of ordeal and judgment when the saints who refuse the beast and its image sing the song of Moses beside it in chapter 15. It is the means of ongoing trade for Babylon in chapters 17–18. These three references could point to the sea as a symbol of chaos or evil or at the very least the necessity of judgment within God's creation.[31] Therefore, the sea existing before the throne of God in heaven could signify the ongoing need for judgment in creation, the ongoing nagging presence of evil in an otherwise perfectly constructed and rightly ordered creation (Rev. 4:2-11).[32] The sea represents, following Bauckham's argument, "the destructive potential which remains to threaten the created universe."[33]

This interpretation seems to be on the right track when one considers that the new creation is described as being without a sea (21:1). Jonathan Moo argues that the absence of the sea signifies the absence of the need for judgment, because chaos and evil have been definitively defeated.[34] The sea is listed among seven elements that are no longer present in the newly created heavens and earth: sea, death, mourning, crying, pain, everything that is cursed, and night (21:1, 4; 22:3, 5).[35] Moo suggests that these elements echo the curse of sin and the entrance of evil into the world in Genesis 3:14-19 and recall certain elements of the primordial chaos at creation. The first and last of these listed elements, night and the sea, especially represent the shadow side of the good creation and the possibility of the emergence of evil (like Noah's replanted

---

31. Jonathan Moo, "The Sea That Is No More: Revelation 21:1 and the Function of Sea Imagery in the Apocalypse of John," in *Novum Testamentum* 51 (2009), 166–167.

32. McDonough argues that the throne room scene functions as "a kind of archetype of the eschaton," Sean M. McDonough "Revelation: The Climax of Cosmology" in *Cosmology and New Testament Theology*, ed. Jonathan T. Pennington and Sean M. McDonough, Library of New Testament Studies 355 (London and New York: T & T Clark, 2008), 182.

33. Richard Bauckham, *The Theology of the Book of Revelation* New Testament Theology (Cambridge: Cambridge University Press, 1993), 53.

34. Moo, "The Sea That Is No More," 166–167: "in his vision of the complete elimination of the sea and night, creation has been brought beyond any threat of future evil, chaos, or judgment."

35. Moo, "The Sea That Is No More," 149, 165.

vine). The utter absence of these elements recalls not just a return, but a renewal of the original state of creation. With the presence of the rainbow the unmaking and making new of the world in the Noah episode is called to mind, but one greater than Noah is here (see Matt. 12:6, 41, 42). With the absence of night and sea, gone too is the need for judgment. John envisions the work of Christ as having the ultimate outcome of restoring the world to a Noachic and even Adamic state, but without the necessity of judgment to rein in evil. John discerns in God and Christ's work of new creation a new Adamic humanity where God will dwell with humanity.[36] God tabernacles with this renewed Messianic-Adamic humanity in the garden-city of New Jerusalem which contains two trees of life (one on either side of the River of Life; Rev. 22:2).

Therefore, we might discern in John's description of the heavenly throne room a proleptic glimpse of the new creation: God, surrounded by all of creation in worship.[37] And yet the presence of the sea and the rainbow signals the persistence of evil in God's creation and God's purpose to do something about it. This may be the meaning of the scroll in the hand of the one on the throne and John's dismay that no one is worthy to open it. The sealed scroll represents the divine plan to get from the good creation tinged with the persistent presence of evil to the final unmaking and making new of the world when judgment shall be rendered unnecessary and God can dwell with a humanity capable of beholding God's face. Once the Lamb is deemed worthy to unseal the scroll immediately the cycles begin careening toward their inevitable conclusion. The three cycles of seven dominate both the structure and the dramatic action from this point onward to the creation of the new heaven and earth. Since these cycles seem to drive the activity of moving from troubled creation to perfect new creation, it is appropriate to see if close scrutiny yields this logic.

---

36. The LXX of Gen. 3:8 uses the term περιπατοῦωτος to speak of God's activity in Paradise (cf. Rev 2:1; 3:4; 21:24), but also notes that Adam and his wife hid from God's presence or face (προσώπου). John uses προσώπου to refer to God's presence and face in ways reminiscent of Gen. 3. In Rev. 6:16, the inhabitants of the earth call on the mountains and rocks to fall on them and hide them from the face (ἀπο προσώπου) of the one seated on the throne. In 20:11, earth and heaven flee from the face of the one seated on the throne (ἀπο τοῦ προσώπου; cf. Gen. 3:8). Finally, the inhabitants of the New Jerusalem are promised that they will see the face of the one on the throne in 22:4.

37. The theophanic presence of God with creation accomplishes the divine goal for creation. Therefore, the throneroom scene is proleptic in this sense too as the theophanic elements of lightning, rumblings, and thunder emanate from the throne (cf. Exod. 19).

Setting the Parameters of the Cycles

Close scrutiny of the entirety of every cycle would require a study more lengthy than the allotted space given here. At the same time, devoting concentrated attention to only one of the cycles would yield incomplete conclusions regarding the thrust and tenor of the cycles conceived as a whole. This interpreter is therefore faced with a conundrum: how to do justice to the epic scope of the Apocalypse while still attending carefully to the text in a limited space. In the interest of both relative brevity and thoroughness, a sensible solution is to take a more wide-angle approach with the cycles, while scrutinizing the conclusion of each cycle. This is a satisfying resolution to the conundrum because one is able to focus in on smaller portions of text while keeping the sweep of the whole in view. A careful reading of the conclusion of each cycle can tell interpreters quite a lot about the trajectory and telos of the cycles and the Apocalypse as a whole.

The only task left before digging into the details of the text is to determine the parameters of the cycles as a whole and of the conclusion of each cycle. Fortunately, there is wide agreement about most of the textual boundaries of the cycles. The cycle of seals begins with Revelation 6:1 and concludes with 8:5.[38] The cycle of trumpets consists of 8:2, 6—11:19. And finally, the cycle of bowls begins in 15:1, continues in 16:1-21, and finally concludes with 18:1—19:8.[39] The conclusion of each cycle is delimited by a recurrence of theophanic phenomena. Therefore, the texts under investigation in the

---

38. There is some discussion of whether Rev. 8:2-5 belongs to the end of the seals cycle or the beginning of the trumpets cycle. See especially the discussion in G. K. Beale, *The Book of Revelation: A Commentary on the Greek Text* (Grand Rapids and Cambridge: Eerdmans and Paternoster, 1999), 445–446.

39. This is probably the most controversial demarcation of the allotted text as it includes material that is not explicitly labeled as a feature of the bowl cycle. However, the final bowl describes the destruction of Babylon, the divine remembrance of "great Babylon," and divine judgment as a "cup." This language occurs in Rev. 16:19 and 18:5-6. Therefore, chapter 18 functions as a kind of close-up to what chapter 16 and the final seal describe from a "bird's eye view." By way of analogy, chapter 18 is the Google Street View to chapter 16's Google Earth. See Davis, "The Relationship Between the Seals, Trumpets, and Bowls," 151–152: "[W]e take it as fixed that the seventh bowl is the immediate prelude to or introduction of the parousia. It is that final number of the series explicitly said to be 'the last' (15:1); it follows immediately after the sixth bowl which depicts the *assembling* for Armageddon; and the next truly sequential event described is the second coming (19:11-21), the *conquest* of Armageddon. In regard to this last contention, it should be observed that: (1) all of chapters 17 and 18 are a 'close-up' describing the fall of Babylon in detail and therefore relates to 16:19, to be placed under the seventh bowl; (2) 19:1-10 is in bulk (vs. 1-8) a response to 18:20 and therefore related to chapters 17-18. Hence, 19:11-21 is the next event described, sequentially speaking, after the seventh bowl."

following chapters shall consist of 8:1, 3-5; 11:15-19; and 16:17-21 [18:1—19:8]. It is to the work of interpreting the rhetorical cosmological meaning of these texts that I now turn.

4

Silence: The Prayerful Endurance and Non-Participation of the Saints

> The Lamb, "as though it had been slain", rides into battle like a warrior, his garment drenched in blood, together with his "called, chosen and faithful ones", to fight against the powers and forces of the world; there seems to be no end to the cries of woe, the slaughter and annihilation. Can this darkness, this wrath that is unleashed from above and from below, these cries of anguish in the face of ever-intensifying plagues, this elegy on the (almost wanton) ruin of all that the world holds precious and enjoyable, be reconciled with the serene, ceaseless hymns of worship before the throne, on the Sea of Glass, beneath the light of the Seven Lamps of the Spirit? How does this carnage fit with the extolling of him who was, and is, and is to come, and who—when the drama is at its climax—"has begun to reign"?
>
> —Hans Urs von Balthasar, *Theo-Drama 2*[1]

In this chapter I will examine the cycle of the seven seals (6:1—8:5) but specifically the climax of the series (8:1-5). This cycle depicts the Lamb unsealing a scroll with seven seals. Each broken seal is accompanied by a scene of divine judgment, sometimes directly inflicted and other times indirectly. I will examine the series as whole in order to set the seventh seal in its proper context before going on to investigate the significance of the seventh seal. The seals cycle in general portrays judgments meted out with increasing intensity upon the earth's inhabitants who are depicted as idolatrous and hostile to the reign of God in the world. The judgments function to essentially tear the

---

1. Hans Urs von Balthasar, *Theo-Drama: Theological Dramatic Theory*, vol. 2, Dramatis Personae: *Man in God*, trans. Graham Harrison (San Francisco: Ignatius, 1990), 34.

world apart, dismantling the inhabitation of idolatry and making way for the rule of God and true worship. John's visions also function, then, as an oblique argument for his hearers to endure in their resistance to the idolatry of the inhabitants of the earth. In their persistent non-participation, they are exempt from the judgments that break down the world around them—it is as if they inhabit a different world. Finally, I will examine the breaking of the seventh seal which is accompanied by silence. I argue that this silence is the specific vocation that John seeks to persuade his audience to take up. This silence is a participation in the judgment and dissolution of the cosmic reality of Babylon-Rome and likewise a participation in the work of new creation effected by the presence of God and the Lamb. In depicting non-participation as an instrument of judgment and dismantling, John is pitting his own rhetorical cosmology (that of new and restored creation) against the cosmic construction of Rome.

Overview of the Cycle of Seven Seals

The First Four Seals Are Broken

The cycle of seven seals begins immediately after John's vision of an idealized totality of creation worshiping the one on the throne and the Lamb.[2] The Lamb had been handed the scroll that only he was worthy to unseal. In chapter 6, the unsealing of the scroll is abruptly set in motion. The cycle of seals begins with four riders on horses riding out in response to a heavenly voice. John repeatedly uses the formulae "I heard" and "I saw" which elsewhere in the Apocalypse often work at cross-purposes (see Rev. 1:12; 5:5-6; 7:4, 9).[3] John hears the voice of each of the four creatures utter the word "come."[4] John then sees four horse-riders riding out in response to each utterance. Each creature is connected to the riding out of one of the horses.

---

2. See Sean M. McDonough, "Revelation: The Climax of Cosmology," in *Cosmology and New Testament Theology*, ed. Jonathan T. Pennington and Sean M. McDonough, Library of new Testament Studies 355 (London and New York: T & T Clark, 2008), 182, who sees the throne room as an "archetype of the eschaton."

3. This is where attention to rhetography can aid interpretation. John's vision report thwarts the senses of his audience (because his own sensory perception has been thwarted) and therefore calls on them to re-see what they have heard and re-hear what they have seen. John's rhetorical cosmology builds a world that is familiar and yet at the same time somehow strange.

4. Various translations render the ἔρχου here as either "come" or "go." The difference can have a significant effect on the interpretation of the action here. If the creatures are saying "come" the horse-riders' source is probably somewhere from outside the throne, if it is rendered as "go" the throne (or at least the heavenly throne room) becomes the source from where the riders are sent.

Many commentators connect the horse-riders with the visions in Zechariah 1:7-11; 6:1-8.[5] Indeed the color schemes (red, sorrel, dappled gray, and white) are reminiscent of John's colored horses in both passages where Zechariah depicts horses and riders or charioteers as agents of divine judgment. Zechariah describes the riders as "those whom the Lord has sent to patrol the earth" (1:10). But in Zechariah their mission is connected with peace (1:11) whereas in John the second, third, and fourth horses "take peace from the earth" and bring woe in various forms (Rev. 6:4ff). Zechariah also envisions four sets of colored horses pulling chariots (Zech. 6:1-3). These charioteers are also portrayed as patrolling the earth in various directions and are connected to the four winds (6:5-8).

It would be quite easy to say that John adopts this colored horse scheme and translates it within his own vision and for his own context. However, there are a few reasons that this might be problematic. First, is the question of whether or not the horses are sent out from God or not. The horses ride out in response to the creature's utterance of ἔρχου. This is variously rendered in translation as either "come" or "go." However, this does not necessarily mean that the horses are directly sent or invited by divine action. As Edmondo Lupieri points out, the four occurrences of the word here, and the three occurrences in Revelation 22:17-20 render yet another sevenfold pattern in the Apocalypse.[6] The final three occurrences of this verb are invocations for the coming of Christ, with the last usage emphasizing and making this fact explicit: "Come, Lord Jesus" (22:20). Therefore, it is just as possible that all uses of this word are invitations for Christ to come and accomplish the divine plan for creation. In this sense, then, the horses would signify not direct divine judgment, but indirect judgment through their resistance to the coming of Christ.[7]

---

5. See David E. Aune, *Revelation 6–16*, Word Biblical Commentary (Nashville: Thomas Nelson, 1998), 390, 393; G. K. Beale, *The Book of Revelation: A Commentary on the Greek Text* (Grand Rapids and Cambridge: Eerdmans and Paternoster, 1999), 372–374.

6. Edmondo F. Lupieri, *A Commentary on the Apocalypse of John*, trans. Maria Poggi Johnson and Adam Kamesar (Grand Praids: Eerdmans, 2006), 142.

7. Contra Beale, *The Book of Revelation*, 378. This is the logic of Hans Urs von Balthasar in *Theo-Drama: Theological Dramatic Theory*, volume 4: *The Action*, trans. Graham Harrison (San Francisco: Ignatius, 1994). The action of God in Christ's saving deed is a sort of Apocalyptic provocation, designed to spur the believer to greater *disponibilitie* while having the concomitant effect of bringing sharper and more focused resistance from the secular. First, for Balthasar, the slain Lamb is God's action in the world, not merely symbolic of it: "The Lamb is God's mode of involvement in, and commitment to, the world," 52. The One who sits on the throne hands everything over to the Lamb (in a kind of liturgy, *traditio*) who then pours himself out as a sacrifice for the world, 53–55. Thus, according to Balthasar's reading, the full flowering of human fulfillment and freedom can only be found by placing oneself in the personhood

Closely related to this interpretive possibility is the second point of difference between John and Zechariah's visions. There seems to be a clear distinction between the first rider and the next three. The first rider is depicted in a way that anticipates images of Christ throughout the rest of the work. The rider on the white horse in Revelation 6 rides out with a bow in his hand, wearing a crown, and rides out with the purpose of conquering. The bow here (τόξον) is not the same word used in 4:3 (ἶρις) to describe the rainbow around the throne, but it is a Greek equivalent translation for the Hebrew word behind it: *qeset*. The Hebrew term refers to both the bow of the warrior and the rainbow.[8] David Aune argues that in 4:3 John probably chose the pagan term so as to avoid confusion that he was referring to a rainbow.[9] However, it is highly probable that the word "bow" here is meant to evoke that Noachic image of the unmaking and making new of the world both in its covenantal and divine warrior connotations.[10] God is depicted as "bending a bow" (τόξον) in the context of divine judgment and vindication in Psalm 7:13 LXX.

Another rider on a white horse appears in Revelation 19:11-16 and is a clear reference to Christ. This rider also has diadems on his head and rides out to conquer his enemies. In 14:14 Christ is introduced as Son of Man and is described as wearing a golden crown and carrying a weapon (possibly a bow).[11]

---

of this slain Lamb and consequently sharing in his victory. However, the handing over of the Father to the Son, and the Son to the world also produces resistance. The key consequence of Christ's atoning work on the cross is not pacification but an intensification of struggle. Resistance comes from those who wish to locate the source of their personhood in something other than the person and mission of Christ. The Apocalypse of Christ provokes the resistance to attempt to construct a worldly kingdom, created according to human means and methods of worldly power, 425. This results in a perverse mimicry of the means and methods of the kingdom, as those who choose to reject the slain Lamb opt instead for the anti-Logos, the beast. The beast is named in worship as fundamentally competitive (Rev. 13:4). The beast receives a mortal wound but is healed (closing the wound unlike the Lamb's wounds which remain open), it performs miracles that Jesus refused to do, and its only link to God is the blasphemy written on its heads and horns, 450–451. These grotesqueries demonstrate that even when attempting to make a kingdom from material other than the Lamb's victory, the strategy still relies on the priority of God's action in Christ.

8. David E. Aune, *Revelation 1–5,* Word Biblical Commentary (Dallas: Word, 1997), 285. The LXX consistently translates *qeset* as τόξον, as do other Greco-Roman writers (See Josephus, *Ant.* 1:103).

9. Aune, *Revelation 1–5,* 286.

10. It is certainly not the case, as Harrington argues, that John here is hoping for a Parthian invasion of and victory over Rome, Wilfrid J. Harrington, *Revelation,* Sacra Pagina 16 (Collegeville: Liturgical, 1993), 89. Such a hope for the defeat of Rome by yet another foreign power through military force flies in the face of the logic of John's Apocalypse which imagines force of might conquered by resolute weakness, the Lamb conquering a beast by being conquered by it.

11. Beale, *The Book of Revelation,* 375.

Christ is also depicted elsewhere in the book of Revelation as a conquering one (see 3:21; 5:5; 17:14). In the letters, the primary image of an ideal and obedient reader is rendered as "one who conquers" (2:7, 11, 17, 26, 28; 3:5, 12, 21). The beast is also imaged as a conqueror of the saints (11:7; 13:7) but the overall usage of the terminology refers to Christ and his followers. It may also be significant that when the best conquers, the verb carries a direct object, while when Christ and his followers conquer the verb often does not carry the direct object.[12] Brian Blount demurs on the possibility of the first rider being Christ because Christ is here envisioned as breaking the seals.[13] However, this does not seem to be an impassable obstacle. A book that so thoroughly thwarts the senses and so masterfully rejects literalist rendering of its imagery would hardly be incapable of depicting a single agent busy with two simultaneous tasks.

A few other loosely connected points indicate that John is not adopting wholesale the horse-judgment vision of Zechariah. The horse-riders are not connected to the four winds as they are in Zechariah 6:1-5. Instead, John connects the four winds with four angels in Revelation 7:1. If John meant to evoke the Zechariah image in a deep way he could have easily connected the horse-riders to the four winds at their appearing or even at 7:1 by saying that the angels were holding back the four winds "which are the four horse-riders." This also might fortify the idea discussed previously that the horse-riders are indirect rather than direct agents of divine judgment. In uncoupling the horses from the four winds, John is uncoupling the idea of the horses as agents sent out from the presence of the throne ("the four winds of heaven going out, after presenting themselves before the Lord of all the earth" Zech. 6:5). In addition to this Beale suggests that another text might also stand behind the seals cycle. Leviticus 26:14-28 portrays divine judgment as increasingly devastating on those who refuse to abide covenant statutes. There are four such announcements of judgment which include drought, sword, death, and famine.[14] The Leviticus background assumes judgment on the specific sin of idolatry (26:1), so this would certainly fit as a background to John's own polemic against the idolatry of the imperial cult.

Overall, in interpreting the images of the horse-riders it is best to approach the images of the first four seals within the total thematic unity of the work itself, rather than letting the intertextuality govern the interpretation alone. John is taking up images given to him from the Hebrew Scriptures, but is

---

12. This fact is noted but its ultimate significance is rejected by Beale, *The Book of Revelation*, 375.

13. Brian K. Blount, *Revelation: A Commentary*, New Testament Library (Louisville: Westminster John Knox, 2009), 124.

14. Beale, *The Book of Revelation*, 373.

recontextualizing them and in some cases giving them drastically different significance.[15] In this case, the general sweep of the work envisions the coming of Christ into history eliciting Satanic and demonic resistance (see especially Rev. 12:1-9, 13-13:10). I argue that the first horse as Christ and the next three as malevolent forces seems to fit well with this scheme.[16] Whether the horse-riders are seen as agents of indirect or direct judgment, the point John makes is that they are to be seen as judgment upon the world.[17] Blount makes this point clear, reminding readers that the voice concerning weights and measures indicating famine comes from the throne and is therefore best understood as the divine voice.[18]

In addition, the fourth rider is said to be accompanied by Death and Hades, while earlier Christ was said to have the keys to Death and Hades. Blount asks whether Christ let them slip out as he made his own escape or whether he even intentionally breaks them out of captivity.[19] Whether as direct or indirect agents of judgment, Christ is loose out among the world where also range Death, Hades, and divine judgment. To them it is given to do their worst, even to those who belong to Christ, because Christ has already faced their worst and has endured and conquered them and their power (5:5, 9). Because of this he is the agent of new creation in the midst of the deconstruction of the first creation or "world." The saints, too, can participate in his victory over the agents of evil with their own endurance and conquering (12:11; 13:10). In this way they are

---

15. These Old Testament images are given, in the idiom of Austin Farrer, "rebirth." Austin Farrer, *A Rebirth of Images: The Making of Saint John's Apocalypse* (Boston: Beacon, 1949).

16. In this case, rather than the four horses seen as operating as one unit, we might see emerge a 1 3 scheme. The three remaining horses after the first might then correspond to other sets of three in the Apocalypse such as the three woes (8:13; 9:12; 11:14) and the three angels flying in midheaven (14:6-11). It is interesting to observe that the schema of "four horsemen" is only a recent development in interpreting this passage. Most patristic and medieval interpretations distinguish the first rider from the subsequent three, seeing the first as a representation of Christ's entry into the world and the general spread of his message. According to Kovacs and Rowland, it was Albrecht Dürer's lumping of the "four horsemen" together that proved an influential catalyst for later scholarship and art linking them together in a continuous chain, Judith Kovacs and Christopher Rowland, *Revelation: The Apocalypse of Jesus Christ*, Blackwell Bible Commentaries (Malden and Oxford: Blackwell, 2004), 93.

17. See the discussion in Lupieri, *A Commentary on the Apocalypse of John*, 143–144 regarding the passive nature of the first three riders: the first conquers but is not shown in the act of killing, the second is said to take peace from the earth but it is the humans who do the killing of each other, and finally the third rider arrives not with an instrument of famine, but with an instrument of measurement. It is finally, only the fourth rider, accompanied by death and Hades that is said to have an active role in killing with sword, famine, and pestilence.

18. Blount, *Revelation*, 127.

19. Blount, *Revelation*, 130.

also seen as participants in Christ's work of new creation. More needs to be said about this phenomenon but it will have to be put aside until we come to the end of the seals cycle.

Taken together, the four horse-riders represent John's vision of the situation of his community and of his world.[20] John clearly sees a deterioration of a world order that may have once been considered stable (hence the image of taking peace away from the earth and a market that once had a sense of equity now being thrown off kilter by famine). This once stable world order now cast into turmoil was the counterfeit world of Rome. John sees in the riders a sense of divine judgment upon this demonic imitation. Through the riders, whether directly or indirectly, God is bringing an end to this world. The elements of plague depicted in the seals (both in the four horse-riders and in the sixth seal) are very similar to the signs of the end of the age in the so called "Little Apocalypses" of the Synoptic gospels (see especially Mark 13:4-8, 24-29; Matt. 24:3-8, 29-33). This parallel suggests that the phenomena accompanying the four riders are signs of the unmaking and remaking of the world through the work of Christ. It is, after all, the Lamb who is unsealing the scroll. Just as in the synoptic accounts so in John's vision, the coming of Christ into the cosmos spells the end of the current configuration of the world. War, famine, the displacement of the cosmic bodies, an earthquake—these are all signs that the end is near for the current arrangement of things in the cosmos.

The main thrust of all of this, then, is judgment. Vindictive judgment is not solely envisaged here; rather this judgment is intended to bring about repentance (see Rev. 9:20-21; 11:13). The fact that the plagues and the judgments do not destroy all of the earth or its inhabitants indicates that there is yet a divine hope that the inhabitants of the earth will turn away from their evil and practice true worship and holiness. However, the fact that the horse riders set out in response to the creatures' calls for the divine coming show that this state of repentance is not present on the earth. Rather than repentance, the plagues evoke further resistance. Instead of justice and righteousness violence, social dissolution, and inequity rule the day—a state of affairs that John knows will excessively affect Christians who refuse the benefits of the idolatrous Roman economy.[21] Resistance to the divine rule will therefore require further judgment because the desired repentance has yet to appear.

---

20. Elisabeth Schüssler Fiorenza, *Revelation: Vision of a Just World*, Proclamation Commentaries (Minneapolis: Fortress Press, 1991), 63, argues that "the first four seals do not portray a sequence of events but instead reveal and highlight the true nature of Roman power and rule."

21. See Beale, *The Book of Revelation*, 381.

THE FIFTH AND SIXTH SEALS AND AN INTERLUDE

It is with this in mind that one expects an intensification of judgment with each new seal until the cycle is brought to its dreadful conclusion. It is somewhat surprising, therefore, that the drama comes to a temporary halt with the fifth seal. John sees the souls of those who had been slain by holding to the testimony and word of God. Blount rightly notes that holding to this testimony is equivalent in John to a non-accommodating and resistant stance towards Roman idolatry and culture.[22] John sees the souls of these who have resisted participation in the Roman system (and consequently its world constructing activity) residing under the altar. Their prayer for deliverance and justice assumes the out-of-joint nature of a world where those holding the testimony of Christ are killed ("how long will it be before you judge and avenge our blood on the inhabitants of the earth?" 6:10). The seals cycle is again demonstrating that its major concern is the state of the cosmos and how this state cannot last long.

The prayer also anticipates the opening of the final seal where the prayers of the saints are said to participate in not only the judgment of the world but also its divine visitation (8:3-5). But already in the vision of the souls under the altar John is making a connection between the saints' prayerful non-participation which leads to death and the idea of bringing the process of the seals to completion (6:9-10).[23] In witnessing the encouragement of those under the altar, John's audience is likewise encouraged to remain steadfast in their resistance to participation in Roman cultic cosmological discourse. The souls are to remain at rest until the full number of their fellow resisters are killed (6:11).[24]

---

22. Blount, *Revelation*, 131.

23. We should probably understand the reference to the future deaths of the saints as a rhetorical image for John rather than a reality for the churches in Asia Minor. Paul Duff makes the case that there is very little evidence of widespread persecution or even serious harassment and that the crisis has its source within the churches (i.e. amongst John and his opponents), Paul D. Duff, *Who Rides the Beast? Prophetic Rivalry and the Rhetoric of Crisis in the Churches of the Apocalypse* (Oxford: Oxford University Press, 2001), 126–127. In support of this is the fact that the only martyr to be mentioned by name in the book is Antipas (Rev. 2:12).

24. John cements a strong connection between worship of and testimony to God and the Lamb and the non-participation in Roman cultic discourse in his use of the word "altar" (θυσιαστηρίου). This term is significant in the OT tradition, where it refers to the altar of burnt offering or incense in the temple, Aune, *Revelation 6–16*, 405. Boll points to the fact that there was a constellation named "Altar" in the southern sky within the Milky Way. Boll argues that the souls clothed in white are stars in the Milky Way covered with this "Altar" constellation, *Offenbarung*, 32--35; see also Malina, *Revelation*, 128–32. While this reading by itself remains largely unconvincing (the altar is located within the heavenly temple, as John depicts in several other places in the Apocalypse) it does remain interesting on the level of

It is not exactly clear how this anticipation of the future deaths of saints relates to the interlude in chapter 7 where the servants of God are to be sealed with what is most likely a seal of protection (7:3; 9:4). It is possible that the seals represent a protection not from Roman violence, but rather from divine judgment.[25] If this is the case we can already see how the cycles, though recapitulating each other, exist as different approaches to one set of events. The three horse-riders after the first rider are envisioned as having some authority from God for the purpose of judgment, but the emphasis is placed on their task as agents of unrighteousness. They represent a dissenting opinion on the cultic cosmological discourse of Rome. Rather than a golden age, it is portrayed by John as a world severely disoriented. It exists in a state of deterioration from the inside as it begins to fall apart in response to those who refuse its foundational assumptions. These same circumstances will be portrayed in the cycles of trumpets and bowls as divine plague judgments, but here they stand as distortions of God's good creation by those purportedly in charge. The sealed therefore are exempt from divine judgment because they bear the signs of belonging to God.[26] Yet it is for this very reason that they are subject to the violence of Rome—the seal marks them out as possessions of another God and another world. Whereas the beast causes all who worship him to receive its mark which designates all who bear it for earthly comfort but divine judgment, God's worshipers bear the seal of protection which separates them out for death in the kingdom of the world but for protection from divine judgment of that world (see 9:4; 13:16-17; 16:2).[27]

If the riders represent the state of disarray of the world under the reign of Rome, and the fifth seal depicts the state of God's servants languishing under this reign, then the sixth seal can finally be understood as direct divine intervention in light of this state of affairs. This seal depicts the beginning of the process of the deconstruction of the cosmos. The first sign of this is the appearance of the earthquake (6:12). This is the first appearance of the earthquake in John's vision, but it will hardly be the last of a motif that suggests the visitation and theophany of God amongst creation. Richard Bauckham argues that the earthquake in the poetic reflection of the tradition of Sinai becomes one of the more crucial images of divine visitation of and intervention

---

the cosmic deconstruction and reconstruction for which I am making a case. The world as construed by Rome is being undone and reconfigured around these divine and heavenly centers (God, the Lamb, the angels, and heaven's temple).

25. See Schüssler Fiorenza, *Revelation*, 66.
26. Blount, *Revelation*, 143; Aune, *Revelation 6–16*, 455.
27. Lupieri, *A Commentary on the Apocalypse of John*, 148–149.

in creation.[28] Bauckham also notices the importance of the earthquake within the four theophanic visions in John's Apocalypse (4:5; 8:5; 11:19; 16:18-21).[29] The earthquake is not present in the vision of God seated on the throne in chapter 4 but makes an appearance in increasing intensity at the other points of the text. This suggests that in the heavenly throne room, as the model of all creation (see the discussion in chapter 3 of this study), everything is as it should be. But when the divine presence visits earth in judgment and rectification things get a bit bumpy. The divine act of judgment and new creation encounters the world with turbulence and turmoil because that world is constructed in an antithetical way to the divine reign.

The earthquake is accompanied by what Beale calls "stock-in-trade Old Testament imagery" in depicting the dissolution of the world.[30] The prophetic tradition is thick with references to the shaking of the earth, the darkening or shaking of the cosmic bodies like the moon, stars, sun, and heavens, and the pouring out of blood (See Isa. 13:10-13; 24:1-6, 19-23; 34:4; Ezek. 32:6-8; Joel 2:10; 30-31; 3:15-16 and Hab. 3:6-11). These texts formed the basis of reflection about the end of the cosmos in other New Testament texts besides the Apocalypse (see Matt. 24:29; Mark 13:24-25; Acts 2:19-20). This makes it likely that the imagery is to be taken figuratively rather than literally, since the same phenomena are applied to disparate events throughout the New Testament (whereas Acts has the imagery anticipate and describe the events of Pentecost, in the gospels Jesus uses the same imagery to describe the *parousia* of the Son of Man).[31] These texts supplied the matrix through which John could interpret his vision for his audience, describing through rhetorical cosmological discourse what he perceives as happening in a hidden way.

These signs in the prophetic tradition signal judgment at God's coming. When John describes the sky being darkened "like sackcloth," he probably has Isaiah 50:3 in the background, where the same wording is used (ὡς σάκκον). The imagery of sackcloth confirms the judgment motif and prefigures another use by John in the cycle of trumpets, where the two witnesses are clothed in sackcloth (Rev. 11:3). This divine judgment is further demonstrated in the shaking and displacement of the stars, mountains, and islands (6:13-14). Beale suggests that these elements signify human or divine powers that can be good or evil in the LXX and OT Pseudepigrapha.[32] John depicts the dissolution of the

---

28. Richard Bauckham, *The Climax of Prophecy: Studies on the Book of Revelation* (London and New York, T & T Clark, 1993), 199–202.

29. Bauckham, *The Climax of Prophecy*, 202–204.

30. Beale, *The Book of Revelation*, 398.

31. See Beale, *The Book of Revelation*, 397–398.

"islands and mountains" as the fall of Babylon, an evil regime resistant to divine rule (16:20).

Another text that stands prominently behind this cosmic imagery is Isaiah 34:3-4. John describes the moon becoming like blood. This sanguinization of the moon causes it to lose its function as a cosmic luminary. Isaiah 34:3-4 connects blood with the melting or rotting away of the heavens and depicts God's sword as "sated with blood" (34:6). The connotations in the Isaiah text are of judgment and sacrifice both in heaven and in the nations of the earth. The judging activity of God is enacted with such an intensity that it dismembers the cosmos. As R. H. Charles puts it, "The world and its wellbeing depend on the faithfulness with which the luminaries of heaven fulfil [sic] their parts . . . When, then, the sun and moon and stars forsook this order, the end of the world was at hand."[33] Another way of stating this is that when the cosmic bodies move from their place, whether from forsaking their orderly place or by divine intervention, one knows that the intervention of God is at hand. Judgment and the displacement of the cosmos go hand in hand.

Another parallel element between Isaiah 34 and this sixth seal is the sky being rolled up as a scroll. Beale suggests that this image depicts the heavens receding in such a way that "its contents are no longer visible."[34] It is probably not incidental that this image is picked up and used by John in the cycle of the sealed scroll. Indeed, this is a significant element of the overall coherence of the seals cycle: the cosmological elements—those markers of stability and intelligibility—are disappearing from knowledge and availability even as the mysterious contents of the sealed scroll are being revealed. At the coming of God, the cosmos loses its place as dominant signifier while the presence of God becomes more and more crucial for understanding what is happening to the whole of creation. The sky-scroll episode is a microcosm of John's logic in the Apocalypse in general.

Whereas Beale concentrates on the imagery as a recollection of the prophetic tradition, there is another interesting layer to attend to in these cosmic signs. Aune posits that for a Roman inhabitant the sky turning black like sackcloth would be perceived as *"auspicia oblativa,* i.e., unsought signs."[35] Sky

---

32. Beale, *The Book of Revelation*, 399. Stars: Judg. 5:20; Dan. 8:10; Deut. 4:19; Isa. 14:12; 24:21; Jer. 8:2; Wis. 13:2; mountains: Dan. 2:44; 4 Ezra 13:6-7; Zech. 4:7; Jer. 51:25; 1 Enoch 18:13; 21:3; 52; 108:4; 2 Baruch 36-40; islands: Ps. 71[72]:10; 96[97]:1; Isa. 41:1; 45:16; 49:1, 22; 51:5; 60:9; Jer. 38:10; Ezek. 26:18; Zech. 2:11; 1 Macc. 8:11.

33. R. H. Charles, *A Critical and Exegetical Commentary on The Revelation of St. John*, vol. 1, The International Critical Commentary (Edinburgh: T & T Clark, 1920), 180–181.

34. Beale, *The Book of Revelation*, 397. This image is also present in *Sibylline Oracles* 3:82.

phenomena like eclipses and darkenings of the sun and moon were perceived frequently as omens and portents. Aune points to the ominous character of such things in Greco-Roman dream interpretation, quoting Artemidorus who characterized a sun "dim or diffused with blood, or hideous to behold . . . [as] inauspicious and evil for all men."[36] The divine theophanic judgment is not the only tradition standing alongside John's vision here, he also has in mind the way such phenomena would be perceived by non-Jewish inhabitants of Rome. Once again we can see the intentionality of John in portraying the entrance of God into the world as the breakdown and deconstruction of the Roman cosmological stability. God's coming in judgment means the breakdown of the Roman cosmological order and along with it the breakdown of the cultic system of sacrifice (see the discussion of the breaking of the contract with the gods in chapter 2).[37]

This cosmic upheaval causes the inhabitants of the earth to, quite literally, head for the hills (Rev. 6:15b). John uses the incredibly long circumlocution "the kings of the earth and the magnates and the generals and the rich and the powerful and everyone slave and free" (6:15) to refer to everyone on the earth (excluding perhaps the followers and worshipers of the Lamb). This vivid imagery portrays the powerful and well-to-do as ones who have benefited from the way the world works according to Rome.[38] But John wants to make clear that this is not simply a critique of the rich and powerful, but exists as a critique of *all* participants in the system of idolatry that constructs and

---

35. Aune, *Revelation 6–16*, 413.

36. Aune, *Revelation 6–16*, 413.

37. See Aune's discussion of "prodigies" or portents in the Greco-Roman world in *Revelation 6–16*, 416–419. Prodigies were understood to be signs of the anger of a god (*ira deum*) and signaled the end of peace with the gods (*pax deorum*). Aune argues that the idea of prodigies in the ancient world were so common that they became a kind of literary form, symbolically indicating upheaval and turmoil. Aune writes, "Phenomena considered to be prodigies included eclipses of the sun and moon (Plutarch *Alex.* 31), the raining of blood and stones, unusual hail, lightning, thunderclaps in a clear sky (Cassius Dio 37.25.2), comets, meteors, earthquakes, and the behavior of birds, the sight and sound of armies in the sky, the sound of clashing arms and horses (Appian *Bell. civ.* 4.1.4), and the sweating, weeping, or moving of statues (Appian *Bell. civ.* 4.1.4)," 417. Aune also argues that all the plagues in the Apocalypse may appropriately fall into the category of prodigy because they are restricted to certain heavenly or terrestrial phenomena, 418–419. The portrayal of these plagues as prodigious in nature is likely not incidental to John's project because, as we will see in the trumpets and bowls cycles, he takes over the plagues of Egypt—specifically not considered prodigies since they are acts of God through Moses—and makes them occur in his own vision without human agency, 418.

38. Robert H. Mounce, *The Book of Revelation*, rev. ed., NICNT (Grand Rapids: Eerdmans, 1998), 152: this imagery emphasizes "that those who might normally have reason to feel secure will be utterly undone."

sustains the Roman cosmological ideology.[39] All who participate in this system are implicated in its condemnation, not just "great ones" but also "slaves" and "poor" (see 18:23; 1:1; 2:20; 3:17; 13:16; 19:18).

There is also a strong connection between the various members of the group listed here and idolatry. This is a characteristic way of cataloguing the enemies of God (see Ps. 2:1-2; Isa. 24:21; *Sibylline Oracles* 3:663; 4 Ezra 15:20; 1 Enoch 38:5; 55:4; 62:1, 3, 6, 9; 63:1, 2, 12; 67:8, 12).[40] John uses this characterization of earth dwellers again when he depicts all who worship the beast participating in its idolatrous economy (Rev. 13:16-17). Further, John portrays these people as hiding themselves in caves and among the rocks of the mountains. Beale points out that this wording is very similar to what is used in Isaiah 2:10, 18-21: "You enter into the rocks and hide yourselves in the earth from the presence of the terror of the Lord . . . But the idols will completely vanish. And they will go into caves of the rocks and into holes of the ground before the terror of the Lord . . . In that day they will cast away to the moles and bats their idols of silver and their idols of gold, which they made for themselves to worship."[41]

That this group of people retreats to these havens demonstrates that they have not turned away and repented from their idolatry. Their resistance persists despite the fact that their world crumbles around them. The presence of the mountains and rocks is another indicator that the world has not been completely dissolved, just severely reorganized. Creation and the inhabitants of the earth flee the presence of the one on the throne, calling to mind the actions of Adam and Eve in hiding from the presence of the Lord when they had sinned (Gen. 3:9).[42] The idolaters call for the mountains and rocks to fall on them, preferring to die along with their world system, rather than face the justice and judgment of the Lamb. It is those who cling to their idolatrous practices and the world it makes possible who are doomed along with it when that world is deconstructed (see Rev. 12:11; 18:4). The idolaters are so wrapped up in their world that they cannot imagine an alternative. Therefore, they conclude with the question "who is able to stand" in the presence of the one on the throne and the Lamb (6:17)?

Their question is answered almost immediately when John reports seeing an uncountable multitude standing before the throne (7:9). This group is to

---

39. See Aune, *Revelation 6–16*, 419, who argues that the phrase for John has a democratizing effect in portraying all those fearful at the arrival of the one on the throne.

40. See Aune, *Revelation 6–16*, 419.

41. Beale, *The Book of Revelation*, 400.

42. Beale, *The Book of Revelation*, 400; Mounce, *The Book of Revelation*, 152.

be understood as the same group of 144,000 sealed from the tribes of Israel (7:4-8). The reconstituted tribes are numbered in a way that demonstrates fullness and completion. John hears the number, understanding that it is the full reconstitution of the people of God, but when he sees this group it turns out to be an expanded vision of God's people from every nation, language, and tribe. This is more than a remnant, it is a vision of hope that there are many who do not belong to the "inhabitants of the earth" and do not face their judgment.[43] That this group is able to stand before the throne and the Lamb signifies that the deconstruction of the world depicted in the sixth seal does not affect them.

How is this the case? We have already above discussed the seals as a signifier of belonging to God over and against the economic mark as the signifier of belonging to the beast. This logic extends all the way to the world that each of these groups inhabit—the discursively constructed cosmology within which each exist. Those who are sealed stand confidently before the throne, praising God and the Lamb for salvation, while the inhabitants of the earth lament the loss of their sturdy world.[44] The people praising God have "come out of the ordeal" and have "washed their robes and made them white in the blood of the Lamb" (7:14). Their resistance to the idolatry of their culture matches the resistance modeled by the Lamb. Just as he was slain, so their garments are washed in blood. On account of their resistance, however, they have somehow been excluded from the judgments visited upon the inhabitants

---

43. The designation of "inhabitants of the earth" represents for John a people hostile to the reign of God as they are depicted at various points as worshiping the beast and not having their names in the book of life; he uses it again in Rev. 8:13; 11:10; 13:8, 12, 14; 17:2, 8. See Peter S. Perry, *The Rhetoric of Digressions: Revelation 7:1-17 and 10:1–11:13 and Ancient Communication,* Wissenchaftliche Untersuchungen zum Neuen Testament: 2. Reihe 268 (Tübingen: Mohr Siebeck, 2009), 224.

44. This is the significance of the four winds being held back until the servants of God are sealed (Rev. 7:2-3). The four winds have their parallel with the horse rider motif in Zech. 6:4-5, but as I argued above John does not connect them directly with the horse-riders. A closer parallel may be found in the appearance of the four winds motif in the "Little Apocalypse" of the Synoptic gospels (Mark 13:27; Matt. 24:31). Here the four winds are connected closely with the shaking and displacement of the cosmic bodies, along with war and famine warnings that sound similar to the language of the seals plagues. In the Synoptic account, the four winds seem to have a gathering function, so that the elect are gathered out of the tumult. However, John's use of the four winds seems to take a different tack. He perceives the four winds as the instruments that will damage the earth, the sea, and the trees (Rev. 7:1-3). The four winds do not gather the elect, rather they are restrained until God's servants are marked out for special protection. It is assumed that once they are marked out the winds can go about their task of damaging the cosmic elements of the earth, the sea, and trees. In John's view, then, God's servants are not taken out of the turmoil, but exist within it, without feeling the effects of the deconstruction of the world. Hence, they must not be a part of that constructed world that is being judged.

of the earth. Somehow their world is not falling apart, even as the plagues dismantle the cosmos.

This interlude or digression between the sixth and the seventh seal is meant to depict the safety and confidence of those in John's audience who buy into his vision of costly witness. Their resistance allows them to absent themselves from the judgment upon the idolatrous cosmic reality. Their refusal to participate in Roman economic activity and discourse has enabled them to stand while judgments and plagues swirl around them.[45] The interlude is thus meant to argue on a visual and emotional level. John wants to comfort his audience—instill faith rather than fear—even as he argues for them to take up a posture of resistance unto death.[46] John wants them to be a separate people in encouraging their resistance to idolatry, so he portrays them as a separate people in that the judgments and plagues do no fall on them.[47]

Instead, the saints are pictured as those who remain in worship in God's temple. Neither the plagues, nor the elements will harm them. John has it this way: "They will hunger no more, and thirst no more, the sun will not strike them, nor any scorching heat" (7:16). Two reasons are given for this status for the saints. First, the one seated on the throne shelters them (literally "tabernacles" σκηνώσει, 7:15). Second, the Lamb will guide them to "springs of the water of life" (ζωῆς πηγὰς ὑδάτων, 7:17). And, third, there will be no more tears. All of these images appear in the vision of the new creation. John hears a voice declare that the home (σκηνὴ) of God is among mortals and that God will tabernacle (σκηνώσει) with them (21:3). The river of the water of life (ὕδατος ζωῆς) also flows through the center of the New Jerusalem (22:1-2, 17). Finally, God will wipe every tear away and crying will be no more in the heavenly city (21:4). Not only are the saints exempt from the turmoil and ordeal of judgment upon the cosmos, they are pictured as proleptically enjoying the benefits of the new creation. The reason for this is God's arrival among them. The interlude comes to an end; the stage is set and all that remains is for the seventh seal to be opened and the final plague to befall the earth-dwellers.

THE SEVENTH SEAL: SILENCE

The silence in heaven that accompanies the seventh seal is a topic of much debate among scholars. One of the reasons for this is that it is unexpectedly

---

45. Perry, *The Rhetoric of Digressions*, 238: "The scenes of protection, worship, prophecy, and witness stand like islands of mercy in a sea of judgment and destruction."

46. Perry, *The Rhetoric of Digressions*, 235–237, 240–241.

47. Perry, *The Rhetoric of Digressions*, 240.

anti-climactic. The interlude between the sixth and seventh seal was devoted to the preparation and protection of those belonging to God from the judgment of God that would damage the earth, the sea, and the trees (7:2-3). This is the most-likely expected content of the seventh seal, yet, like so many other times in the Apocalypse, expectations are thwarted. This has led some scholars to suggest that the seventh seal has no content and is just a container for the series of trumpets that follows.[48] My own approach will be to view the silence as a multivalent image denoting a range of ideas from judgment to liturgy and prayer to the new creative work of God. The silence is a part of the events that occur when the seventh seal is broken[49] which go to make up the whole of the content of the vision. I will make this case below and then conclude by drawing together what this means for John's overall strategy of rhetorical cosmology.

Silence is first of all a contrast to the bombastic auditory imagery John has utilized in the seals cycle up to this point.[50] The sudden absence of noise after the crescendo of sounds marks this off as something different within the cycle. This seal is not simply built into the series, but represents some sort of break within the sequence. It is not just the next element; it is set off as special. Therefore, we may regard the silence not as just another part of the ongoing process, but rather the pinnacle of the cycle. If the cosmos John has been describing up to this point has been characterized by an abundance of sounds, that world has abruptly been stilled or halted. The events that accompany this unsealing are not an inevitable unfolding of the regular progression of history. The audience should understand them rather as the height of the divine work, the event of divine visitation and intervention. This is borne out by the theophanic imagery about which I will say more later.

The silence lasts, according to John, for about half an hour (ὡς ἡμιώριον). There is no more mention of half an hour in the Apocalypse, but the period of one hour appears in several other places (17:12; 18:10, 17, 19).[51] These specific instances of an hour refer to the undoing of the kingdom, rule, and prosperity of Babylon.[52] Therefore, we should probably understand the half hour in a similar

---

48. See, for example, George Eldon Ladd, *A Commentary on the Revelation of John* (Grand Rapids: Eerdmans, 1972), 122.

49. The half-hour of silence implies that it is not the full event of the seventh seal.

50. John includes depictions of noises like voices as loud as thunder (6:1), crying out with a loud voice (6:10; 7:2, 10), and a great earthquake (6:12).

51. This designation of one hour as the undoing of Babylon's economic prosperity is also connected with the idea of silence (18:22-23).

52. There is another possible aspect of the "hour" that may bear significance for the Johannine literature more broadly. The Gospel of John portrays and gives special emphasis to the event of Jesus' death as his "hour" (John 2:4; 5:25, 28 (?); 7:30; 8:20; 12:23; 13:1; 16:21, 25; 17:1). If there is a connection

way: a finite and delimited period of time of ambiguous length that stands in for the undoing of the reign of a regime hostile to God and the Lamb.[53] However, the specific designation of half an hour as opposed to one full hour probably means that this silence does not represent the full judgment or divine activity.[54] The silence represents half of this phenomenon, but the audience should expect more in order to complete the divine activity. This is how we should understand the content of verses 3-5, as the supplement to the half-hour of divine silence.

There are a range of things the silence could signify for John. One option first put forth by Charles is that the silence makes it possible for the prayers of the saints to be heard before the throne of God.[55] Charles supports this interpretation by referring to the Babylonian Talmud (*b. Ḥag.* 12b), which depicts companies of angels who praise God ceaselessly by day, but are silent by night "because of the glory of Israel." The angels are silent, in other words, in order to enable the prayers and praises of Israel to rise before God's throne. Bauckham declares this interpretation as "the correct interpretation."[56] However, there is no indication in the text that God is incapable of hearing the prayers of the saints, even over the din that has preceded this silence.[57] Indeed, quite the opposite seems to be true in Revelation 6:11 where the prayer of the saints under the altar is given a response.

Aune prefers and proffers a liturgical understanding of the silence. He points to the silence that is to be maintained in the presence of God during and in the incense offering of the temple cult (Ps. 62:1; Hab. 2:20; Testament of Adam 1:12).[58] In Greek ritual also, silence was a liturgical prelude to prayer (which fits the order John presents here).[59] Beale also notes a scheme where this silence could be understood as a reference to part of the daily sacrifice ritual in the temple as portrayed in the Mishnah (*m. Tamid*).[60] This liturgical act is

---

here, it would signify that the undoing of the world as an orientation set against God happens in the crucifixion. The hour of Jesus death is the hour of the Lamb's costly witness which undoes the idolatrous world. See the discussion of "one hour" in chapter 6, below.

53. Contra Bauckham, *The Climax of Prophecy*, 83. See also Blount, *Revelation*, 157, who argues that each of John's subsequent uses of the concept of half denote "either the judgment/destruction of those who have persecuted God's people (11:9, 11) or the salvation of those whose witness endures (12:14)."

54. See James L. Resseguie, *The Revelation of John: A Narrative Commentary* (Grand Rapids: Baker Academic, 2009), 142.

55. Charles, *The Revelation of St. John* 1, 223-224.

56. Bauckham, *The Climax of Prophecy*, 70.

57. See Aune, *Revelation 6-16*, 507.

58. Aune, *Revelation 6-16*, 508.

59. Aune, *Revelation 6-16*, 508.

convincing especially in light of the overall liturgical flavor of the Apocalypse. It is indeed a document that John intends to be read aloud in the gathered worship of local church communities. If the reader was a good narrator, the sounds would be emphasized, and therefore so would the silence, thus heightening the anticipation of what would come next. In the gathered worship setting, when the silence is read, the audience participates in that silence by listening along.

The liturgical aspect of the silence is incomplete, however, without acknowledging the importance of judgment and silence. Beale points to Habakkuk 2:20 and Zechariah 2:13 as instances of the prophetic encouragement of silence due to God's presence in the holy (and heavenly) temple from which God executes judgment on the ungodly (idolaters).[61] In addition to this, Zephaniah 1:7 evokes temple imagery in telling the people to be silent because God intends to slay them like a cultic sacrifice.[62] Judgment emanates from the divine throne in the heavenly temple. In Isaiah 41:1, the prophet commands the people to listen in silence to God's indictment of them.[63] A period of silence preceded divine judgment which comes down from the throne in Wisdom 18:14. Silence is the seemingly inevitable posture of those on earth who face divine judgment.

However, John portrays the silence in heaven and not on earth. Though this does not cancel out the centrality of the notion of judgment in this text it should perhaps redirect its significance.[64] Beale also points to a tradition in the Targums of Ezekiel 1–3 where the cherubim, who constantly praise and thank God, fall silent in order to hear the revelatory word from God.[65] This image

---

60. Beale, *The Book of Revelation*, 452. Beale goes so far as to place this silence within an overall structure of Revelation as a reflection of the order of the temple liturgy: "(1) trimming of the seven lamps (Rev. 1–3), (2) slaying of the sacrificial lamb (Rev. 5:6), (3) pouring out of the sacrificial blood at the base of the altar (Rev. 6:9), (4) offering of incense, during a time of silence and prayer (so Luke 1:10; cf. Rev. 8:1, 4-5), (5) the burnt offering and drink offering (Rev. 16:1), and (6) singing of psalms (19:1-8)." There are of course interesting parallels here. However, this schema glides over large swaths of important features of the Apocalypse, and hymns litter the entire landscape of the text, not just in 19:1-8. It is likely therefore that the temple liturgy connections remain on the level of allusion rather than representation. It is more likely that the liturgy recalls early Christian worship rather than temple liturgical rites, but see Margaret Barker, *The Revelation of Jesus Christ: Which God Gave to Him to Show to His Servants What Must Soon Take Place (Revelation 1.1)* (Edinburgh: T & T Clark, 2000), who argues that the earliest Christians carried on the memory of the first temple liturgical tradition.

61. Beale, *The Book of Revelation*, 447.
62. Beale, *The Book of Revelation*, 447.
63. Beale, *The Book of Revelation*, 449.
64. See Beale, *The Book of Revelation*, 448.
65. See Lupieri, *A Commentary on the Apocalypse of John*, 153.

is itself situated in a context of judgment because the cherubim hand burning coals to the seraphim so that they can cast them down on the wicked and "destroy the sinners."[66] Beale connects this image with the four living creatures in Revelation 4–5. The living creatures ceaselessly praise God, so if there is silence in heaven this implies that they have fallen silent. Beale suggests that they have fallen silent "to listen to God declare his verdict of final judgment on the wicked."[67] Under this aspect, the silence refers to all of heaven waiting with bated breath to hear the final pronouncement of the word of God.

That heaven waits silently for the judging word of God is convincing. However, this cannot be the sole function of the silence, for judgment is not the final divine purpose in John's vision. Judgment is the avenue to new creation. Therefore, it is not surprising that silence carries these new creation connotations as well. A return to primeval silence at the end of all things is envisioned in 4 Ezra 7:30. As was in the beginning, when the Spirit hovered and darkness was all around and there was silence (4 Ezra 6:39) so in the end there will be a seven-day silence (see 2 Baruch 3:7).[68] In Wisdom 18–19, silence is connected to both God's judgment and defeat of Egypt and God's work of new creation. A quiet or gentle silence precedes the judgment of the firstborn (Wis. 18:14) before God's word leaps down like a fierce warrior from the royal throne into the land marked for destruction (18:15). This final plague of judgment on the firstborn clears the way for Israel's liberation (19:1-2). Perhaps most fascinating is the way that this exodus is spoken of in terms of new creation: "The whole creation began to take on a new shape in its very nature. It once again submitted to your commands" (19:6 CEB). These events indicate the transformation of the cosmos and are likened to the way someone up-tunes the string of a harp, playing the same melody in a different key (19:18-21). The plagues punishing the false worship of Israel are in another place depicted as the beginning of the new creation (11:17-18).[69] In these intriguing parallels, we can see how John, too, puts together these concepts of silence, judgment, and new

---

66. Beale, *The Book of Revelation*, 451.

67. Beale, *The Book of Revelation*, 452. Beale also connects this imagery to Midr. Rab. Exod .29:9 that portrays the ophanim and seraphim silencing their praise of God when God revealed the law on Sinai.

68. See Harrington, *Revelation*, 103; Blount, *Revelation*, 158. In this text specifically the focus is on the lack of human voice, both before the creation of humans and after the death of all humans.

69. This connection among silence, the plagues of judgment, and new creation solidifies the connection between the seals cycle and the cycles of trumpets and bowls (the latter two are clearly constructed on the plagues in Exodus). If the plagues are seen as catalyst and initiation of the new creation, then this also begins to confirm my own reading of the cycles portraying a rhetorical cosmological transformation.

creation. Here is more confirmation that the half-hour of silence anticipates something more.

This something more comes in the form of an angel holding a golden censer standing before the altar (Rev. 8:3). This is the same altar mentioned in Revelation 6:9 under which the saints cry out to God for judgment on their murderers (6:10).[70] These prayers have already been heard, but the time has come to respond to them with action. The angel is given a great quantity of incense to offer with the prayers of the saints (see 5:8 where the incense is equated with the prayers of the saints).[71] There is some question as to whether the incense is to be understood as alongside the prayers of the saints or as the prayers themselves. Robert Mounce favors the latter option, arguing for a dative function that clarifies that the incense consists of the prayers.[72] This reading is to be preferred because it makes more sense in light of 5:8. The angel[73] offers the incense-prayers on the altar that is before the throne and they rise before God, signifying their acceptability to God (8:4).[74]

Next the angel takes the censer and fills it with glowing embers from the altar. Presumably the glowing embers are a mixture of the fire-materials, the prayers, and incense. The prayers of the saints have risen to God in the smoke, but the source of the prayers is their presence on the altar of incense (8:3). Therefore, the embers that are cast down on earth contain the prayers that were offered to God on the altar. Most scholars see a parallel in Ezekiel 10:2-7 where a man in linen (most likely an angel) is commanded to take fiery coals in hand and spread them over the city in judgment.[75] However, that passage does not contain the theophanic phenomena that the Apocalypse reports. Whereas Ezekiel envisions the coals as having a judging function, the coals for John seem

---

70. Beale, *The Book of Revelation*, 454–455.

71. Aune, *Revelation 6–16*, 513, does not believe the prayers should be metaphorically understood as the incense, but that the incense rises with the prayers.

72. Mounce, *The Book of Revelation*, 174. Contra Blount, *Revelation*, 165, who argues that it is a dative of advantage meaning the incense is offered with the prayers in order to present the prayers in the best possible light for the best chance at divine acceptance. This is not convincing since the smoke signifies that the offering is acceptable as well as the fact that the saints sacrifice is portrayed in 6:9-10 as sharing in Christ's sacrifice, a sacrifice that is without question acceptable before God.

73. Beale takes note of the representative function of the angel in the letters at Rev. 1:19, *The Book of Revelation*, 455.

74. On the acceptability of the rising smoke of the sacrifice see Mounce, *The Book of Revelation*, 175. Beale argues that incense is always associated with sacrifice and therefore the rising of the prayers reveals the acceptability of the sacrifice, and that the sacrifice typified in the prayers of the saints share in Christ's perfect and prior sacrifice, *The Book of Revelation*, 456–457.

75. Aune, *Revelation 6–16*, 515; Mounce, *The Book of Revelation*, 175.

to have a closer tie to God's presence in the world. John sees and hears "peals of thunder, rumblings, flashes of lightning, and an earthquake" when the angel throws the coals upon the earth (Rev. 8:5).

The combination of atmospheric disturbances and an earthquake occurs thrice in the Apocalypse, each time at the end of one of the cycles of seven. Aune notices this, but argues that each occurrence of these elements serves a different function.[76] However, as we have argued above, there is a kind of parallelism and recapitulative logic to all of the cycles, and therefore we should imagine these elements serving similar purposes. These elements are allusions to the Sinai theophany (Exod. 19:16-18)[77] and are common tropes in Jewish and early Christian writings used to depict the presence of God and the end of the cosmos.[78] Thus the incense-prayers hurled down from the altar in heaven to the earth somehow are implicated in bringing or accompanying the presence of God on earth. Mounce argues that this means "God is about to answer the prayers of the saints," but the presence of God on earth, which points forward to the telos envisioned at Revelation 21:3-4, suggest that God already has answered their prayers. The world has been unmade, the silence preceding judgment and new creation has been experienced, and God's presence is among God's creation and people. This, for all intents and purposes, could be the end. In fact, if the text were to be sewn up so that the next passage was 21:1, most readers would be none-the-wiser.[79] We can therefore confidently say that this seventh seal of silence and prayer is one aspect of the end.[80] It remains for us to parse out the significance of that fact.

Conclusion

The opening of the seventh seal represents for John the end and goal of history.[81] But this presents a paradox, for at first blush it seems anti-climactic,

---

76. Aune, *Revelation 6–16*, 517.

77. Beale, *The Book of Revelation*, 458; Mounce, *The Book of Revelation*, 175.

78. Beale, *The Book of Revelation*, 458.

79. Blount, *Revelation*, 158: "It only *appears* as if the moment of new creation does not follow directly upon the period of silence narrated at 8:1 . . . the narration that follows 8:1 recapitulates the events that have already happened (the seals episodes) from a different eschatological perspective (trumpets) . . . The next chronological step (after John finishes relating God's intervening acts of judgment) will be the creation of the new heaven and the new earth. The silence of 8:1 is therefore properly positioned (in real time) just before that moment. Only because of John's method of narrating his visions does the silence seem to be separated from the new creation. That separation is a literary fiction that gives John more 'time' to make his point. As far as eschatological real time is concerned, 8:1 moves chronologically right to 21:1."

80. See Beale, *The Book of Revelation*, 452, 457–458.

and even, for the most part, devoid of content. The silence in heaven represents an absence of the sound phenomena that had characterized the seals cycle to this point. Indeed, the end of the seals cycle just leads to another cycle and so it seems as if the end has not been reached at all. However, as we have seen, this silence forms a multivalent constellation of images ranging from prayer to judgment to new creation. At the end of this silence John presents a vision of the theophany of God, a theme that constitutes the heart and *telos* of his entire vision. Thus, as paradoxical as the silence and prayer is at the seventh seal, in depicting God's presence in creation it represents the accomplishment of the divine goal for history.[82]

This means that silence and prayer are connected intimately with what John sees is the divine work of the end. The silence is a time of offering prayer. The angel at the altar takes the prayers of the saints and offers them before the throne. These prayers are the prayers of the martyr-saints who rest under the altar. Therefore, the prayer offered within this silence is not any garden variety of prayer, it is prayer voiced from a place of resistance to idolatrous practices of imperial cult and economy. Those who pray under the altar are those who were killed for non-participation. Therefore, the prayer that is offered as a pleasing sacrifice to God is prayer from those who refuse to compromise with Roman society. For John, "martyrdom is true prayer" and the church is most witnessing to the imminent visitation of God when it is standing apart from the discourse of cult and economy in such a way that it is being killed.[83] The church's experience of that silence is its experience of prayer as separation.

The silence also provides a liturgical pause in which to literally be patient (Rev. 1:9; 2:2, 3, 19; 3:10; 13:10; 14:12). The half-hour of silence creates a liturgical space and time for the endurance of the saints. Here the judgment

---

81. There is a sense in which all of the events leading up to the seventh broken seal are just anticipations of the contents of the scroll. After all, how could the scrolls contents be disclosed while it is still sealed? It is not until the seventh is broken that the meaning of the scroll is revealed. This is significant for my reading as it underscores that the plagues and judgments are oriented toward the unmaking and remaking of the world by the divine presence. All judgments up to this point are preparations for that vision and conclusion. See Aune, *Revelation 6–16*, 507; Bauckham, *The Theology of the Book of Revelation*, 80.

82. This is how this imagery has been translated at times in later Christian interpretation. For example, Bede viewed the silence as the quiet of Christ's rest after the crucifixion which is followed by the resurrection. Similarly, Ignatius of Antioch, Valentinus and Milton connect the imagery to the salvific event and the beginning of everlasting rest accomplished through the work of Christ. On this see Kovacs and Rowland, *Revelation*, 108.

83. Lupieri, *A Commentary on the Apocalypse of John*, 154. See also Perry, *The Rhetoric of Digressions*, 240–241: "This is martyr ecclesiology."

connotations resonate clearly. The silence signifies the need to wait on God's judgment of the unrighteous and idolatrous economic practices that sustain the Roman world. By providing this interval of silence, John invites his audience into the possibility of non-participation in their culture of idolatry. God and the Lamb are about to dismantle the world of the cult and the economy, and in this period of quiet the church both anticipates that activity and beckons it closer. Just as heaven's praise falls silent, so the church is to wait expectantly for the divine word of judgment that will spell the end of the Roman constructed cosmos and usher in God's new creation. Participation in this silent anticipation of judgment is the "little power" that belongs to those of the church in Philadelphia (3:8).[84] It is not much, but it is enough to somehow participate in the judgment of the cosmos.[85]

That the saints do participate in the unmaking and remaking of the world is evident from the image of the prayers of the saints being cast down as the burning coals upon the earth. These prayers of non-participation, which John encourages all Christians to pray (6:11) have gone up to the throne and now return back to earth, effecting the meteorological and seismic phenomena that signal God's visitation and new creation. These prayers somehow participate in the unmaking of the cosmos.[86] John's argument here is that if his hearers will remain steadfast in the endurance and resistance to the cult and economy, and the world it constructs, then their resultant suffering will have a role to play in the dismantling of that world. Their prayers, which are to be martyr-prayers, will participate along with the coming of God in unmaking the Roman cosmological reality. The church's non-participation in the idolatrous cultic economy is intended to introduce a sense of anomie for those who worship the beast, both within the church and in the wider culture. This is the apocalyptic

---

84. Indeed, the church in Philadelphia is one of two churches that are not reprimanded in the letters by Jesus (the other being Smyrna). Yet it is only the Philadelphian church that is portrayed as "having kept my word of patient endurance" as a completed fact (with the aorist ἐτήρησας). Because they have already kept this word of endurance they will be be kept (τηρήσω) from the "hour" (ὥρας) of trial that is coming upon the whole world to test "the inhabitants of the earth" (3:10). This "little power" of endurance is mighty when one considers that it enables one to inhabit a new world (3:12) even as the old one comes to a cataclysmic end.

85. Another parallel from the Wisdom of Solomon sheds light on the unlikely power of prayer. Moses is depicted as limiting the effect of divine anger on the people of God by taking up the weapons of prayer and incense (Wis. 18:21). The passage continues, "He stood strong against the fury. In doing so, he limited the damage that was done. He showed that he was your servant. He overcame divine anger not by bodily strength or by the power of weapons" (18:21-22, CEB).

86. See Harrington, *Revelation*, 104: "their prayer, which had gone up to God (8:4), returns to the earth, causing things to happen on earth."

word that John speaks into the midst of his congregations. If they will but hold out, their witness will begin to effect the breakdown of the world, and will participate in the dismantling of the world of Rome. Their resistance plays a role in the judgment and new creation at God's coming.

Far from being devoid of content, then, the prayerful silence of the seventh seal sheds light on how John understands the mission of his hearers. They are to participate (in the judgment and new creation) by not participating (in the Roman cosmological discourse of cult and economy). God's judgment has removed the rocks and mountains from their sturdy foundations, it has altered the heavenly bodies, and has sent the sky skittering off like a tightly wound scroll. Now God's presence with creation orients the new creation. The one on the throne now resides in the center of creation, sheltering from the scorching sun and orienting the entire creation around the throne and the Lamb (7:15-17). By their participation through endurance and prayer in the undoing of the world, the saints have also come to share in the construction of the new creation.[87] In this way, silence is paradoxically filled with the praises of God, just as the darkness is paradoxically filled with the abundance of God's light. Silence is only considered an absence from the point of view of the world that is being judged and dismantled. From the viewpoint of those who are living proleptically in the new creation, it is the content of witness. Silence is not just holding out from the culture. It is the activity that makes space for the new creation and true worship.

Without giving his audience time to bask in the victory of this vision, John ushers them away to the next series of visions and plagues. This is the end and yet not the end. There is more in his vision that he wishes them to see. There is yet another aspect of the judgment and new creation that they must understand if they are to understand their mission. For their ministry of silence and prayer is not their entire vocation. In silence they practice non-participation in the worship of the beast through cult and economy. But they must also participate in true worship of God and the Lamb. The trumpet blasts function as summons to worship, calling John's audience to the next aspect of their vocation: praise.

---

87. See Wis. 18:24 where Moses is depicted as wearing a robe on which could be seen "the whole of the universe."

5

Praise: Narrating the Emergence of God's Reign and the New Creation

The Son of God has made the darkest place of human history the most luminous place in the universe. Everything is dim beside it. Ten thousand suns gathered into one, would be blackness itself compared to the unspeakable glory of the cross of Christ. The cross is the great, suffering, infinite, crowning glory of God. It is the mighty, struggling, dying effort to do what omnipotence can not do; to accomplish the impossible; to cause infinite justice and infinite mercy to kiss each other over the brow of a doomed [person], and folding their arms about [her], lift [her] to a new possibility. To the amazement of a moral universe, it is done. Infinite love, infinite suffering bring it to pass. A door of hope is opened for [humanity]. A possibility is set before us. There is light for darkness, purity for impurity.

—Phineas F. Bresee[1]

The cycle of trumpet judgments follows immediately upon the conclusion of the seal judgments. This means that John's hearers would understand them to be closely related to each other, for their close proximity and John's use of intercalation in rhetorical composition indicates association. The trumpets cycle should not be understood as a progression from the seals judgments. Rather, they depict the same set of judgments and plagues seen under a slightly different aspect. The fact that both cycles end with the same goal of theophany suggests this. In the seals cycle, John was primarily concerned with spelling out the vocation of resistance for the church amidst the judgments on Roman

---

1. Ernest Alexander Girvin, *Phineas F. Bresee: A Prince in Israel, A Biography* (Kansas City: Pentecostal Nazarene Publishing House, 1916), 359.

cosmological discourse. The prayers of the saints that appear at the end of the cycle are the prayers for vindication on account of their endurance in this mission. In the trumpets cycle, John seeks to emphasize a different facet of the divine work of dismantling the cosmos: how the church's resistance makes possible the repentance of the nations. Therefore, these textual units should be understood to be happening simultaneously. While the literary nature of the text necessarily takes chronological time and progression, the theological and symbolic nature of the text demonstrates that these cycles are two layers of the same path to the end. Therefore, one rightly understands that the next event in history after the last broken seal is not the first trumpet, but the presence of God at the last judgment and new creation.[2]

Overview of the Cycle of Seven Trumpets

In many ways, John modeled the cycle of seven seals on the so-called "little apocalypse" of the Synoptic Gospels. Now in the cycle of seven trumpets he turns to different source material from which to organize the presentation of what he sees. The trumpets cycle, along with the bowls cycle after it, is reminiscent of the plagues that befall Egypt in Exodus 7–11.[3] In that account, God demonstrates the utter lack of power and authority of the Egyptian deities by causing the stability of the cosmos—over which these deities were supposed to have supervision—to crumble and disintegrate.[4] Now with the cycle of trumpets John envisions the work of God and the Lamb as doing the same work of unmaking, but also making new. If the world of Babylon (Rome) is constructed and sustained by a cosmological discourse that sees Caesar and the gods at the center of a new and golden age, John rejects this world by lifting the veil on its unrighteousness, impurity, and corruptibility. The world has been created by God and is affirmed as good through praise (Rev. 4:11). But seeing how the divine authority and intention for creation is distorted and disordered by the corrupt Roman cosmological system of cult and economy, John seeks to demonstrate how God will unmake that world in order to bring it back to its original and renewed purpose.

---

2. See G. K Beale, *The Book of Revelation: A Commentary on the Greek Text* (Grand Rapids and Cambridge: Eerdmans and Paternoster, 1999), 472–473; Brian K. Blount, *Revelation: A Commentary* New Testament Library (Louisville: Westminster John Knox, 2009), 166.

3. The Exodus narrative (Priestly account) recounts ten plagues, but two Psalms have it as seven plagues (representing the Yahwistic tradition). Blount argues that John is following the Yahwist and that this focus on exodus also implies liberation, Blount, *Revelation*, 166.

4. See Beale, *The Book of Revelation*, 465–466, 481; John J. Davis, *Moses and the Gods of Egypt* (Grand Rapids: Baker, 1971).

After the theophanic vision that ends the cycle of seals, John reports that he sees seven angels with trumpets. The image of trumpets has significance both in the Old Testament tradition and in the Greco-Roman world. In Jewish tradition, the sounding of a trumpet could signify a variety of phenomena. One key aspect of a trumpet blast was to announce the arrival of the Day of the Lord (Zech. 9:14; Zeph. 1:14-16; Apoc. Abr. 31:1; 4 Ezra 6:23; Sibylline Oracles 4:124). The earliest Christians took this image over and applied it to the *parousia* of Christ (1 Thes. 4:16; Matt. 24:31; 1 Cor. 15:52; Didache 16:6).[5] Therefore, with the image of trumpets, the audience should already be anticipating the arrival of the divine. Just as the outset of the seals cycle was the arrival of the rider on the white horse (in our reading an image of the entrance of Christ into the world), so too the cycle of trumpets begins with an image that suggests God's entrance onto the world stage.

Beale suggests another important aspect of trumpets for Jewish tradition: judgment. The trumpets announce the imminence of God's judgment about to be visited on the world of idolaters. In the Life of Adam and Eve 22:1-3, a trumpet blast signals the imminence of God's "sentence" and "judgment" on Adam and Eve, even as they hide from God's presence (compare with Rev. 6:17).[6] This judgment can at times carry a militaristic overtone, with the sense of the divine preparing to go to battle against the enemies of God's people (Josh. 6; Judg. 7:16-22; Jer. 4:5-21; 42:14; 51:27; Ezek. 7:14; Hos. 8:1; Joel 2:1; Zeph. 1:16).[7] G. K. Beale suggests that the Exodus plague background as well as the trumpet motif of judgment implies that the trumpets cycle is primarily about judgment and not a series of actions designed to evoke repentance. Instead, the punishments only harden the resistance of the people upon whom they fall (Rev. 9:20-21).[8] While it is true that the Exodus background carries with it Pharaoh's increasing hardness of heart, there is another tradition in which God gives the Israelites favor in the eyes of their Egyptian neighbors (Exod. 11:3). Perhaps this suggests a dichotomy of action and attitude between rulers and subjects, but this dichotomy does not seem to be present in John's vision. Additionally, it is only after the scourge of the plague is removed that Pharaoh hardens his heart in the Exodus narrative, while in the trumpets cycle the people refuse to repent even in the face of the plagues (Rev. 9:21). This heightens the sense of obstinacy of the inhabitants of the earth as compared to the Egyptian

---

5. David E. Aune, *Revelation 6–16* Word Biblical Commentary (Nashville: Thomas Nelson, 1998), 519.

6. See Beale, *The Book of Revelation*, 471.

7. Beale, *The Book of Revelation*, 468.

8. Beale, *The Book of Revelation*, 466–469.

regime, but it would also demonstrate that even a people so stubborn can turn and change. Therefore, the fact that John even mentions the possibility of repentance must imply that it is at least one of the intended outcomes of the trumpet plagues.[9]

Trumpets in Jewish tradition also signal the announcement of kingship. After the plagues liberate the people of Israel from bondage in Egypt, they are summoned by an extremely loud trumpet blast (Exod. 19:16). The trumpet as summons to the mountain carries with it a concomitant image of theophany and divine presence as ruler and king (19:6). The image of trumpets already, then, anticipates the climax of the trumpets series when authority and kingdom is handed over from the world to God (Rev. 11:15-19). Beale points to a text in Philo where the Feast of Trumpets imagines God as warrior destroying factions in cities and in the universe and establishing a reign.[10]

In the Greco-Roman world, the sounding of a trumpet was sometimes considered a sign of the wrath of divine anger or a "prodigy."[11] Prodigies often consisted of cosmic irregularities and damage, and so were often harbingers of divine wrath. If the cosmos, which were sustained by the gods, were coming apart and acting erratically it was a sign that the world was about to be rearranged in some way. Dio, utilizing the form of prodigy report, claims that the sound of a trumpet was heard before the eruption of Vesuvius in 79 CE.[12] David E. Aune also indicates that Plutarch held that the Etruscan diviners viewed the trumpet sound as a prodigy heralding a new age.[13] Therefore, within John's cultural milieu, a series of seven trumpets accompanied by a series of disasters and plagues on a cosmic scale would be an unmistakable sign that the world was standing under judgment, and the foundations and sureties of that world were being removed. That the judgments fall on a certain group of people that worship a certain way, and not on others who worship the one on the throne and the Lamb, would indicate that the gods that were thought to sustain the world were no longer in charge. John is demonstrating that

---

9. Blount, *Revelation*, 166–167, argues that John's visions are based on the ethical premise of witness with the goal of causing those who see—both inside and outside the church—the public witness he calls for to take the warnings seriously and change their ways. See also Robert H. Mounce, *The Book of Revelation,* rev. ed., New International Commentary on the New Testament (Grand Rapids: Eerdmans, 1998), 176–177, who also sees in the partiality of the judgments (only one third is affected) an ultimate purpose of garnering repentance.

10. Beale, *The Book of Revelation*, 470.

11. Aune, *Revelation 6–16*, 518–519, cf. 416–419.

12. Aune, *Revelation 6–16*, 520.

13. Aune, *Revelation 6–16*, 519.

their oversight of the world had failed and that therefore, they were no longer worthy of worship.

The First Six Trumpets

The first angel sounds the first trumpet and the action resumes, bringing with it an immediate sense of trauma. The sign accompanying the first trumpet blast is hail and fire mixed with blood hurtling down upon the earth (Rev. 8:7). This image is culled from the seventh Egyptian plague (Exod. 9:13-35) where God sends thunder, hail, and lightning to the ground. Joel 2:31, which also depends on the Egyptian plague tradition, includes blood and is probably a source for John's meditation here. In the Exodus plague, the hail strikes trees and the vegetation of the field (Exod. 9:22-25). John sees the plague damaging the earth, trees, and green grass. Beale argues that famine is in view here, since fire is said to do the major damage.[14] However, there is no mention of food or crop shortage here. With the third rider in the seals cycle, John has no problem mentioning specific crops that are affected by plague and pestilence, so the absence of a specific food crop here should give us pause before associating this with famine. If this text resembles anything in the seals cycle, it is closer to the image of the four winds that were assigned to damage the earth, the sea, and the trees (Rev. 7:1).

More significant than famine here, is the image of blood pouring from the sky. Blood is another element in Roman prodigy lists, and therefore signals wrath, judgment, and cosmic disintegration.[15] The Sibylline Oracles reference fire and blood as a sign of the eschaton (5:377-378). Mounce argues that the blood refers to a blood red storm in the sky that hurtles down hail and fire.[16] This fearsome sight should cause those who see it to tremble with fear and turn from wicked activity. Elsewhere John portrays blood as a fitting punishment for the crime of shedding the blood of the saints (Rev. 16:6). Therefore, blood is God's way of pronouncing an end to the system that sheds the blood of the resistant saints. As Blount writes, "Rome wants blood: God will rain it down until its people drown in it."[17]

John reports that the plague destroys a third of the earth and trees and all of the green grass. This measure of a third is more than the measure of one fourth used in the seals cycle (Rev. 6:8) but is still less than total destruction. Therefore, again John's hearers are to understand that there is still time to repent and

---

14. Beale, *The Book of Revelation*, 475.
15. Aune, *Revelation 6–16*, 519.
16. Mounce, *The Book of Revelation*, 178.
17. Blount, *Revelation*, 168.

turn to true worship. One-third may refer to a passage in Ezekiel 5 where the population of Jerusalem is divided into thirds and given different punishments. Beale also points to Zechariah 13:8-9 where two thirds of the people of Israel are cut off and a third is preserved.[18] If this text is in mind, John is reversing the measures of judged and saved, perhaps holding out a greater hope for a larger remnant to turn and repent.

The second trumpet is accompanied by something like a great fiery mountain being hurled into the sea (Rev. 8:8). Much of the description of this mountain sound like the tragic eruption of Vesuvius in 79 CE. Dio reports that the sound of a trumpet was heard before the eruption, thus connecting it with the sign of a prodigy.[19] The Sibylline Oracles contain a description of the Vesuvius eruption as filling the heavens and destroying cities and people (4:130-134). It is possible that such a traumatic event in the empire provided inspiration for John's vision report as he hunted for words and images to describe what he saw. A mountain burning with fire could have evoked the fear and horror that the eruption caused the people affected by the disaster (Pliny the Younger's eyewitness account reported people praying for death; compare with Rev. 9:6).[20]

The mountain may also stand in for a kingdom. Jeremiah 51:25 refers to Babylon as a "destroying mountain" that "destroys the whole earth" (compare with Rev. 11:18). God promises to make Babylon a "burned out mountain." The mountain in John's vision is on fire and so probably stands under judgment. Jeremiah 51 also contains the image of a trumpet being sounded among the nations and a symbolic image of a scroll of Babylon being tied to a stone and sinking down never to rise again (51:24, 63-64). Beale argues this connection of imagery of stone and mountain to Babylon forms the basis for this mountain image and likewise the stone image in Revelation 18:21.[21] The mountain being cast down also recalls the imagery from 6:14 where every mountain was removed from its place. Though this mountain has special significance as a regime hostile to the reign of God, its demise is seen as part of the volatile cosmic reconfiguration.

The mountain's fall affects the sea (the one part of the created order conspicuously absent from the first trumpet judgment) in that a third of it becomes blood and a third of the sea life is killed and a third of the ships are destroyed. This is probably an allusion to Exodus 7:20 where Moses turns the

---

18. Beale, *The Book of Revelation*, 475.
19. Aune, *Revelation 6–16*, 520.
20. Aune, *Revelation 6–16*, 531.
21. Beale, *The Book of Revelation*, 476.

Nile to blood, but it would also bring to the Greco-Roman mind the idea of a prodigy.[22] Again, the cosmic signs signal the end of the stability of the cultic system. This is further confirmed by the detail that the plague destroyed a third of the ships (Rev. 8:9). The word for ships (πλοίων) occurs in the Apocalypse only here and in the economic critique of 18:19. Beale, following the lines of his famine interpretation for the whole of the trumpets cycle, argues that this image refers to "the picture of a cutback in resources that were formerly plentiful."[23] However, this seems to be instead a direct judgment of God upon the Roman economic system, a system that relied heavily upon the sea for its economic prosperity.[24] Ships are the only human-made things that are destroyed in the trumpets cycle.[25] That John singles the ships out suggest that he is making a clear call for his churches to extricate themselves from the idolatrous Roman economy. In his vision of a third of the ships being destroyed, John gives his audience a preview of a concept he will expand later in the Apocalypse.

The third trumpet vision pictures a great star "blazing like a torch" falling on and making bitter a third of the rivers and springs of water (8:10-11). The vision probably refers to the effects on one-third of the rivers and springs caused by the star falling, as it would be impossible for one star to fall on a third of the rivers. This star probably refers to a fallen angel who has been judged, as is the case in 1 Enoch 18:13 and 21:3. Edmondo F. Lupieri draws attention to the fact that the word torch (λαμπὰς) is used only here and at Revelation 4:5. This could signify a similarity between this fallen angel and the torches that burn before the throne which are the seven spirits of God. If this is true, the angel would seem to have a semblance of cosmic authority and oversight, and its fall therefore compromises the stability of the cosmos (specifically here the waters).[26]

---

22. Aune, *Revelation 6–16*, 520.

23. Beale, *The Book of Revelation*, 477.

24. See G. B. Caird, *A Commentary on the Revelation of St. John the Divine*, Harper's New Testament Commentaries (New York: Harper & Row, 1966), 114. See also Jonathan Moo, "The Sea That Is No More: Revelation 21:1 and the Function of Sea Imagery in the Apocalypse of John," Novum Testamentum 51 (2009), 160.

25. Edmondo F. Lupieri, *A Commentary on the Apocalypse of John*, trans. Maria Poggi Johnson and Adam Kamesar (Grand Rapids: Eerdmans, 2006), 157.

26. There is no evidence for a star or a constellation named "Wormwood" or "Absinthe," Aune, *Revelation 6–16*, 521. This point sheds light on the weakness of the overall approach taken by Malina and others that the visions are solely sky phenomena to be interpreted on an astrological conceptual level, see Burce J. Malina, *On the Genre and Message of Revelation: Star Visions and Sky Journeys* (Peabody: Hendrickson, 1995); Franz Boll, *Aus der Offenbaung Johannis: Hellenistische Studien zum Weltbild der Apockalypse*, ΣΤΟΙΧΕΙΑ 1 (Leipzig: Druck und Verlag B. G. Tuebner, 1914). The fact that John can

The water is not poisoned, but merely made bitter. The eschatological transformation of fresh water to bitter is depicted in 4 Ezra 5:9. The association with death is probably symbolic in that the water has been altered from its original intent. It is no longer good for drinking and is therefore a symbolic depiction of death. Wormwood, according to Jeremiah 9:15 and 23:15, is the fitting punishment for idolatry, making the water impure as punishment for the pollution and impurity of worshiping false gods.[27] John's mention of springs of water made bitter here would call to mind for readers the previous image of the Lamb leading his people to the springs of the water of life (Rev. 7:17). It also anticipates the image of the water of life flowing in the New Jerusalem as a reward for the faithful enduring ones (21:6; 22:1; 22:17). Once again, then, the people facing judgment seem to be in a different cosmic reality than those belonging to God. Whereas the people of God are invited (in the present tense) to come and partake of the water of life (22:17) the inhabitants of the earth must swallow bitter swill. God's people and the inhabitants of the earth are not pictured as dwelling in different spaces, but their experience of the cosmic reality differs radically, according to John. This theme will emerge later in the trumpets cycle and in the bowls cycle as well (see Rev. 9:4).

When the fourth angel blows the fourth trumpet, a plague of darkness strikes a third of the light produced by the sun, moon, and stars (8:12). This plague has a thick, multivalent tradition within the Old Testament. The prophets describe the Day of the Lord as a day of darkness rather than light (Amos 5:18; Joel 2:2; Isa. 13:10). Amos 8:9, where God declares that the sun will set at noon and darken the world in the midst of the day, may account for the awkward imagery that John uses of a third of the time of daylight rather than the intensity of the light being diminished by a third.[28] The ninth Egyptian plague also stands in the background (Exod. 10:21-23). God causes darkness to fall over Egypt for three days and nights. This plague, like many of the Exodus plagues, was designed as a judgment of the false Egyptian gods.[29] The darkness casts shadows over the sun god Ra and demonstrates the superiority and authority of the God of the Israelites. The Exodus narrative is suggestive

---

name and narrate the activity of a star that does not appear on a star-map means his vision encompass more than just star-interpretation—he is dealing with the nitty-gritty of the entire cosmic enterprise, from sea creatures and ships to rocks and trees.

27. Blount, *Revelation*, 169–170; Beale, *The Book of Revelation*, 479.

28. See Aune, *Revelation 6–16*, 522; Mounce, *The Book of Revelation*, 181. For a different opinion see Beale, *The Book of Revelation*, 481.

29. See John J. Davis, *Moses and the Gods of Egypt* (Grand Rapids: Baker, 1971); Beale, *The Book of Revelation*, 481.

in another way in that the darkness is also said to not affect the Israelites, who enjoyed normal light where they lived (Exod. 10:23). This calls the mind the exemption of the plagues for those who have been sealed as belonging to God in the Apocalypse. Again, it is as if they inhabit a different cosmos even as they reside alongside their neighbors. Finally, as Aune points out, it is probably more than coincidental that the fourth trumpet deals with matters that were created by God on the fourth day of creative work in Genesis 1:14-19.[30] God created the luminaries and is recalling their light as judgment for Rome's distorted cosmological administration.[31]

The Vesuvius eruption might have been called to an ancient audience's mind at the mention of diminishing daylight. Dio reports that the ash cloud in the sky darkened the sunlight for a period of several days. Pliny the Younger's eyewitness report confirms this daylight darkness.[32] The darkening of the sun as in an eclipse could have been considered a prodigious sign of coming disaster, as Herodotus reports an eclipse as producing "night instead of day." Lucan describes an eclipse in terms of veiling the sun in "gloom" and causing "mankind to despair of daylight."[33] John probably means to evoke this despair producing darkness as a sign that the cosmic structure is unstable and altering in a drastic way. The Roman imperial cultic discourse that constructed this cosmic reality is losing its hold on the cosmos.

After the fourth trumpet is sounded the tone of the judgments shifts. First there is a brief interruption of the series when an eagle (or vulture—the word ἀετοῦ can be translated as either) flies in midheaven announcing three "woes" to the "inhabitants of the earth."[34] This and the fact that the final three trumpets are

---

30. Aune, *Revelation 6–16*, 523.

31. See the discussion in Beale, *The Book of Revelation*, 483–484, where Beale discusses later rabbinical sources that demonstrate the turning away from the covenantal and spiritual principles upon which the world was created causes the celestial bodies to darken. These sources are of course later than Revelation, so there is no way to make any certain connection to the reflection of the celestial bodies in Revelation. However, the theological principles are built from the same foundational materials: "Celestial intervention is a sign demonstrating that people are judged for having violated the covenantal and moral order that God has established on earth." Here we might argue that the covenantal and moral order being broken is the Noachic covenant, which was understood as binding for all people, Jews and Gentiles. It is in the Noachic covenant that blood of sacrifice becomes sacred (Gen. 9:4-6), and therefore something only to be devoted to God. The Roman sacrificial order, and the economy that sustains and proliferates that order, is in violation of that covenant. I owe these insights to my colleague and friend René Such Schreiner.

32. Aune, *Revelation 6–16*, 523.

33. Both Herodotus and Lucan quoted in Aune, *Revelation 6–16*, 522.

34. "Inhabitants of the earth" is the technical terminology in the Apocalypse for idolaters.

given more detail and length suggests that John is working with a 4 3 pattern, perhaps taking on a separate tradition of three woes and connecting it with the trumpet judgments to make seven. In Revelation 9:12, the trumpets are referred to as "woes" only. The three woes turn from plagues against natural and cosmic phenomena to plagues visited on humans. The plagues afflict the unsealed, but Beale suggests that the unsealed can be both without and within the boundaries of the church (compare with 22:18).[35] All who compromise with the idolatry of Roman culture in Asia Minor are subject to the judgments of God unleashed in this cycle.

When the fifth angel sounds a trumpet John sees a fallen star open the Abyss and unleash a horde of demonic locusts (9:1-3). Aune is reticent to identify this angel as Satan, but Beale thinks this image could be another way of portraying the way Satan was cast down from heaven to the earth.[36] Satan is said to both be cast out of heaven (12:9) and ascend out of the abyss (11:17; 17:8), so this could be a way of combining these two images. Regardless of the identification, the idea that the angel is fallen (πεπτωκότα) rules out identification with any of the angels in good standing (compare with the angel of 10:1 who also comes down to earth, but is said to descend, καταβαίνοντα). Fallen angels are seen as disobedient stars in Jewish tradition, and their place is often construed as captivity in the abyss or darkness, as Jude 13 has it: "wandering stars, for whom the deepest darkness has been reserved forever," (NRSV).[37] The off-kilter nature of the stars represents their out-of-joint status within God's creation; they are shaken because they are not grounded in God's righteous intent for the cosmos.

The angel unlocks the abyss which darkens the sun and the air (Rev. 9:2). That ideas of a return to the primeval state of creation are in John's mind is evident from the fact that ἀβύσσου is most often translated in the LXX or the Hebrew *tehom*. At the beginning of creation, God's spirit hovers over the primordial *tehom* (Gen. 1:2) and then again at the deluge in the time of Noah—that constant catalyst for John's imagination as well as symbol for God's

---

35. Beale, *The Book of Revelation*, 485–486.

36. Aune, *Revelation 6–16*, 525; Beale, *The Book of Revelation*, 492.

37. Beale also brings up a passage from Testament of Solomon which is striking for our purposes. 20:14-17 says, "good angels do not fall like stars from heaven because they 'have their foundations laid in the firmament'; but 'demons' appear as 'stars . . . falling from heaven . . . dropped like flashes of lightning to the earth' because they have no such foundations," Beale, *The Book of Revelation*, 492. Fallen angels are able to be shaken because they are not grounded in the goodness and righteous intention of God's cosmic design. Their fall represents the fallen status of all cosmic designs that do not match the creative work of the one God.

unmaking and making new of creation—the fountains of the *tehom* burst forth to flood the earth (Gen. 7:11). In Revelation, God is allowing or giving power to the fallen angel to unleash the powers of chaos onto a crooked world system in order to unmake it and remake it. The concept of given authority, here as elsewhere, establishes in the mind of the audience that God is still in full control of events.[38] God and the Lamb have full authority over Satan's realm and are using Satan and his minions against themselves. There is evidence of a logic that G. B. Caird calls the "self-destroying power of evil."[39] This recalls the Johannine Jesus' opinion of power and authority, "You would have no power over me if it were not given you from above" (John 19:11 NRSV). In that text Pilate has been given authority to crucify Jesus, an action that ultimately thwarts the imperial kingdom that Pilate represents.

Demonic locusts rush out of the abyss to attack people who do not bear the seal of belonging to God on their forehead (Rev. 9:3-5; compare with 7:2-3). This image recalls the Egyptian plague of locusts in Exodus 10:15, but these locusts act in bizarre fashion. Instead of attacking the crops, they are told to attack humans.[40] Once again, the sealed of God are exempt from this plague, protected by the sign that designates them as belonging to the God rather than to the beast. The ones who do not bear this seal bear the full force of the locusts' torment. Beale argues that some unbelievers may become believers during this time, but that it is only because they have already been sealed by God's prior action.[41] This interpretation seems forced and appears to be a way to shoehorn in reformed theology on predestination. This reading fits within Beale's overall approach to the plagues that sees their function solely as judgment and ruling out repentance. Much more satisfactory is to understand that those who bear the mark can turn away and receive the seal. In fact, this is the goal toward which the church's witness is geared. The resistance of those who are sealed is to demonstrate the new world that emerges as given when the fallen world breaks apart. Certainly John envisions that both those in and outside the church can

---

38. See Beale, *The Book of Revelation*, 493; Mounce, *The Book of Revelation*, 187; Blount, *Revelation*, 174–175: "Here is the irony: evil will be unleashed, but evil will be made to act as God's judgment tool. The demonic, bestial forces that rise up from the bottomless pit will target and destroy the very humans who do evil's satanic, beastly bidding."

39. G. B. Caird, *A Commentary on the Revelation of St. John the Divine*, Harper's New Testament Commentaries (New York: Harper & Row, 1966), 114.

40. This probably urges against a reading of the trumpet plagues as indicating famine, as in Beale's reading.

41. Beale, *The Book of Revelation*, 496: "Of course, there are unbelievers who become believers throughout this time, but they are the ones who have been 'sealed' beforehand by God's decretive will. In fact, they became Christians as a result of the sealing activity directed toward them."

bear the mark of the beast, but just as certain can all those who repent bear a new identity mark. Even Jezebel has been given time for repentance (Rev. 2:21; compare 2:5, 16, 22; 3:3, 19; 11:13).[42]

It is not necessarily that the ones bearing God's seal escape the trials mentioned in the book. It is probably better that readers understand that those who belong to God also "come out of the great ordeal" but they experience the trials as good news and as liberation (7:14). After all, it is not their world which is being torn asunder, for they are being led by the Lamb to the springs of the waters of life; the scorching heat does not burn them. Their cosmological discourse enables them to live in God's good creation and to bear witness to that reality. The cosmic judgments and signs are not a terror to them, but rather signs of their deliverance.[43] Even while the sun and sky are darkened they walk in the light of God and the Lamb (22:5).[44] It is again, as though they exist in a different cosmic reality, even though they reside alongside their neighbors.[45]

The unsealed on the other hand suffer loss and torment at the stinging power of the locusts, whose stinging power is said to have the authority of scorpions (9:3, 5, 10). The people seek death but cannot find it (9:6), an image that calls to mind the people calling for the rocks and mountains to fall on them (6:16). Begging for death in the midst of severe suffering and so much cosmic demolition recalls imagery from Job 3.[46] Intense suffering causes Job to not only seek death but to go so far as to evoke a reversal of creation. He does not just wish for death, he wishes for someone to proclaim the day as darkness

---

42. See Blount, *Revelation*, 184–185.

43. See Mounce, *The Book of Revelation*, 187.

44. Once again the Johannine gospel parallel is instructive: " 'Now is the judgment of this world; now the ruler of this world will be driven out. And I, when I am lifted up from the earth, will draw all people to myself.' He said this to indicate the kind of death he was to die . . . Jesus said to them, 'The light is with you a little longer. Walk while you have the light, so that the darkness may not overtake you. If you walk in the darkness, you do not know where you are going. While you have the light, believe in the light, so that you may become children of light.' " (John 12:31-36 NRSV)

45. Cf. the reference from Pss. Sol. 15:4-9 as quoted by Aune, which also contrasts those who bear the mark of God and those who bear the mark of destruction on their forehead: "He who performs these things shall never be shaken by evil: The flame of fire and the wrath against the unrighteous shall not touch him, When it goes forth from before the Lord against sinners, to destroy the substance of sinners. For the *mark of God* [τὸ σημεῖον τοῦ θεοῦ] is upon the righteous for salvation . . . And those who act lawlessly shall not escape the judgment of the Lord: As by their enemies skilled in war shall they be overtaken, For the *mark of destruction* [τὸ γὰρ σημεῖον τῆς ἀπωλείας] *is upon their forehead,*" Aune, *Revelation 6–16*, 530, emphasis original.

46. Indeed, the probing theological questions of Job seem to be standing quietly in the background of much of the cycle of trumpets, see Beale, *The Book of Revelation*, 484, 498; Wilfrid J. Harrington, *Revelation*, Sacra Pagina 16 (Collegeville: Liturgical), 109; Blount, *Revelation*, 176.

and gloom rather than as light (Job 3:3-4).[47] Here we see a hint of where John places the focus on these plagues and judgments. These plagues are intended to judge the people for idolatry, but the ultimate goal is cosmic deconstruction and reconstruction. The divine hope in subjecting the world to destruction is that those who suffer the effects of the destruction will also call for the end of the cosmos and thus participate in its end and anticipate the arrival of the new.[48] Even in this gruesome image of people seeking death John sheds the gospel light on God's ultimate intention in judgment.[49]

One more thing can be said about the fifth trumpet plague. The king of the demonic locusts is the angel of the abyss (the angel that fell into it or the angel that comes up from it?) and is called Abaddon or Apollyon (Rev. 9:11). It is probably best to understand this king of the demonic locusts as the fallen angel that opened the abyss.[50] Apollyon comes from the Greek ἀπολλύμι meaning "to destroy." The same Greek root stands behind this word and the name of Apollo the sun god.[51] The emperor Domitian, who was probably Caesar at the time of John's writing, considered himself to be an embodiment of the god Apollo. John's sense of irony is on display here. The emperor is the demonic king and ruler, and oversees an army of destroyers, and is named destroyer himself (see 11:18).[52] This man goes about dismantling the very world he claims

---

47. See the discussion of the meaning of Job's curse of the day and of creation in J. Gerald Janzen, *Job*, Interpretation (Atlanta: John Knox, 1985), 61–71.

48. For a thorough, book-length treatment on the question of the concerns for the repentance of the nations see Allan J. McNicol, *The Conversions of the Nations in Revelation*, Library of New Testament Studies 438 (London: T & T Clark, 2011). While I read a more widespread vision of conversion than McNicol does, his treatment of the question across scholarship is judicious and charitable.

49. Again, this runs against Beale's reading of the plagues as solely judgments that rule out repentance and only seek to harden the hearts of the inhabitants of the earth, Beale, *The Book of Revelation*, 499. For a different opinion see Elisabeth Schüssler Fiorenza, *Revelation: Vision of a Just World,* Proclamation Commentaries (Minneapolis: Fortress Press, 1991), 72: "John writes this grotesque and brutal vision not for cruelty's sake but rather for the sake of exhortation to repentance." See also Bauckham's extensive discussion of the conversion of the nations, Richard Bauckham, *The Climax of Prophecy: Studies on the Book of Revelation* (London and New York: T & T Clark, 1993), 238–337. Bauckham argues that the Lamb's mission and the purpose of the church's witness is to convert the nations and bring them into the kingdom reign of God. He writes, "It is to all the nations of the world that the seven Spirits are sent out, in order, through the prophetic witness of the church, to win the nations to the worship of the true God…the sacrificial death of the Lamb and the prophetic witness of his followers are God's strategy for winning all the nations of the world from the dominion of the beast to his own kingdom," 336–337.

50. See Pablo Richard, *Apocalypse: A People's Commentary on the Book of Revelation*, trans. Phillip Berryman, The Bible & Liberation Series (Maryknoll: Orbis, 1995), 84.

51. Beale, *The Book of Revelation*, 503–504.

52. Blount notes that the locust was one of Apollo's symbols, *The Book of Revelation*, 179.

to rule as provider, protector and sustainer.[53] Rather than a Roman golden age, or *Roma Aeterna* (as inscribed on the Temple of Venus and Roma constructed by Hadrian), John sees a reign of destruction that must itself be destroyed so that a new creation can emerge as given. Once again, the self-destructive property of this evil regime is forefront in John's vision.

The sixth trumpet brings a series of visions beginning with the altar of incense calling for the release of four captive angels who had been bound at the Euphrates River (9:13-14). That these angels are bound implies that they were rebellious angels that were imprisoned for their disobedience (see 20:2). John uses a definite article which suggests that these angels are supposed to be familiar to his audience, though these angels do not seem to have a role in the text beyond this episode. The Euphrates image anticipates its counterpart in the sixth bowl plague, where the river will be dried up to make way for the invading kings of the east, probably an image of the feared Parthians (16:12). The Euphrates served as the boundary line between the Roman and Parthian empires. Part of the imagery surrounding Roman cultic cosmological discourse involved the idea of the well-ordered cosmos at Rome's recovery of the standard from the Parthians.[54] John is here stoking the paranoia and fear of Rome in order to deface that imagery of the perfect cosmos.[55] But Rome should not fear the Parthians, John is arguing, they should rather fear the God who is in control of the undoing of their world. They should fear the worship of that God, since it is the altar that speaks the loosing of judgment. Another indication of the cosmic undoing with this trumpet is the Edenic connotations that the Euphrates River carries (Gen. 2:14).[56] Again, the Parthian image calls the fear to mind, which John then redirects to the judging activity of God.

The judgment that follows this image is conveyed by John in terms that recall the Greek and Roman mythological tradition of a Chimaera, a fearsome hybrid creature slain by Bellerophon.[57] An army of these gruesome creatures, numbering two hundred million, is unleashed upon humanity, killing a third

---

53. Resseguie argues that the human faces on the locusts mean that evil always needs human cooperation, James L. Resseguie *The Revelation of John: A Narrative Commentary* (Grand Rapids: Baker Academic, 2009), 149.

54. Recall the discussion in chapter 2 regarding the Prima Porta statue.

55. Blount, *Revelation*, 182. See also Beale, *The Book of Revelation*, 514, for a discussion of how the demonic horses resemble imagery evocative of the Parthians.

56. Lupieri, *A Commentary on the Apocalypse of John*, 165.

57. Creatures that were heroically subdued are now returning in defiance of Rome's glorious narrative and tradition. Cf. the discussion of the "war of myths" between John and Rome in Wes Howard-Brook and Anthony Gwyther, *Unveiling Empire: Reading Revelation Then and Now*, The Bible and Liberation Series (Maryknoll: Orbis, 1999), 223–235.

of the population. These horrific creatures, John reports, kill with three specific elements: fire, smoke, and sulfur emanating from their mouths (Rev. 9:18). This image recalls the cosmic judgment inflicted on Sodom and Gomorrah, cities in the prophetic tradition indicted for their worship of idols and their unjust economic practices (Isa. 3:9-4; Jer. 23:9-19; Ezek. 16:44-54). The phrase "proceeding out of their mouths" (ἐκπορευομένου ἐκ τῶν στόματι αὐτῶν) refers to the lies and deceit of the beast and his minions—all who propagate the sustaining discourse of the unjust world. But this phrase is also used by John to signify God's judgment (Rev. 19:15), and, perhaps most strikingly, it is used of the fire that comes from the mouths of the two witnesses in 11:5.[58] John again sees judgment under two aspects here. First, there is the demonic and evil destructive force that judges the idolaters and tears their world apart. But second, this vision is somehow connected to the vocation of the Lamb and the saints. The dismantling of the world is a scourge to the inhabitants of the earth, but it is something longed for and even participated in by those who worship God.

After a third of the population of humanity is killed, John reports that the surviving humans did not repent from "the works of their hands" (9:20). This is stock and trade terminology for idolatry, as is the notion that the people continued to participate in murders, sorceries, fornication, and thefts (see 2:14, 20-22; 21:8; 22:15).[59] Even after the horror and judgments faced, they continue to worship idols made of earth materials like silver, gold, bronze, and wood. John specifically mentions that these idols cannot hear or walk, employing phraseology from classic prophetic idol-polemic (see Isa. 6:9-10; 44:6-20; Ps. 115:3-8; Wis. 15:15-17). These terms also have significance for his own particular rhetorical purposes. John has already perceived the true God as the one who hears and responds to the prayers of the martyrs under the altar. But John also portrays Christ as the one who "walks" among the churches (Rev. 2:1; 3:4). The gods of Babylon (Rome) have demonstrably failed—the world they were supposed to oversee and sustain has disintegrated—while the true God Jesus Christ, who is bringing his world into being anew, is one who is actively at work and involved with his people.

What are interpreters to make of this lack of repentance? Is it, as Beale suggests, indicative of the fact that the plagues were never meant to induce repentance in the first place? Do they have, in his terminology, a "damning effect" rather than a "redeeming effect"?[60] Once again, Beale seems to be

---

58. See Beale, *Revelation*, 511.
59. See the texts cited by Beale, *The Book of Revelation*, 519.
60. Beale, *The Book of Revelation*, 517. See also Aune, *Revelation 6–16*, 541.

shoehorning in a reformed theology of predestination into the imagery of Revelation. He argues,

> The "plagues" were never intended to cause the vast majority of idolaters to "repent" of worshiping demons, but only have the effect that "those not having the seal of God" remain in their hardened condition (cf. 9.4). These plagues will have a redeeming effect only on a remnant of compromisers inside the church and idolaters outside the church, who, it will turn out, will have been sealed beforehand and finally benefit from its protective function.[61]

This ignores the overwhelming evidence that the primary goal of the work of the Lamb is the conversion of the nations. Richard Bauckham has argued convincingly that the sevenfold use of variations of the fourfold designation "all tribes, languages, people, and nations" represents John's emphatic conviction of universal salvation (5:9; 7:9; 10:11; 11:9; 13:7; 14:6; 17:15).[62] Bauckham then notes that the first occurrence of this form is closely associated with the work of the Lamb (5:9). This fact, coupled with the fact that the 28 elements of all the nations of the world correspond to 28 appearance of the word "Lamb" in the Apocalypse, suggests "that the ultimate purpose of the Lamb's conquest is to win all the nations of the world . . . for his kingdom."[63] It follows that the prophetic witness (practiced in prayer, as I demonstrated in the previous chapter, and praise which is addressed in this chapter) of those who follow the Lamb participate in this mission.[64] Though at this point the breakdown of the cosmos does not induce repentance, it does not mean that the repentance and conversion of the nations is not the ultimate goal envisioned by John (Rev. 11:13; 21:24-26; 22:2).

An Interlude of Witness and Repentance

Just as in the seals cycle, John places a lengthy interlude between the sixth and seventh trumpet (10:1—11:14). This digression gives John's audience to take a breath in the midst of the terrifying imagistic rhetoric that he has been piling up in the trumpets cycle. The audience would expect to see the third woe follow

---

61. Beale, *The Book of Revelation*, 517.
62. Bauckham, *The Climax of Prophecy*, 326.
63. Bauckham, *The Climax of Prophecy*, 336. See Rev. 11:15.
64. Bauckham, *The Climax of Prophecy*, 337; Blount, *Revelation*, 184–185; Brian K. Blount, *Can I Get a Witness? Reading Revelation through African American Culture* (Louisville: Westminster John Knox Press, 2005).

quickly on the heels of the first two, but they get instead a vision of a mighty angel with a scroll, a vision of the temple, and a vision of two witnesses. In the midst of the terrors John puts before them, the audience gets a glimpse of their own mission and vocation. The interlude serves to strengthen and encourage the audience as it prepares for what it expects will be the third and greatest woe.[65]

The first interlude vision involves the descent of a mighty angel from heaven (10:1). This angel bears features that resemble both the one seated on the throne and the Lamb. The angel is wrapped in a cloud (1:7) and over his head is "the rainbow" (ἡ ἶρις; 4:3).[66] This rainbow reminds John's audience what is at stake in the trumpets cycle and in the Apocalypse as a whole: the unmaking and making new of the world. In addition to this the angel is described as having the voice of a lion (λέων 10:3; see also 5:5), a face like the sun (see 1:16)[67], and brass feet (see 1:15; 2:18). In the angel's hand is an open "little" scroll (see 5:1). This close association with features of God and the Lamb leads Beale to believe that this is a manifestation of God as "the Angel of the LORD."[68] It is in fact better to understand this angel as the angel in the chain of succession that Bauckham identifies at the beginning of the Apocalypse: from God to Jesus to the angel to John (Rev. 1:1).[69]

The presence of the scroll brings the seals cycle into the trumpets cycle, again demonstrating that these visions are recapitulative.[70] The fact that the scroll is opened should remind the audience in the midst of the terrifying

---

65. See Peter S. Perry, *The Rhetoric of Digressions: Revelation 7:1–17 and 10:1–11:13 and Ancient Communication*, Wissenschaftliche Untersuchungen zum Neuen Testament: 2. Reihe 268 (Tübingen: Mohr Siebeck, 2009), 139, 235–237, where the rhetorical function of *parekbasis* in the ancient discourse is emotional and designed to minimize fear and maximize confidence.

66. The definite article clearly marks this reference to rainbow as "the rainbow" around the throne in heaven, Beale, *The Book of Revelation*, 524.

67. The cosmic description of the angel should not be overlooked. In the midst of the dismantling of the Roman discursive world, God's messenger stands out as a shining cosmic body, undarkened by plague or judgment. The significance of this and other similar imagery in the Apocalypse will be unpacked in chapter 6.

68. Beale, *The Book of Revelation*, 522–523, 525.

69. Bauckham, *The Theology of the Book of Revelation*, 81: "The scroll must be opened by the Lamb before it can be given to John to eat. So the scroll is taken from the hand of God by the Lamb (5:7), who opens it (6:1, 3, 5, 7, 9, 12; 8:1). It is then taken from heaven to earth by an angel (10:1-2), who gives it to John to eat (10:8-10)." See also Aune, *Revelation 6–16*, 555, who argues that the identification of the angel as "another" mighty angel demonstrates this the image is not Christological.

70. Bauckham makes a convincing case for the identification of the sealed scroll and the little scroll as one image, *The Climax of Prophecy*, 243–257. See also Aune, *Revelation 6–16*, 558 who suggests that the scroll is not pictured simply as opened but "unsealed."

breakdown of their world that there is good news ahead. The scroll is opened and unsealed and the good news of the presence and victory of God pictured at the breaking of the seventh seal offers comfort to those afflicted ones awaiting the seventh trumpet blast. After John ingests the scroll he is sent out to prophesy once again concerning many peoples, nations, languages, and kings (10:11). That is, he is sent back out to the work of witness, to the continued work of not only pronouncing judgment but also converting and bringing the nations to repentance.

The next interlude vision John reports is his experience of measuring the temple (11:1-2). John is given a reed or a rod with which to measure "the temple of God, the altar, and those who worship there" (11:1 NRSV).[71] The reed is a surveyor's tool of measurement. It is striking that the only other occurrence of a reed in the Apocalypse is when an angel measures the New Jerusalem with one (21:15-16). That John is measuring the temple, altar, and worshipers with a reed portrays the worshipers as already dwelling proleptically within the renewed creation. This image is sharpened by supplementing the image of reed with the image of a rod or shepherding staff. Jesus promises in the letter to Thyatira that those who conquer will be given an iron rod with which to rule over the nations (2:27). This promise, like all the promises in the letters, is a gift pertaining to the new creation. The shepherding rod image occurs again at 12:5 again with reference to the nations. Blount makes the case that the shepherding image occurs in connection with the defeat of the nations. In 19:15 the nations are struck down and then shepherded with a rod of iron. Blount writes, "the judgment is reconstructive, not punitive."[72] Again, the conversion of the nations (within the context of unmaking and making new the creation) is in view here. Finally, it is significant to notice that the outer court—the court of the gentiles—is not measured.[73] This area is not characterized by the worship of God and therefore it is designated for destruction for 42 months. This demonstrates once more the dismantling of the place and location of those outside the worshiping community and the protection and stability of those inside the worshiping sphere.

The third interlude vision John reports is the prophetic work, death, and resurrection-ascension of the two witnesses (11:3-14). The identity of the two

---

71. This is almost certainly a reference to the heavenly temple and altar, which have been prominent in the text to this point, and make a reappearance later in the chapter. The earthly temple had been destroyed by the time John wrote the Apocalypse, see Blount, *Revelation*, 203–204.

72. Blount, *Revelation*, 203.

73. Though the measuring of the temple is never actually pictured in the Apocalypse (Aune, *Revelation 6–16*, 603) interpreters can safely assume the action is implied to have taken place.

witnesses is a subject of quite lively debate among scholars.⁷⁴ Suggestions of specific identities range from Enoch and Elijah (who were both "taken" up in Scripture), to Moses and Elijah, Jesus and John the Baptist, to John the Baptist and James the brother of Jesus (as a renewal of the priestly and Davidic-royal line).⁷⁵ The particular identity of the witnesses may be less important than their symbolic value as examples for the churches that John is calling upon to take up the prophetic vocation of witness as resistance.⁷⁶ However, I want to suggest two options not discussed thus far in scholarship that could clarify the imagery and its rhetorical function for John.

First, the only two named witnesses in the Apocalypse are Jesus and Antipas (1:5; 3:14; 2:13). Both of these witnesses witness unto death. The connection to Antipas is made stronger in the sense that the two witnesses in Revelation 11 are called "my two witnesses" (τοῖς δυσὶν μάρτθσίν μου) and Antipas is called "*my* faithful witness" (ὁ μάρτυς μου ὁ πιστός μου). If this connection is meant by John's usage of the two witnesses, it could be meant as an image that brings all of John's audience into close association with the work of Jesus as witness. Antipas in this construal stands in for any or all of the hearers of the Apocalypse—they stand next to Jesus. John is encouraging his audience to endure until death, just like Jesus and Antipas, with the knowledge that they too can overcome death and conquer the world.⁷⁷

Second, the two witnesses are also called "two lampstands (δύο λυχνίαι) that stand before the Lord of the earth" (11:4 NRSV). This imagery recalls the image of the churches from the letters where the churches are the "seven lampstands" (ἑπτὰ λυχνιῶν). Aune points to the Jewish tradition of two witnesses as a guarantee of the truthfulness of testimony (Num. 35:30; Deut. 17:6; 19:15; 1 Kgs. 21:10; see also Matt. 18:16; 26:59-60; John 8:17; 2 Cor. 13:1; 1 Tim. 5:19; Heb. 10:28).⁷⁸ This image of two witnesses then would go to show "the truthfulness of the Christian testimony" and represents the overall "witness of the people of God."⁷⁹ Bauckham too sees the two witnesses as representative of "the whole church."⁸⁰ In my opinion, it is preferable to see

---

74. See Antoninus King Wai Siew, *The War Between the Two Beasts and the Two Witnesses: A Chiastic Reading of Revelation 11:1—14:5*, Library of New Testament Studies 283 (London and New York: T & T Clark, 2005), 214–249.

75. See Aune, *Revelation 6–16*, 598–603; Barker, *The Revelation of Jesus Christ*, 194.

76. Aune, *Revelation 6–16*, 602.

77. Perry, *The Rhetoric of Digressions*, 103, 227.

78. Aune, *Revelation 6–16*, 602. See also Bauckham, *The Climax of Prophecy*, 274.

79. Aune, *Revelation 6–16*, 602–603.

80. Bauckham, *The Climax of Prophecy*, 273, see also 274.

the two lampstands as the two faithful churches from the letters. The churches of Smyrna and Philadelphia who are portrayed as "faithful until death," and as having "kept my word of patient endurance" (Rev. 2:10; 3:10 NRSV). These two are the only churches who are not encouraged to repent. Rather they are engaged faithfully in the prophetic witness and endurance of resistance of the culture that John is calling for all the churches to embody. That these two churches are portrayed in the letters as both undergoing affliction for a limited period of time (2.10) and as being kept from the time of trial that is coming upon the inhabitants of the earth (3.10) further strengthens the bond with the image of the witnesses who are killed and yet vindicated. In portraying these two churches as the faithful witnesses whose vocation brings an end to the world and participates in the new creation, John is calling all of his churches to take up that prophetic vocation of witness as resistance.

The witnesses are commissioned to prophesy for 1,260 days (42 months). Their vocation is characterized as a "torment" such that the inhabitants of the earth celebrate and exchange gifts when the witnesses are killed (11:10). The fire that comes out of their mouth recalls the demonic horses that are sent to kill a third of humanity (9:17-18), their own witness participating in the plagues of judgment upon the inhabitants of the earth. Their testimony disrupts the social order and cosmic reality to the point that it becomes a "torment" to those on the earth. This is the same word (βασανισμὸς) used for the torment brought upon the inhabitants of the earth by the demonic locusts (9:4-6, 10). Therefore, once more John is making associations between the vocation of prophetic witness and the destruction of the world—the witness participates in some way in God's work of unmaking the world. The witnesses refusal to compromise or collude with the idolatrous inhabitants of the earth is seen as the catalyst or cause for the breakdown of the idolaters' world. Though the witnesses are killed, they are eventually resurrected by God's Spirit and invited to "come up here" (11:12 ἀνάβατε ὧδε)—the same invitation John received to the throne room of heaven at the beginning of his vision (4:1 ἀνάβα ὧδε). Though the church will suffer on account of its enduring witness, it will be and is vindicated in that it is invited to participate in the heavenly reality.

Without this interlude of the temple worship and the two witnesses John's audience would have trouble understanding their own role and vocation in the midst of the trumpet plagues.[81] John's pause gives them a chance to make the intimate connection between their own work and the work of God and the Lamb to unmake and make new the world. Their witness and worship

---

81. Perry, *The Rhetoric of Digressions*, 102.

participates in this work of cosmic destruction, but it also brings about the repentance of the nations. At the vindication of the witnesses an earthquake kills a tenth of the city, but nine-tenths repent and give glory to God.[82] Seven thousand are killed, but sixty-three thousand glorify God. The remnant is not a minority but a majority! This vision sets up the imminent seventh trumpet, during which the audience anticipates the final end and judgment.

The Seventh Trumpet: Praise

Once again, the climax of the series is anti-climactic. John's audience is expecting the third woe, but he reports neither the death of the rest of the sinners, nor the complete dissolution of the cosmos. Instead, the seventh trumpet blast brings with it voices in heaven proclaiming a hymn (11:15). The loud voices in heaven (which may be taken to be representative of the voices of all worshipers) declare that "The reign of the world (τοῦ κόσμου) has become the reign of our Lord and of his Messiah, and he will reign forever and ever." The shouting voices are probably meant to evoke the practice of *acclamatio* in the Greco-Roman context, a shouted or sung utterance that was often used to express praise or appreciation. It was also used by Roman soldiers to hail Caesar as Imperator.[83] The shouts of the Lord having reign and dominion signal that Caesar's empire is over and so is the discursive cosmos over which he reigns. These loud voices also should be understood as the flip side of the coin of "silence." This hymn of praise is the positive content that the silence enables. If the silence is the endurance of resistance that brings an end to the world, praise is the counter-vision of the world that brings the new creation into expression. We should not be alarmed that the voices are heard in heaven rather than on earth, for heaven is the place around the throne, where the multitudes of worshipers are found. To them it is given to participate already in the new creational realm, and therefore they are pictured and heard as being already before the throne.[84] Pablo Richard argues convincingly that any time praise is depicted in the Apocalypse the reading and hearing community makes an appearance as actively present.[85]

Interpreters should not miss the significance of the terminology "has become." The dismantling of the cosmic reality of the idolaters through the

---

82. See Schüssler Fiorenza's discussion of this repentance, *Revelation: Vision of a Just World*, 79.

83. David Seal, "Shouting in the Apocalypse: The Influence of First-Century Acclamations on the Praise Utterances in Revelation 4:8 and 11," *JETS* 51.2 (2008), 341.

84. See Aune, *Revelation 6–16*, 638.

85. Richard, *Apocalypse*, 83.

work of God and the patient endurance of those who worship the Lamb is precisely what lets the new reign of the Lord and his Messiah to emerge as given. Authority has changed possession, from the rule of the world, construed as the human realm "that had been in opposition to God and in conflict with his purposes,"[86] to the rule of God, where all creation has now been brought to proper orientation around the throne (this is confirmed by the presence of the elders, who were earlier said to be "around the throne" 4:4). These elders join the hymn with a contribution of their own, giving thanks (εὐχαριστοῦμέν) for God taking great power and beginning God's reign (11:17).[87] God is described in their hymn as the one who is and who was. This recalls the threefold designation for God who "was, and is, and is to come" used elsewhere in the Apocalypse (1:8; 4:8) and parodied grotesquely in reference to the beast ("was, and is not, and is about to ascend from the abyss and go to destruction" 17:8, 11). But here God's future coming is left out of the formula. This signifies that the arrival of God upon the earth and in creation has taken place (just as it had in the seventh seal). God is no longer named as the coming one because God is fully present.

The elders' hymn continues by citing the rage (ὠργίσθησαν) of the nations. Aune connects this to a motif in Jewish tradition that depicts the resistance of the people to God's enthronement or the reign of the Messiah (Ps. 98:1; Exod. 15:14).[88] How should we understand this image as John employs it? The rage of the nations makes perfect sense if we consider it, as Beale does, as a step back in the eschatological process. The rage of the nations against the reign of God is due to the deterioration and breakdown of their world order. Roman cultic discourse had established Rome as the benefactor to both imperial center and margins, but the Christian witness of non-participation threatened this status quo. To refuse sacrifice was to refuse the gods and Caesar, and with them to refuse the world that they caused to be and sustained. The non-participation threatened the whole system of sacrifice to and benefits from the gods, therefore the nations' rage is directed at God's coming reign embodied

---

86. Aune, *Revelation 6–16*, 638.

87. This is the only expression like this in the New Testament and it suggests the possibility of a Eucharistic acclamation in the setting of public worship (see Didache 10:4). However, David R. Carnegie cautions against reading this thanksgiving in too technical a sense, since there does not seem to be a meal involved at this moment in the text, "Worthy is the Lamb: The Hymns in Revelation," in *Christ the Lord: Studies in Christology Presented to Donald Guthrie*, ed. H. H. Rowdon (Downers Grove: Inter-Varsity, 1982), 244–245. However, if we understand the cycles as recapitulative then the end of the trumpets cycle should lead directly into the wedding feast motif at Rev. 19.9.

88. Aune, *Revelation 6–16*, 643–644.

in the Christians' witness of non-participation. The divine rage in return, therefore, is the judgment that seeks to dismantle this world that pits itself against God's saints. It is a punishment that fits the crime[89] and a "majestic antithesis."[90]

The end brings a time of judgment. Just as in the seals cycle the prayers of the saints and the silence of their non-participation were used as instruments of judgment and re-arrangement of the world, so now the praise of the saints participates in that same vocation. The hymn makes present the reality of a world where God's reign sets things where they belong: the dead are judged, the slaves of God receive their reward, and the destroyers of the earth are themselves destroyed.[91] If the cults of Rome construct a world that places Roman priorities and prerogatives at the center of the cosmos,[92] then the hymns of the Apocalypse also construct a reality within which to live. They are counter-constructions, songs of resistance to Rome's way of shaping and shepherding the world.[93]

In the reality that the hymn narrates God's slaves are rewarded. These are identified as the prophets and saints, all who fear God's name (11:18). The prophets and saints are those who have endured in the costly testimony of Jesus Christ. They have maintained their innocence by worshiping God and resisting collusion with the culture of idolatry around them (see 19:10). The slaves of God are all who belong to God—they bear the seal rather than the mark. The group envisioned here is the whole church, all of whom bear the prophetic vocation of witness to Christ.[94] Therefore, even those who repent from their former idolatries are rewarded at the final trumpet.[95] Part of this

---

89. Mounce, *The Book of Revelation*, 227; Beale, *The Book of Revelation*, 615.

90. This phrase is from H. Lilje quoted in Mounce, *The Book of Revelation*, 227.

91. See Klaus-Peter Jörns, *Das Hymnische Evangelium: Untersuchungen zu Aufbau, Funktion und Herkunft der Hymnischen Stücke in der Johannesoffenbarung*, Studien zum Neuen Testament 5 (Gütersloh: Gütersloher Verlagshaus Gerd Mohn, 1971), 97–108.

92. See Franz Tóth, *Kult als Wirklichkeitskonstruktion*, Martin Luther Universitat, Halle Wittenberg, 2005.

93. Blount, *Revelation*, 95–98. See 97: "The kingdom of the world—it has to be Rome—becomes the kingdom of God and the Lamb instead. They, not Caesar, will reign forever." One is reminded of the Andrew Bird lyric from "Opposite Day": "Those who can't quite function in society at large / They're going to wake up on this morning and find that their in charge / While those the world's set up for / Who are really doing quite well / Are going to wake up in institutions / In prison or in hell," Andrew W. Bird, "Opposite Day," *Andrew Bird & the Mysterious Production of Eggs* (Chrysalis Music Group, 2005).

94. Beale, *The Book of Revelation*, 616–617.

95. Schüssler Fiorenza, *Vision of a Just World*, 79.

reward is participating in the reign of God and the Lamb. God's slaves, with God's name upon their foreheads, will worship God and will "reign forever and ever" (22:3-5). Aune is correct to point out that this reward is an umbrella term for life in the new creation, but it should not be missed that the saints will participate in the administration and governance of that new creation.[96]

The final reality that the hymn makes clear is that the divine work of unmaking and making new at the seventh trumpet involves "destroying the destroyers of the earth." This is another instance of the punishment fitting the crime, or the ancient tradition of *lex talionis*.[97] What is most striking about this image, however, is the final surprising revelation that it is not God who has done the destroying of the earth, but the beast, Babylon, and all of their minions. This is perhaps John's most unique contribution to the prophetic tradition (or indeed, as Bauckham says, John's contribution which is the *climax of* the prophetic tradition). God is the judge, but it is the Roman mismanagement, ill governance, and idolatrous fornication that have destroyed creation (see 19:2).[98] This is an example of John's persistent logic that evil is its own judgment; it is its own destruction (see 17:15-18).[99] Beale is correct in pointing to Jeremiah 28:25 ("the destroyed mountain which destroyed the whole earth") as a pattern for John's vision of judgment[100], but John is recasting that image as much as he is reusing it. It is the demonic behind the idolatry of Rome that has ruined the earth, and God's activity of judgment falls not upon the earth *per se* but rather upon those beings which ruin it.[101] God's destruction of the destroyers paves the way for new creation, for the world to be restored and healed.

After this hymn, John reports another vision that includes theophanic phenomena—"flashes of lightning, voices, thunder, an earthquake, and great hail" (Rev. 11:19). This image should send audiences back to the theophany at the end of the seals septet. This further cements the idea that these cycles recapitulate, building significance as they layer one on top of the other. This theophanic imagery emerges in concert with a vision of God's heavenly temple and the ark of the covenant seen within it. The ark represents God's gracious presence with creation and also God's provision of atonement.[102] The presence

---

96. Aune, *Revelation 6–16*, 644–645.

97. Aune, *Revelation 6–16*, 645–646.

98. Howard-Brook and Gwyther, *Unveiling Empire*, 221.

99. See Rev. 13:4 where the combative nature of the beast leads to its undoing. Every time the beast and its armies seeks to fight against God it comes to utter ruin (17:14; 19:19-21; 20:7-10).

100. Beale, *The Book of Revelation*, 616.

101. See Harrington, *Revelation*, 126.

of God with creation is seen most clearly in the worship of the people of God. In worship, those who follow the Lamb live, as it were, in a different world. Whereas the silence at the end of the seals cycle represented the saints' refusal to participate in the world building rhetoric of the Roman cult and economy, praise functions as the other side of silence. Praise is the positive content for which silence clears a path. Silence participates with the divine in bringing the Roman cosmological construct to an end. Praise participates in the divine work of new creation. Amidst the loud and terrifying sounds, and the images of carnage and utter destruction, shouted singing voices pierce the chaos, and share the news of God's coming new creative work. Praise narrates that work and brings it into the present.[103]

Conclusion

The climax of the trumpets cycle makes clear that worship is closely connected in the divine takeover of authority and power.[104] The worship of those who follow the Lamb participates in an intimate way in the regime change that is at the heart of John's vision. Like a news reporter on the scene of an event, praise reports the end of the reign of the world and the beginning of the reign of God and the Messiah. But it has become clear at the end of both the seals and the trumpets cycle that both silence and praise are necessary for the saints of God to remain faithful to their costly witness. Silence is necessary in that it is the absolute refusal of the Roman discursive cosmological construction. This silence effects the end of the world. The refusal to participate ushers in the destruction of the system of the inhabitants of the earth. Silence, then, leads to a chaotic and unstable place—refusal, like the eschatological earthquake, denies one firm footing in the world.[105] The cosmic bodies are darkened in the

---

102. Beale, *The Book of Revelation*, 619.

103. See Leonard L. Thompson, *The Book of Revelation: Apocalypse and Empire* (New York and Oxford: Oxford University Press, 1990), 64, 71–73; Stanley P. Saunders, "Between Blessing and Curse: Reading, Hearing, and Performing the Apocalypse in a World of Terror," in *Shaking Heaven and Earth: Essays in Honor of Walter Brueggemann and Charles B. Cousar,* ed. Christine R. Yoder et al. (Louisville: Westminster John Knox, 2005), 151.

104. For the idea that the idea of power is at the center of worship in the Apocalypse see James Chukwuma Okoye, "Power and Worship: Revelation in African Perspective," in *From Every People and Nation: The Book of Revelation in Intercultural Perspective,* ed. David Rhoads (Minneapolis: Fortress Press, 2005), 110–126.

105. Howard-Brook and Gwyther, *Unveiling Empire*, 210: "When the sky is rolled up, the non-worshippers try to hide, but those who worship the Lamb experience it as 'providing shelter from hunger, thirst, and the scorching heat of the sun.' And yet the worshipers still have to live facing their neighbors in the world whose sky has been darkened and rolled up like a scroll."

churches' refusal to abide by Caesar's "light." But praise is also necessary as the positive counterpart to that refusal. John does not envision sheer negation in response to Rome—his critique is not pure critique. Instead, refusal opens space for reception. The deconstructive work of God is but a prelude to the new creative work of God, and both are a gift for which the church rightly gives thanks. Silence and praise are the means for the church to participate in this divine gift. The angel stresses the importance of both these activities when he tells John to "Worship God. For the testimony of Jesus is the spirit of prophecy" (19:10). Silence and praise are the necessary activities for remaining faithful witnesses to the work of God to bring salvation to the nations and restore creation to its divine intention. It is at the climactic moment of the cycle of the bowls where John will connect these two activities most acutely.

6

Silence and Praise: Economic Non-Participation and Narrating the New Creation

The point that apocalyptic makes is not only that people who wear crowns and who claim to foster justice by the sword are not as strong as they think – true as that is: we still sing, 'O where are Kings and Empires now of old that went and came?' It is that people who bear crosses are working with the grain of the universe. One does not come to that belief by reducing social processes to mechanical and statistical models, nor by winning some of one's battles for the control of one's own corner of the fallen world. One comes to it by sharing the life of those who sing about the Resurrection of the slain Lamb.

—John Howard Yoder, "Armaments and Eschatology"[1]

The bowls cycle does not follow immediately upon the end of the trumpets cycle. Therefore, unlike the relation between the seals and trumpets, the connection between the bowls and trumpets is harder to trace structurally in the text. However, the bond is cemented when one looks at the literary similarities. Both are modeled quite extensively on the Egyptian plagues. Both sets of judgments are concerned with very similar themes and elements. And both cycles are concerned with a constellation of judgment, praise, and wrath.[2] This similarity confirms that the bowls cycle is a recapitulation of the trumpet cycle rather than a progression of further judgment. Given the close structural

---

1. John Howard Yoder, "Armaments and Eschatology," in *Studies in Christian Ethics* 1.1 (1988), 58.

2. Indeed, at least the last in this list of similarities could be applied to all three judgment cycles. This serves to cement the link among all three and demonstrates their status as recapitulative.

relation between the seals and the trumpets, all three cycles should be seen as a threefold meditation on a singular event of judgment. Elisabeth Schüssler Fiorenza employs a helpful image when she argues that the trumpets and bowls "seem to refer to the two written sides of the scroll" (see Rev. 5:1).[3] One of the key differences between the bowls and the trumpets seems to be the extension of wrath and judgment. Where the trumpets dealt judgment to a third of the cosmos and human population, there is no such limit placed on the effect of the bowl judgments. For example, in the trumpets cycle a third of the sea became blood and killed a third of the sea-life; in the bowls cycle the entire sea turns to blood and kills every living thing in the sea. This intensification should not be seen as a progression of judgment, however. Instead, in keeping with the idea that the cycles recapitulate each other, the intensification of wrath should be understood as the same judging activity seen under a different aspect.[4] John's focus in the trumpets cycle was the witness of the saints and its potential to produce repentance—hence the limits on the destructive activity. Here, the focus lies not on repentance but on the obstinacy of the earth-dwellers and the fittingness of the judgment that dismantles the idolatrous world. The bowl plagues are called "the last" (ἐσχάτας) and the completion (ἐτελέσθη) of the wrath of God (15:1). This does not exclude the idea of repentance/ It simply means that John is emphasizing a different aspect of the divine judgment in this vision cycle.[5]

There is a liturgical flavor overall to the bowls plagues that may have been latent in the seals and trumpets but is made more emphatic here. The bowls are called "phials" (φιάλας) which are the customary instrument for pouring out libations in cultic practice.[6] Similarly the verb "to pour out" (ἐκχέετε) is used for the pouring out of the sacrificial blood by the priest at the base of the altar in the sanctuary (Lev. 4:6-7, 17-18, 25, 30, 34; 8:15).[7] The shedding of the saints' blood and the pouring of plagues from bowls as fitting judgment are both seen under the aspect of sacrifice and liturgy. Perhaps this is the reason John provides

---

3. Elisabeth Schüssler Fiorenza, *Revelation: Vision of a Just World*, Proclamation Commentaries (Minneapolis: Fortress Press, 1991), 70.

4. See Schüssler Fiorenza, *Vision of a Just World*, 92–93, who argues that the same judgment is depicted in the bowls as in the trumpets, but the bowls depict the specific effects of the judgment against the worshipers of the beast. This is true to a certain extent but, as we have seen, all the plagues have been directed at the obstinate idol-worshipers, while not seeming to harm the saints.

5. Contra G. K. Beale, *The Book of Revelation: A Commentary on the Greek Text* (Grand Rapids and Cambridge: Eerdmans and Paternoster, 1999), 825–826.

6. David E. Aune, *Revelation 6–16*, Word Biblical Commentary (Nashville: Thomas Nelson, 1998), 883.

7. Beale, *The Book of Revelation*, 813.

no interlude as he does in the previous two cycles. The images pile onto one another with terror and quick pace, with no need to stop because at this point in the liturgical performance of the text there is no doubt about the close relation between the saints' sacrifice and the demolition of the cosmos.[8] The bowls cycle is unique in that, after the seventh bowl has been poured out, John takes a closer view of the effect of the fall of Babylon two chapters later. For our purposes, then, the bowls cycle extends from 16:1-21 and then continues in 18:1—19:8. The seventh bowl, which envisions the fall of Babylon, is described in 16.17-21 and then illustrated in much richer detail in 18:1—19:8.[9]

Overview of the Cycle of Seven Bowls

The bowls cycle begins with a loud voice from the temple, belonging to God or Christ, instructing the seven angels with bowls to pour them out upon the earth (16:1). It becomes clear very quickly that John is using the earth here as synecdoche for the entire cosmos as the angels pour the bowls not just on the earth, but in the water and in the air as well.[10] These bowl judgments are meant to judge the whole world. The judgment begins when the first angel pours the first bowl onto the earth and painful and searing sores appear on the flesh of those who bear the mark of the beast (16:2; see also 13:4, 8, 12, 15). This plague is based on the Egyptian plague of boils (Exod. 9:9-11) and so sets the stage for the rest of the cycle which is heavily influenced by the Exodus plagues. The focus on the mark of the beast is the shadow side to what John has presented in the previous two cycles of plagues. In the seals and trumpets judgments, those who bore the seal of God were protected from the plagues. Now the plagues are directed at their specific target, not indirectly, but directly.

---

8. Brian K. Blount, *Revelation: A Commentary*, New Testament Library (Louisville: Westminster John Knox, 2009), 302–307 identifies an interlude at 16:13-16 but it is not a liturgically colored interlude.

9. See Robert L. Thomas, "An Analysis of the Seventh Bowl of the Apocalypse," *The Masters Seminary Journal* 5.1 (1994): 73–95.

10. In depicting the bowls as judgment on the earth more broadly construed, John may even be presenting an image of the judgment on the four basic elements of the world, see Franz Boll, *Aus der Offenbarung Johannis: Hellenistiche Studien zum Weltbild der Apockalypse*, ΣΤΟΙΧΕΙΑ 1 (Leipzig: Druck und Verlag B. G. Teubner, 1914), 63–67; Joseph Freundorfer, "Die Apokalypse des Apostels Johannes und die Hellensitische Kosmologie und Astrologie: eine Auseinandersetzung mit den Hauptergebnissen der Untersuchung Franz Bolls: 'Aus Der Offenbarung Johannis'," *Biblische Studien* 23.1 (1929) 32–33; Aune, *Revelation 6–16*, 899; Blount, *Revelation*, 293. Against this interpretation see Adela Yarbro Collins, *Cosmology and Eschatology in Jewish and Christian Apocalypticism*, Supplements to the Journal for the Study of Judaism 50 (Leiden, New York, and Köln: Brill, 1996), 107–108; Adela Yarbro Collins, "The History-of-Religions Approach to Apocalypticism and the 'Angel of the Waters' (Rev. 16:4-7)," *CBQ* 39.3 (1977), 374–379.

Those who participate in the idolatrous economy of Rome are singled out. The mark of the beast may not be physically visible, but the boils reveal on the skin what was once secret.[11]

The second angel pours out the second bowl on the sea, turning it to blood (16:3). This judgment is parallel to the second trumpet, but here the whole sea is transformed rather than one-third of it, and all of the sea creatures die rather than a third. This plague should not be seen as a supplement to the trumpet judgment. Instead, interpreters should understand that the plague that marked off a third of the sea for judgment emphasized the possibility of repentance in the midst of judgment, here the emphasis falls on total judgment. When the two aspects of this judgment are seen together the audience understands that the total world system (here characterized by the chaos of the sea[12]) is under judgment, but that they can still repent and be protected amidst the destruction of the cosmos.

When the third angel pours the bowl of judgment into the rivers and springs of water they become blood (16:4). This is again an intensification of a plague found in the trumpets cycle. The difference between the two plagues lies not in just its intensity however, but also its outcome. When one-third of the rivers and springs were affected in the trumpets cycle they became bitter. Now however, all the rivers and springs are turned to blood. G. K. Beale connects both the plague of the sea and the plague of the waters to economic suffering. This is a foretaste of the demise of all who make their wealth through maritime commerce that will be portrayed dramatically in Revelation 18.[13] The waters turning to blood would have been understood as a prodigy or sign of the anger of the gods in the ancient world (see Cicero, *De div.* 1.43.97; 2.27.58).[14]

The "angel of the waters" then breaks out into a doxological hymn, praising God for just and fitting judgments. The idea of an angel of the waters assumes the ancient cosmological understanding where the elements and phenomena of the created world are overseen or represented by angels (see 1 Enoch 60:12-22; 61:10 69:22; 75:3, 2 Enoch 4-6; 19:1-4; 1QH 1:8-13).[15] The angel uses the modified three-fold name of God ("one who was, and is, and is to come"). But whereas in the trumpet cycle this name was modified by leaving off "is to come," here "is to come" is substituted with "holy one" (Rev. 16:5). Once

---

11. James L. Resseguie, *The Revelation of John: A Narrative Commentary* (Grand Rapids: Baker Academic, 2009), 210.

12. Beale, *The Book of Revelation*, 815.

13. Beale, *The Book of Revelation*, 816–817.

14. Aune, *Revelation 6–16*, 884.

15. Aune, *Revelation 6–16*, 884.

again this modification of God's name signifies that God is present on earth (a reality that will be made clear by the end of the cycle with the theophanic phenomena). God's judgments through the bowl plagues are equivalent to God's entrance into the world. God is, in the prophetic idiom, "the Holy one, in [the world's] midst" (see Isa. 12:6; Hos. 11:9; Ezek. 20:41; 28:22).[16] The angel declares the blood judgments as fitting (ἄξιοί) because the inhabitants of the earth had poured out the blood of the saints.[17] The punishments depicted here are retributive justice for the murder of the saints, but they are also more than that. The plagues are also a dismantling of the cosmic reality that makes the killing of the enduring saints a possibility. The judgment envisioned by John is oriented toward the goal of remaking the cosmos in such a way that the murder of the righteous is unthinkable.

The altar responds to the angel's declaration of praise by affirming the truthfulness and justice of God's judgments (Rev. 16:7). This appearance of the altar means that it is present in each of the three cycles (6:9; 9:13). The image of the altar and the voices emanating from it always signify the petition of the slain who are found under the altar. In a sense, all of the judgments in all of the cycles are an outworking of the justice and vindication of the sacrificial slain beneath the altar.[18] In the seals cycle, the altar symbolized the endurance of the saints and the costly ethic of non-participation in idolatry even unto death (6:9). In the trumpets cycle, the altar participated in the judgment of those on earth in the release of the demonic riders (9:13). Once again, John is hinting at the profound connection between the church's costly witness and the dismantling of the cosmos—their worship as witness has a role in bringing an end to the Roman world system. It is worth noticing that both the angel's hymn and the altar's response are things that John has "heard" (καὶ ἤκουσα).[19] It could be that John is once again utilizing the discrepancy between what is seen and what is heard in the Apocalypse. John has seen the destruction of the cosmos, but when John attunes his ear to gain further insight into this vision he hears worship. Just as the conquering lion exists as a slain lamb, and the 144,000 is actually an

---

16. Aune, *Revelation 6–16*, 886, points to a great deal of inscriptional evidence that indicates a cult of Hosios and Dikaois in Asia Minor. This cult associated these deities with Zeus and Apollo, among other deities. The naming of God in worship as holy in just, could be a purposeful refutation that the gods of the Romans are being defeated. Their world is being torn asunder by the true just and holy God, who is at work to remake the creation into a place of purity and peace and righteousness.

17. For the fittingness or deserving nature of the Exodus plagues see Wis. 11:16; 16:9; 18:4; 19:4.

18. Beale, *The Book of Revelation*, 820.

19. Blount, *Revelation*, 298–299.

uncountable multitude, so the destruction of the cosmos is heralded not with terror but praise.

The correspondence of bowls and trumpets continues when the fourth angel pours the forth bowl out upon the sun (16:8).[20] The difference comes in the fact that the trumpet plague darkens the sun while the bowl plague causes fire to scorch people on the earth. This plague had previously been in John's mind when he describes the worshipers before the throne of God as being exempt from being struck by the sun and scorching heat (7:16; see Isa. 49:10). This image continues John's emphasis on the difference in cosmic experience between the idolaters and the saints. Those who have the seal of God are protected; those who bear the economic mark of the beast are ruined. Those who worship God and the Lamb are led to the springs of water of the New Jerusalem; those who worship the beast have their springs of water turned to blood. Those who follow the Lamb are shielded from the sun's scorching rays; those who are deceived by the beast and false prophet are burned by intense heat. In all of these ways, it seems that John's vision of the crumbling of the cosmos is experienced in different ways by the two groups of people.

This is due to the way that John employs rhetorical cosmology—it is not simply literal, but is more than symbolic. It is above all a theo-political way of stating that the gods and myths that sustain the Roman way of structuring the world are bankrupt and impotent and the God of creation is cleansing that creation to make it habitable for the holy. This sheds light on why the people undergoing the plagues blaspheme the name of God who has authority over the plagues (Rev. 16:9). They blaspheme because they do no recognize the sovereignty of God over the shape and form of the world.[21] If they were to recognize God's authority over the plagues, it would mean repentance and the end of the preferred arrangement for them—Rome's imperial center would be radically de-centered and all the familiar anchors and signposts that structure the world would be revoked. The economic security that comes with the idolatrous cultic practice of Rome is too strong a draw, and so the inhabitants of the earth that do not repent choose to be demolished with the cosmos.

John's reflection on the dueling sovereignties of God and the beast continues when the fifth bowl is poured out upon the throne of the beast (16:10). The throne of the beast is an analeptic image that brings the audience back to 13:2 where John reported that the dragon (Satan) gave his throne and

---

20. Pouring the bowl out upon the sun is more evidence that the voice from the temple instructing the angels to pour their bowls out upon "the earth" intended that the bowl plagues affect the entire created order.

21. Beale, *The Book of Revelation*, 823.

great authority over to the beast. Therefore, the image carries even further back to a reference in the letter to Pergamum concerning "Satan's throne" (2:13). Beale argues that this throne is to be equated with Pergamum as "the center of Roman government and of the imperial cult, which was ultimately under Satanic control."[22] Other scholars suggest that the throne refers to Rome.[23] However, it is better not to regard the throne of Satan as having a locative sense at all. Steven J. Friesen argues that Satan's throne does not refer to any archaeological reality dug up at Pergamum, nor does it refer to Pergamum as the center of the imperial cult in Asia (since there was no such "center" of the cult—especially in the Asian province) but that it instead refers to "external hostility from mainstream society."[24] Satan's throne refers to Satan's reign as embodied in the mundane Roman culture of idolatry—a culture that carried with it its own sense of cosmology. Pouring out the bowl of judgment on the throne of the beast should carry the sense of dispossessing the beast and the dragon of authority over the earth. Especially given the occurrence of authority in the previous verse and the investiture of the beast with the dragon's authority in chapter 13, John seems to be saying that the devil and the beast have lost their control over the order of the cosmos.

This loss of control is demonstrated when the beast's kingdom (see 11:15) is plunged into darkness. Darkness stands in contrast to the light of the new creation, where both God and the Lamb function as the cosmic luminaries (21:23; 22:5; see also 18:1). Once again the Egyptian plague of darkness is in the background, as is the fourth trumpet judgment (Exod. 10:21-29; Rev. 8:12). Since the plagues can be attributed more or less directly to the work of the Lamb, there may be a connection between the darkness of the plague and the darkness that accompanies the crucifixion in the Synoptic gospels (Mark 15:33; Matt. 27:45; Luke 23:44).[25] Indeed it is the work of the slain Lamb on the cross that has put into effect this entire series of judgments on the world

---

22. Beale, *The Book of Revelation*, 824; see also Resseguie, *The Revelation of John*, 212.

23. See Aune, *Revelation 6–16*, 889; R H. Charles, *A Critical and Exegetical Commentary on The Revelation of St. John*, vol. 2, The International Critical Commentary (Edinburgh: T & T Clark, 1920), 45; Robert H. Mounce, *The Book of Revelation*, rev. ed., New International Commentary on the New Testament (Grand Rapids: Eerdmans, 1998), 297; Wilfred J. Harrington, *Revelation*, Sacra Pagina 16 (Collegeville: Liturgical, 1993), 165; Blount, *Revelation*, 301.

24. Steven J. Friesen, "Satan's Throne, Imperial Cults and the Social Settings of Revelation," *Journal of the Study of the New Testament* 27.3 (2005), 365.

25. It may be more than coincidental that John's gospel does not report this darkness at the crucifixion, perhaps because of John's emphasis of Jesus as light (John 1:4-5, 9; 8:12) and the crucifixion as the site and event of the glory of God (17:1-2). The interplay of light and darkness in John mirrors perhaps what is going on in the Apocalypse on a cosmic scale. The beast and all of his followers dwell in a darkened

and has enabled the saints to conquer (Rev. 5:9-10; 12:11). There may also be a connection between the Johannine Gospel's understanding of "the hour" of crucifixion and the "hour" of Babylon's demise (John 2.:4; 5:25, 28 (?); 7:30; 8:20; 12:23; 13:1; 16:21, 25; 17:1; Rev. 17:12; 18:10, 17, 19).[26]

Once again, John portrays the people as suffering in the darkness and yet continuing to blaspheme and refusing to repent (Rev. 16:11). John reports that they refused to repent of their deeds (ἔργων). This word when applied to the earth-dwellers connotes the work of idolatry (2:6; 3:1-2; 3:15; 9:20; 16:11; 18:6), but when applied to those who worship the true God refers to proper worship and faithful endurance against the influence of the Roman cult and economy (2:2, 5, 19, 26; 3:8; 14:13). God judges according to these deeds or this work and consequently the question at judgment is one of worship (2:23; 20:12; 22:12). The earth-dwellers in their stubborn refusal to quit these deeds of false worship demonstrate that they are still turning to the gods of the Roman cult and economy to shore up their quickly disintegrating world. Their blasphemy in refusing to speak the truth about God's diagnosis of the condition of the world is their ultimate undoing.

The sixth angel pours the sixth bowl on the river Euphrates. In the trumpets cycle the Euphrates functioned as the border marker between Rome and Parthia, but it also carried Edenic resonances (9:14). Here the Edenic resonances may be latent, but the description of the location from whence the kings come as "where the sun rises" (16:12) could carry some of the same primordial overtones.[27] The bowl plague dries up the Euphrates, providing a multivalent image for John's purposes. First, the image of rivers drying up is a common response of creation to God's arrival (Isa. 50:2; Hos. 13:15; Nah. 1:4). It also is a motif that signifies the miraculous passage of a victorious army (Exod. 14:21; Josh. 3:17; see also Isa. 11:15).[28] John probably merges these two images in his own vision which pictures the river dried up for the arrival of the kings of the east. Isaiah prophesies the drying of the Euphrates, a prophecy which is fulfilled when Cyrus diverted the river and crossed over in order to defeat Babylon (Isa. 44:27-28). God's use of Cyrus, who came "from the east" (41:2), was a means of liberation for God's people and judgment upon Babylon (44:26-28; 45:13).[29]

---

kingdom, while those who follow the Lamb live in the light emanating from the Lamb and God (Rev. 21:23; 22:5).

26. See the discussion below.

27. See Edmondo F. Lupieri, *A Commentary on the Apocalypse of John,* trans. Maria Poggi Johnson and Adam Kamesar (Grand Rapids: Eerdmans, 2006), 241.

28. Aune, *Revelation 6–16,* 891.

After the Euphrates runs dry, John sees demonic spirits proceeding from the mouths of the dragon, the beast, and the false prophet (Rev. 16:13). The concept of things emerging from the mouth is used often by John to refer to language, whether it be the deceitful language of the beast that leads to harm and death (9:18-19; 12:15-16; 13:6) or the word of witness put forward by the Lamb and his followers (1:16; 11:5; 19:15). That these demonic spirits are spirits of deceit and lies concerning the beast is evidenced by the fact that the second beast is referred to here as the false prophet. David Aune traces a connection between this occurrence and the mention of false prophets in 1 John 4:1.[30] The false prophet is one who denies Christ is from God and came in the flesh. This is equivalent in the Apocalypse to denying the work of the slain Lamb, who was crucified and was sent by God to ransom many people through his blood.

These demonic spirits are said to be like frogs. John's vision returns to the storehouse of imagery from the Egyptian plagues. Beale suggests that the frogs represent the empty croaking of loud and meaningless speech.[31] He is drawing this interpretation from Rabbinic evidence that is most likely later than Revelation, therefore the connection seems dubious. In addition, the Rabbinic reflection on "undisciplined speech" seems to not reflect the contextual concerns of John's audience. Theirs is not a wisdom setting that needs a midrashic reflection on "idle talk." John's audience is rather situated in the midst of a cosmic battle, and the options for speech are not "disciplined or loose" in the context of community relations, but "true or false" in the context of witness within their broader culture. Much more satisfactory is the alternative suggestion Beale presents, which is that the frogs represent the deceptive influence of the cult for John "because they were one of the two Egyptian plagues that Pharaoh's magicians were able to reproduce through their deceptive arts (Exod. 8:7)."[32]

This echo of the Egyptian magicians is probable because the demonic frogs perform signs (σημεῖα) that deceive the kings of the earth to join with the beast in his battle against the Lamb and his followers (Rev. 16:14). These signs are mentioned elsewhere by John in connection with the work of the second beast (or false prophet) to deceive the inhabitants of the earth and cause them to bear the economic mark of the beast (13:13; 19:20). Therefore, the signs of these demonic spirits blind the earth-dwellers judgment and persuade them to participate in the cultic economy and its cosmological discourse.[33]

---

29. Beale, *The Book of Revelation*, 827.
30. Aune, *Revelation 6–16*, 894.
31. Beale, *The Book of Revelation*, 832–833. See also Mounce, *The Book of Revelation*, 299.
32. Beale, *The Book of Revelation*, 832.

These signs were very likely special effects produced in various cult ceremonies, demonstrating with "smoke and mirrors" the power of the gods of Rome.[34]

These signs of power and deceit go out to deceive the kings of the whole world (οἰκουμένης). It seems that John is being intentionally vague, or perhaps even he isn't certain of the meaning of what he sees at this point. Are the kings of the whole world distinct from the kings of the east mentioned earlier? Are the kings of the east and the kings of the earth on the same side or are they working at cross-purposes?[35] John does not address this question and we can probably never confidently possess the answer. What can be said about these kings? John seems to be beginning a political-theological reflection that he will carry through to the end of the work. This reflection is on the role of kings in the world of Rome and the newly created world of God (see 17:16-18; 18:3, 9; 19:18; 21:24). Edmondo Lupieri draws attention to the wording that suggests that the evil spirits are poured out like liquid on the kings of the earth, in a kind of Satanic parody of the anointing ritual for a king. Lupieri writes, "Satan intends to anoint his own kings with an evil spiritual unction and set himself and them in opposition to God and his Anointed."[36] Beale argues that this instance of the gathering of the kings already anticipates the image of the kings turning against the economic and religious system of Babylon and destroying it.[37] To this image he adds the notion found in Targum Jeramiah 51:36, 41-44 that the drying of the Euphrates accompanies a judgment on Babylon with the result that kings and peoples become disloyal to Babylon.[38]

John seems to have no role for kings in the world because ultimately he has no role for the world. The world is passing away, and with it so must the

---

33. Mounce, *The Book of Revelation*, 299: "The evil spirits come out of the *mouths* of the unholy triumvirate, suggesting the persuasive and deceptive propaganda that in the last days will lead people to an unconditional commitment to the cause of evil."

34. About the connection of cultic liturgy and the perception and projection of cosmic power Scherrer writes, "Thunder and lightning are associated with Jupiter as symbolic of his authority and divinity, and hence have been imitated by rulers. Plutarch, for example, criticizes rulers who imitate God's thunders (Gk βροντάς), lightnings (Gk κεραυούς) and sunbeams (Gk ἀκτινοβολίας) . . . There are numerous references in Domitian's court power Martial, for example, to both Jupiter (*Epigrams* 8.39; 9.11; 9.3; 9.91) and Domitian (6.10; 7.99, 9.39; 9.86) as Thunderer," Steven J. Scherrer, "Signs and Wonders in the Imperial Cult: A New Look at a Roman Religious Institution in the Light of Rev. 13:13-15," *JBL* 103.4 (1984): 599–610, 605.

35. Harrington sees all of the kings as being on a joint venture, *Revelation*, 166. Beale understands the two terms to be synonymous, *The Book of Revelation*, 834.

36. Lupieri, *A Commentary on the Apocalypse of John*, 243.

37. Beale, *The Book of Revelation*, 828.

38. Beale, *The Book of Revelation*, 829.

reign of kings. And yet he sees hope in that these kings might turn against Babylon and their logic of competition might speed the dismantling of "the city" and its cosmology. Once this is the case, the kings are welcomed into the New Jerusalem and its cosmic reality. John's political theology is this: as long as kings buy into the corrupt and idolatrous economic system of Rome, they will be doomed to face its demise along with it. But since the cosmos is passing away, and since they even seem to have some small role in its passing, they can be participants within the new cosmic reality. But to participate as a king in the new creation, one must walk by the light of the glory of the Lamb and the one on the throne. Kings only remain kings who exist under the kingship of the Lamb (Rev. 19:16). John therefore does not leave room for a temporary "secular" political arrangement while awaiting the kingdom come.[39]

After this brief reflection on political theology, there is an interruptive exhortation from Christ to believers. Aune identifies it as an interpolation belonging to the second edition of the book.[40] But this need not be the case as it can also function as a warning to remain vigilant before the seventh bowl and final judgment and new creation.[41] In the context of the great battle of the day of God, the Almighty Christ, who is coming like a thief, conditionally blesses the hearers if they are found watching and remaining fully clothed. This exhortation hearkens back to Christ's letter to the church in Sardis (3:1-6). There Christ describes himself as a thief and refers to the few faithful in Sardis who have not soiled their clothes with idolatry and will walk with him dressed in white. This interjection referring to clothing sets up an important theme for John going forward, for what one is found to be wearing at the final assize plays a big part in how one will be judged.[42] The dueling conceptions of fine linen in chapter 18 and 19 are a perfect example of the two options John lays out for his audience. One can either wear the fine linen of the luxurious and idolatrous economy of Rome (18:12, 16) or be dressed in the fine linen of righteous deeds (19:6, 14). But to dress in the wealth of Rome is also to dress in the emperor's new clothes. To accommodate to the culture of idolatry is for John to be caught naked. This concept of nakedness may recall the imagery of the nakedness and shame in Eden (see Rev. 3:18; Gen. 2:25; Tg. Ps.-J. Gen 3:10; Apoc. Moses 20:4).[43] With this eschatological warning, perhaps functioning like

---

39. See Steven J. Friesen, *Imperial Cults and the Apocalypse of John: Reading Revelation in the Ruins* (Oxford: Oxford University Press, 2001), 213.
40. Aune, *Revelation 6–16*, 896.
41. Beale, *The Book of Revelation*, 837.
42. For this clothing theme throughout the Apocalypse see Rev. 1:13; 3:18; 4:4; 12:1; 17:4; 19:13, 14.
43. Aune, *Revelation 6–16*, 897.

the interludes between the sixth and seventh elements of the seals and trumpets, the stage has been set for the final bowl of judgment.

The Seventh Bowl: Silence and Praise

John's vision of the bowls cycle had set up the seventh bowl to be a battle. In the sixth bowl the kings of the earth were gathered in order to fight the battle of the day of God Almighty. Before the eschatological interjection from Christ, these armies were depicted as being gathered by the evil spirits of the unholy trinity of the dragon, the beast, and the false prophet. However, when John returns to the image after Christ's macarism it is instead God (with the use of the divine passive third person singular "he gathered") who seems to be in charge of gathering them at the stage of battle.[44] While the nations rage, it is God who is ultimately in control, ordering and directing everything according to the divine intention for unmaking and making new. This is also evidenced by the fact that John refers to the battle with the definite article (τὸν πόλεμον), as if to designate it as "the [well-known] war of the end."[45] An image of a designated final battle is found in the Qumran War Scroll 1QM 1:10 in which the "sons of light" will march out to defeat a coalition made up of "all nations" (15:1; 16:1).[46] The battlefield to which God gathers his opponents is called in Hebrew *Harmageddon*. This is another vague reference from John. It is possible that it is a familiar image to his audience. There is no exact location that can be pointed to on a map called *Harmageddon*. Suggestions range from the mountains near the plain of Megiddo to a city of Megiddo. Most intriguing is the possibility that it is a reference to Mount Carmel which is in the vicinity of the plain of Megiddo. If this is the case, John may be referencing Elijah's contest with and defeat of the prophets of Baal during the reign of Ahab and Jezebel (1 Kgs. 18:19-46).[47]

---

44. Blount, *Revelation*, 306.

45. Beale, *The Book of Revelation*, 835. Cf. Aune, *Revelation 6–16*, 896.

46. Aune, *Revelation 6–16*, 895–896. For the intriguing notion that the Apocalypse itself is fashioned as a Christian "War Scroll" see Richard Bauckham, *The Climax of Prophecy: Studies on the Book of Revelation* (London and New York: T & T Clark, 1993), 210–237.

47. Beale, *The Book of Revelation*, 839–840. Another intriguing suggestion is put forward by Day who argues that the reference point is Zech. 12:11 because that is the only other occurrence of Megiddo in an apocalyptic context. John seems to be concerned with the Hebrew identity of the location so it is probable that he is working within the prophetic tradition for this image. John also alludes quite strongly to Zech. 12:10 at the beginning of the Apocalypse (Rev. 1:7), see G. K. Beale and Sean M. McDonough, "Revelation," in *Commentary on the New Testament Use of the Old Testament*, ed. G. K. Beale and D. A. Carson (Grand Rapids and Nottingham: Baker Academic and Apollos, 2007), 1090. This case is strengthened by the fact that the oracle in Zech. 12 begins with the designation of God as the one "who stretched out the heavens and founded the earth" (12:1 NRSV). The fact that the oracle is set within the

Wherever this battle is to take place, and whatever sources stand behind John's vision of it, the most striking thing about it is that it never actually takes place. This is strangely the case with every occurrence of the battle motif in the Apocalypse. Whenever John's imagery suggests the build-up to a battle he never follows through with actually describing the battle (Rev. 19:11-21; 20:7-9). The closest John's audience comes to actually witnessing a battle scene is where the sword proceeding out of the mount of the rider on the white horse kills a group of inhabitants of the earth, but this is interposed with the image of their death as being eaten by birds (19:21). In 13:4 the beast is named as inherently antagonistic in the people's worship: "who is like the beast and who can fight against?" The dragon and the beast are constantly making war on God and God's people (12:17). But God, it seems, never resists the beast in combat. It is possible that John perceives that for God to do so, God would be stooping to the same level and fighting within the same plane as the dragon and the beast. Instead, God responds by pulling the cosmological rug out from under the beast. Without the beast's cosmos, which he protects by constantly making war, the beast is powerless. No cosmos, no authority. The cosmos is not the battlefield on which God combats the beast, rather the cosmos is what God unmakes and makes new in order to defeat the beast.

This is the logic of the seventh bowl. The angel pours the seventh bowl into the air (ἀέρα). The air is associated with the demonic spirits (Rev. 9:2; see also Eph 2:2). But the reference to air also completes the series of the four basic elements of the cosmos from ancient Greek natural philosophy: earth (Rev. 16:2), water (16:3, 4, 12), fire (16:8), and air (16:17). The bowl plagues have affected all four of the major elements considered constitutive of everything in the cosmos. The entirety of existence as the ancients knew it has been undone.[48] Rather than a battle John reports the unmaking and making new of the cosmos. After this he hears a voice from the throne in the temple declare, "it is done" (γέγονεν, 16:17). God's judgment has been consummated in that it has reached the ends of the cosmos and the telos of God's purposes for the judgment (ἐτελέσθη, 15:1). Just as the work of Christ was finished at the cross

---

context of God as creator means that John could have turned to it for a resource for his mediation on the battle as set within a vision of creation and new creation. See John Day, "The Origin of Armageddon: Revelation 16:16 as an Interpretation of Zechariah 12:11," in *Crossing the Boundaries: Essays in Biblical Interpretation in Honour of Michael D. Goulder*, ed. Stanley E. Porter, et al. (Leiden: Brill, 1994), 315–326.

48. For further discussion of this idea, both for and against this interpretation see Boll, *Offenbarung*, 63–67; Freundorfer, "Die Apokalypse des Apostels Johannes," 32–33; Aune, *Revelation --16*, 899; Blount, *Revelation*, 293; Yarbro Collins, *Cosmology and Eschatology in Jewish and Christian Apocalypticism*, 107–108; Yarbro Collins, "The History-of-Religions Approach," 374–379.

in John's gospel (τετέλεσται, 19:30), so now Christ's work has been worked through the entire cosmos—his sacrifice has meant the undoing of the world and the entrance of God's reign over the new creation.

John builds upon this image of the unmaking and making new of the world when he turns for the final time to theophanic imagery. The coming of God into the area of creation is once again seen as the final judgment and outworking of the divine plan for creation (see Isa. 29:5b-6; 30:30). God's entrance on the world stage is accompanied by lightning, voices, thunder, earthquake, and great hail. The hail is so terrible for those on earth that they curse God, even at the end remaining resistant to the reign of God Almighty.[49] Aune remarks that the response of the people is strange, given that the hail would have been understood as a sign of the anger of the gods. This disruption in relation with the gods would normally require "diagnosis and repair."[50] Instead, the people respond with curses. John may be twisting the idea of a prodigy to conform to his own understanding of the contest of cosmological visions and therefore a contest between the gods of Rome and the true God. The negative response may be due to their understanding that their gods are being defeated; the beings and practices that sustained their comfortable way of life are being destroyed.

Once more John envisions the foundations of the earth shaking and being removed, stating that "every island fled away and no mountains were to be found" (Rev. 16:20 NRSV). John's vision emphasizes that the entrance of God signals the entrance of the new creation, and with it the disintegration of the first. The earthquake that accompanies the theophany of God is both a sign of God's presence and an instrument of judgment on the world of idolatry. Among apocalyptic usage of earthquake imagery, only John envisions the earthquake causing the fall of cities.[51] This may be due to several local earthquakes being fresh in the cultural memory of Asia Minor, such as the catastrophic earthquake in Sardis in 17 CE and the severe quake in Laodicea in 60 CE.[52] But John's point is probably overwhelmingly theological. The first city that falls is Babylon, here designated as "the great city" (ἡ πόλις ἡ

---

49. If this is the depiction of the final judgment and the end of history and the beginning of new creation, it is striking that John does not seem to emphasize a literal understanding of the end. Hail the size of John's description would almost certainly kill anyone on whom it falls, but this does not seem to be the case here, Aune, *Revelation 6–16*, 902. Those resisting God's reign and new creation are around at least long enough to curse it, and possibly longer than that (Rev. 22:15).

50. Aune, *Revelation 6–16*, 902.

51. Bauckham, *The Climax of Prophecy*, 205.

52. Bauckham, *The Climax of Prophecy*, 206.

μεγάλη) splitting into three parts. John's use of great city may be a reference to the prophetic work of Jonah who was called to Nineveh "that great city" (τὴν πόλιν τὴν μεγάλην, LXX) several times (Jonah 1:2; 3:2; 4:11). In Jonah, too, the prophetic vocation was to declare God's judgment on account of wickedness, and just as in the Apocalypse, the message of Jonah does not envision repentance of the king or people (3:4). And yet repentance does come when the people believe God will indeed overthrow Nineveh (3:5). Perhaps this imagery of the great city is a precursor, then, to John's vision of the repentance of the peoples and kings in the new creation. Only after the people realize that their cosmos has been overthrown can there be repentance and entrance into God's heavenly city (Rev. 21:24-25; 22:2).[53] Therefore, the cosmic judgments do not rule out repentance. Rather, for John, they make it possible. This is true for Babylon (Rome) but also for the cities that participate in the "Babylonian world system."[54] Thus, at the earthquake that accompanies God's arrival, the cities of the nations fall along with Babylon.

The Economic Critique of Chapter 18 and The End of the Cosmos

Though this theophanic event marks the end of the bowls cycle, John does not end his reflection on the fall of Babylon there. The seventh bowl is expanded and viewed in greater detail in Rev. 18:1—19:8. In this section, John focuses on the earth-dwellers' response to the demise of the great city and the role that the saints play in this great divine drama of judgment, unmaking, and new creation. John's primary purpose in the chapter is an economic critique of Roman trade. But as we have seen, for John there is very little distinction between the discussion of economic issues and the discussion of cosmology.[55] In expanding the vision of the dismantling of the cosmos with an economic critique, John is making clear that the end of the Roman economy means the end of the Roman world system. Therefore, it is appropriate to look, albeit

---

53. Joseph L. Mangina, *Revelation,* Brazos Theological Commentary on the Bible (Grand Rapids: Brazos, 2010), 213: "the city descending is for the sake of the city doomed, or at least for the sake of its inhabitants." It is noteworthy that Mangina also connects the images of Babylon and Nineveh as I do.

54. Beale, *The Book of Revelation,* 843.

55. Oliver O'Donovan, "History and Politics in the Book of Revelation," in *Bonds of Imperfection: Christian Politics, Past and Present,* Oliver O'Donovan and Joan Lockwood O'Donovan (Grand Rapids: Eerdmans, 2004), 40: "Trade is a kind of cultural promiscuity by which one power exploits and drains the resources of many others. John is certainly to be counted among those who have seen mercantile enterprise as a tool of imperialism. The tyranny of the beast in chapter 13 was exercised through the market."

briefly, at how John portrays the fall of Babylon in order to understand more fully how John completes his rhetorical cosmology through the three cycles of seven.

John's economic critique begins with the arrival of another angel, who is described as being so luminous that he illuminates the earth (18:1).[56] The angel, as herald of the fall of Babylon (18:2-3), is also functioning as a cosmic luminary, much like God and the Lamb do in the new creation. This makes clear that the advent of the reign of God and new creation spells the end of the Roman economy *and* cosmological discourse. That John places this cosmic imagery up front demonstrates that it is a point of emphasis for him. Babylon's kingdom languishes in darkness while the kingdom and glory embodied by the descending angel sheds light on both the bankruptcy of the city of Babylon and on the splendor of Christ's coming kingdom.

John next hears God's voice from heaven calling for "my people" to "come out of her." John employs the prophetic form of the "summons to flight" and personifies Babylon as a whore[57] who is about to be punished (see Jer. 51:45; 50:8 [LXX 27:8]; 51:6 [LXX 28:6]; Isa. 48:20; 52:11).[58] This summons to flee is not intended literally by John, as if the people are supposed to leave their homes and live out in the wilderness (see Rev, 12:6, 14; 17:3). Instead, John intends that his audience extricate themselves from participation in the political, economic, and cultic structures of Roman society.[59] The invitation to come out is an invitation to be transferred from one cosmic reality to another. Though physically they

---

56. Beale's argument that the angel refers to Christ is not convincing because John uses the adjective "another" to describe the angel, *The Book of Revelation*, 892–893. On the other hand, Blount clarifies the connection between God and the Lamb and the angel in that the divine passive is employed to demonstrate that it is God who lights up the earth by means of the angel, *Revelation*, 325.

57. This language of "whore," which feminizes evil and privileges the male dominant gaze is problematic because while attempting to lob rhetorical missiles at Rome, it ends up making women collateral damage. Blount's discussion of this phenomenon is helpful, as is his suggestion that in using this text constructively (in preaching or theological writing) some other image or metaphor that doesn't demonize or disparage women, arguing, "There ought to be a way to target the evil of empire without exposing women to such rhetorical and potentially real collateral damage," *Revelation*, 309–310. I might add also the use of "whore" rather than "harlot" is intentional here, because the latter does not by definition carry negative overtones concerning the function of a prostitute. "Harlot" romanticizes and provides a use and place for the prostitute in society. John's critique, as I have argued, has no interest in reserving a place or function for the whore of Babylon in the world; she serves no useful role in John's political theory, and therefore "whore" seems more in keeping with his critique. I am grateful to one of my students, Marsha Thrall, for helping me think through these ideas.

58. David E. Aune, *Revelation 17–22*, Word Biblical Commentary 52c (Nashville: Thomas Nelson, 1998), 990–991.

59. Beale, *The Book of Revelation*, 898–899; Aune, *Revelation 17–22*, 991.

are to remain in the world and in the cities where they live, in every other way they are to live, as it were, in another world. It is only from this wilderness that one can view the judgment and unmaking of Babylon (17:3). Following this summons to the people of God the divine voice continues to indict Babylon, declaring that the city and its economic system will be brought to ruin (18:5-8).

The rest of John's economic critique in chapter 18 is one of the more evocative sections in the Apocalypse. John narrates imaginatively and in great detail the response of those on the earth who had a great stake in the success of Rome's economic system and cosmological discourse—their comfort depended upon the stability and eternality of the world of Rome. John intends this critique for those both inside and outside of the church community. Anyone who participates in the luxury of the Rome's cultic economy stands under John's scrutiny and condemnation.[60] Those who participate in the Roman economy participate in the world that economy constructs. Therefore, when God dismantles that world piece by piece those who have tied their hopes to the continuance of that world will mourn and wail at its demise.

John depicts three distinct groups who mourn the loss of their system of trade. First the kings of the earth lament with shouts of "woe!" (οὐαί) concerning God's judgment of the "great city" (18:10). Next the merchants of the earth cry out in dismay because no one will be able to purchase their cargo anymore. Finally John envisions all those who participate in sea trade, shipmasters and sailors alike, as being utterly ruined by God's judgment upon the economy. John's use of "sea" is multivalent here, referring to both the sea as means of trade as well as to its more primordial sense of being the object of chaos and the source of the beast. John connects the cosmological aspects with the economic aspects of the sea in order to portray the relation between Rome's economic practices and the world those practices construct and assume.

One significant facet of the lament of these three people groups is their repetition of the concept of "the hour" that has brought their city to desolation (18:10, 17, 19). John frequently employs the concept of the hour of God's judgment in the Apocalypse (3:3, 10; 9:15; 14:7, 15; 17:12(?); see also 8:1). It is likely that John put this concept on the lips of the kings and merchants and sailors. However, we have also seen how John has connected the work of cosmic unmaking and making new in the cycles with the work of Christ on the cross. The death of the slain Lamb has provided an image of victory as cosmic upheaval that has proved very productive for John. Therefore, we should also understand this reference to the hour as an evocation of how the gospels,

---

60. See J. Nelson Kraybill, *Imperial Cult and Commerce in John's Apocalypse,* Journal for the Study of the New Testament Supplement 132 (Sheffield: Sheffield Academic, 1996), 100.

and especially John, speak of Christ's "hour" of death (Matt. 26:45; Luke 22:14; Mark 14:35, 41; John 2:4; 5:25, 28 (?); 7:30; 8:20; 12:23; 13:1; 16:21, 25; 17:1). The enduring witness of the slain Lamb constitutes the hour that Babylon's economic and world system has been overthrown and cast into the primordial sea, never to be seen again (Rev. 18:21).

Another striking feature about the economic critique is the way that John sets up pairs of opposites. The first pair of opposites is the goods that one owns and seeks after. John lists the cargoes with which the merchants of the earth participate in trade and make their living (18:11-13). John concretizes the image of wealth and cooperation with the idolatrous culture and economy. John's target is not simply a vague notion of evil desire. Instead, he singles out specific items that crystallize the concept of luxury and success in his context.[61] One of the cargoes listed is fine linen (βυσσίνου). This clothing adorned the wealthy and was a sign of luxury.[62] But those who participate in the system that traffics in this linen will be brought to ruin. John contrasts this cargo with the "fine linen" (βύσσινον) worn by the saints, which is described as the wedding garment of the bride-city of the Lamb—the new creation (19:8). John explains that this fine linen which clothes the saints is "the righteous deeds" (δικαιώματα) of the saints. The word John employs here is complex. The term usually refers to a judgment or decree in the LXX, and this seems to be the meaning of John's usage of it at 15:4 ("sentence of judgment/condemnation").[63] Additionally, the δικαι- terminology is used elsewhere in the Apocalypse only with reference to God as actor. For this reason, Beale argues that it may be better to understands John's reference as "just judgments on behalf of the saints."[64] But the genitive function makes more sense as a subjective rather than an objective construction. Therefore, John envisions the just judgments of the saints as somehow participating in the just judgments of God (see 16:7; 19:2)—they correspond to God's diagnosis of and rectifying activity in the world. The righteous judgments of the saints should be seen as equivalent to their endurance and non-participation in the culture of idolatry. Their patience and non-participation is itself a judgment of the cosmos and a participation in the divine activity of bringing the world to its end.

---

61. For the best treatment of the historical and social significance of the list of cargoes see Bauckham, *The Climax of Prophecy*, 350–371.

62. Bauckham, *The Climax of Prophecy*, 354.

63. Aune, *Revelation 17–22*, 1030–1031.

64. Beale, *The Book of Revelation*, 936, cf. 937. See also Mounce, *The Book of Revelation*, 348, who argues that the gift of God is the privilege of being clothed in the fine linen and not the fine linen itself.

John presents another contrasting cargo in the image of the slaves and human souls that the merchants of the earth exchange (18:13). The exchange of human lives represents for John the grossest cruelty and moral debauchery of the Roman cultic economy. It is estimated that there were about ten million slaves in the Roman Empire during the first century and the region of Asia Minor was one of the regions most heavily mined for the Roman slave trade.[65] Concerning John's disgusted attitude toward the slave trade Bauckham argues, "It is a comment on the whole list of cargoes. It suggests the inhuman brutality, the contempt for human life, on which the whole of Rome's prosperity and luxury rests."[66] John opposes this image of trafficking in human life, the image of God's slaves who have been ransomed (1:5; 5:9). The slaves of God are those who have been liberated from the slavery and oppression of the Roman world system. Instead of existing as enslaved to the idolatrous economy and cult of Rome, they bask in the freedom of God's new creation. Both of these pairs of contrasting cargoes suggest that John imagines and urges for his audience an alternative economy. Not only are they to refuse participation in the Roman cultic economy, they are to positively participate in exchanges that have their source in the justice of the New Jerusalem.

The final pair of opposites John deals with in the economic critique is the contrasting images of silence and praise. Once again aural phenomena are prominent among John's vision report, reminding interpreters that this writing has its setting in the liturgy. John depicts the desolation of Babylon with the threefold repetition of the absence of sound (φωνή, 18:22-23).[67] The city has fallen silent at the hour of God's judgment just as there was silence in heaven for about half an hour at the climax of judgment and new creation in the seals cycle (8.1). For these images John draws heavily on Jeremiah 25:10 but recontextualizes the imagery to have special significance within his own narrative. The first silence is the absence of musical sounds coming from harpists, singers, flutists, and trumpeters. On one level, John is demonstrating that the cultural artistry of the music of Rome typified by sound of skilled musicians will be absent.[68] But John also intends to remind his hearers of the liturgical aspect throughout the entire Apocalypse. The trumpets that herald the coming presence of God, the singers who sing praise around the throne, the harpists who play in praise of the Lamb, all of these things that characterize the new creation will be entirely absent in Babylon (Rev. 5:8; 8:6; 14:2-3; 15:2).

65. Aune, *Revelation 17–22*, 1002–1003.
66. Bauckham, *The Climax of Prophecy*, 371. See also Blount, *Revelation*, 334.
67. Cf. Mangina, *Revelation*, 211.
68. Mounce, *The Book of Revelation*, 338.

The true praise of God will be the only musical sound after the judgment, and it will leave Babylon bereft of all musical merriment.[69]

The second absence of sound that John reports is the sound of artisans plying their trade (18:22). Beale argues that this is another instance of the *lex talionis* motif employed by John elsewhere in the Apocalypse, arguing that since Rome removed Christian workers from the marketplace and from their productive lines of work, therefore God will in turn take away from Babylon the ability to produce a living.[70] This argument is not convincing, because as I argued earlier, it is unlikely that there was any widespread or systematic persecution of Christians at the time John wrote the Apocalypse. Beale's reading also ignores the fact that John in fact wants his audience to cease their participation in the economic practices of Rome. In portraying the absence of these sounds of commerce in Babylon, John is implying their presence elsewhere (just as he does with the other sounds).[71] Though the sounds of artisans and hand-mills have ground to a halt in Babylon, the implication is that they are present in the new creation. Ironically, it turns out that the saints were the driving force of culture and artistry in the pagan city that deemed itself the center of culture and artistry. The saints have come out of the city, and along with them so has the cultural and creative vitality.[72]

The third absence of sound John portrays is the absence of the voices of the bride and groom. The celebratory sounds at a wedding are signs of happiness and joy, but also of future hope and vitality.[73] Once more John's imagery is multivalent as Babylon is devoid of this celebratory vitality, but John is also

---

69. Contra Aune, who draws a parallel with the passage in Syb. Or. 8:113-119 which critiques all musical accompaniment for ritual activity, *Revelation 17–22*, 1008. John is not against liturgical music as he portrays it again and again as an integral part of the identity of the saints and the new creation.

70. Beale, *The Book of Revelation*, 919–920.

71. There is another absence that is not represented by a sound, but carries the same logic as the other three absences. The angel declares that the "light of a lamp"(φῶς λύχνου) will not be found in the city. Yet this same language is used to speak of the churches as lampstands (λυχνίαι) and of the light provided by the Lamb (λύχνος) in the new creation (Rev. 1:20; 21:23; 22:5).

72. This interpretation demonstrates a certain similarity to texts generally contemporary with the Apocalypse. Both Acts and the Epistle to Diognetus are concerned to show the cultural benefits that Christianity brings to the Greco-Roman world (Diognetus 5:1-6.10). For this understanding of the purpose of Acts, see C. Kavin Rowe, *World Upside Down: Reading Acts in the Greco-Roman Age* (Oxford: Oxford University Press, 2009). Christians are not to be feared or disparaged, but are to be understood as a preserving element for the world. John may share some of these assumptions, but rather than a preserving function, the saints' vocation is to participate in the end of the unjust world and the ushering in of the new creation. The goodness of culture and artistry is still a product of the saints for John, but rather than a preservative of the world it functions as that which brings it to its end.

73. Aune, *Revelation 17–22*, 1009.

thinking ahead to the next image he will put before his audience: the marriage of the Lamb. The theophanic arrival of God and the new creation, which is for John equivalent to the marriage between the Lamb and the heavenly city, is characterized by "voices" (φωναὶ, 4:5; 8:5; 11:19; 16:18). Therefore, it is not surprising that destitute Babylon is characterized as being deprived of these voices. In the new creation, the bride and bridegroom celebrate the perfection of God's redemption, while in Babylon there is only the sound of silence. Absence in Babylon implies presence in the new creation, while absence in the new creation (see the list of seven things that will be absent from the New Jerusalem; 21:1, 4; 22:3, 5) implies presence in Babylon.[74]

Out of the dead silence emerges raucous noise. John contrasts the absence of sound and voices in Babylon with the "great sound" (φωνὴν μεγάλην 19:1; see also 19:5-6). Thunderous voices sing in praise of God, both for the judgment of the world system of Babylon and for the arrival of the presence of God and, with God, the new creation. The sounds of praise and of the voices of bride and groom characterize the new creation. The shouts of ἀλληλουϊά from the worshipers function almost like a play on the soundalike οὐαί of the merchants, demonstrating John's "brilliant deployment of assonance designed to bring opposing 'still-lives' of despair and joy into sharpest relief."[75] The worship depicted in this scene, like all the hymnic liturgies of the Apocalypse, narrates the activity of God. Here God's activity is described in terms of unmaking and making new the entire universe. The demise of Rome's economic system is described in cosmic terms. The whore who has "destroyed" (ἔφθειρεν) the earth has been brought to naught (see 11:18). "Eternal Rome" is depicted as a burning city emanating eternal smoke (19:3).[76] The praise that narrates these events is not just the idle chatter of bystanders. Instead, John portrays praise as participation in the work of God. Just as the silence of the saints participates in ending the contractual arrangement between Rome and her gods, so too John understands the praise of God's people as a participation in the new creation. Their praise is the presence of the new creation at the seam in the universe where "the reign of the world" becomes "the reign of the Lord and of his Messiah."

---

74. See Resseguie, *The Revelation of John*, 231.

75. Harry O. Maier, *Apocalypse Recalled: The Book of Revelation after Christendom* (Minneapolis: Fortress Press, 2002), 155.

76. Beale, *The Book of Revelation*, 929.

Conclusion

John's portrayal of the divine work of unmaking and making new at the pouring out of the seventh bowl brings together the two images he has been working with throughout the three cycles in the Apocalypse. Once John has reached the third and last telling of the recapitulative vision, he has been able to state and restate his rhetorical purpose. His political vision is a cosmic vision. The judgment and defeat of Rome requires that the world that sustains and makes Rome possible must be dismantled—the world of idolatry must be unmade. The presence of God is the event that ushers in the new creation and the heavenly city, as demonstrated by the theophanic elements that accompany the end of each cycle. However, the unexpected aspect of the Apocalypse is that the theophany is a Christophany (1:7; 19:11-16). The one who conquered the world by the cross is the one who ushers in the new creation and the transition from the reign of the world to the reign of God. The work of the slain Lamb is God's means of bringing the impure and idolatrous world to an end. The Lamb is also God's instrument of new creation.

Consequently, John's call is for those who follow the Lamb to participate in his work, his faithful witness and endurance (19:10). The saints participate in the Lamb's witness by the two activities John has been explicating in the cycles: silence and praise. These activities are liturgical, political, and cosmological. Silence and praise constitute the saint's alternative cosmological discourse. Through silence and praise John builds his own vision of rhetorical cosmology, over against the imperial cultic cosmological discourse. Both silence and praise are necessary discursive vocations for the people of God living in the midst of the discursive world constructed by the Roman cultic economy. The bowls cycle finally brings into focus the importance of both. They are important because they function together to participate in the judging and renewing work of God—one negatively, one positively.

The non-participation or endurance of the saints is envisioned as silence. It brings the Roman cosmology to an end by introducing a break in the cosmological contract between Rome and her gods. Refusing sacrifice is a refusal of the gods who sustain "eternal Rome." This creates a vicious cycle in which the lack of praise given to the gods of Rome causes a lack of sustenance and care for the cosmos that Rome constructs, which in turn causes a further lack of faith in the gods. John's vision of the silence of the saints portrays the breakdown of the cosmos for the purpose of clearing the way for and evoking the repentance of the nations. With the loss of a world only two responses remain as possibilities: repentance leading to worship, or blasphemy leading to torment and suffering.

Silence envisions the participation of the saints in the demolition of the world of idolatry. This demolition is necessary for the emergence of the renewal and purification of the creation. The work of bringing in the new creation belongs to God, but John envisions a role for the saints as well. Their task is praise. Praise is the work of the saints to narrate the new world that God is bringing into existence. The constant feature of the hymnic liturgies in Revelation is their narration of the activity of God. The singers of these hymns should not be seen as passive observers. The worshipers in the Apocalypse do not function like a Greek dramatic chorus, standing off to the side while lobbing commentary in the general direction of the action. In the Apocalypse, praise is at the heart of the dramatic action. Worship functions for John as its own particular cosmological discourse. The worshipers sing of the activity of God and in doing so bring its presence into their midst. On the other side of the saints' vocation of silence, which negates the Roman world, is their work of praise, which enables them to participate in the new heavens and new earth, even in the midst of the house where they are gathered for worship—a house that is situated within a neighborhood of a city brimming with idolatrous pagan worship. Finally, praise participates in the new creation because it is one of the defining features of the new creation. The new creation has no temple because it is itself conceived of as temple-like (21:22; see also 21:15-21).[77] At the climax of the bowls cycle John finally brings the two images of silence and praise together to show how the saints participate in the work of God and the Lamb to unmake and make new the entire cosmos.

---

77. For discussion of the New Jerusalem as a city-temple see Beale, *The Book of Revelation*, 1109–1111.

7

Toward an Apocalyptic Political Theology

> The self-descriptive moment [of ecclesiology] then leads out to a missionary horizon, where the church encounters the 'other' that is summoned into the church, the world that God is redeeming. It is on this missionary horizon that political theology arises. Political theology is not ecclesial self-description directly, but a description of the world as it appears on this horizon, prepared for the church's mission by the Holy Spirit that runs ahead of the church.
> —Oliver O'Donovan, *The Ways of Judgment*[1]

In the preceding chapters I have argued that John's cosmological apocalyptic discourse has functioned to portray and encourage participation in the divine work of the unmaking and making new of creation. The participation in this work is the endurance and witness of the saints to the conquering activity of the slain Lamb, which for John is the spirit of prophecy (Rev. 19:10). In the silence of non-participation in the idolatrous world-building discourse of the Roman cultic economy, the saints have a role in breaking the contract between the inhabitants of the earth and the gods that sustain their world system. The patient hold-out of the saints endangers the stability of the cosmic reality of Rome, calling into question the solidity and permanence of the arrangement, and thus introducing a sense of anomie into their culture. John envisions that their prayers for divine vindication of their costly witness, offered on the altar of heaven, are cast down on the earth. This vocation of the saints participates in the divine judgment and dismantling of the world system of Rome.

---

1. Oliver O'Donovan, *The Ways of Judgment*, The Bampton Lectures, 2003 (Grand Rapids: Eerdmans, 2005), 239.

But John does not just call his audience to the work of pure critique. Enduring non-participation clears the way to envision an alternative. Bearing witness to the shape of this alternative is the work of praise. In praise of the acts of the one on the throne and the Lamb, the saints articulate the new world and reign that is coming to bear on their present place and time. The singing of the saints bears witness to, in Brian Brock's terminology, "the world of praise in which all human life is comprehended within God's work—and thus is renewed."[2] This is not just a future hope but also a present reality—John sees the city descending from God in heaven as an ongoing reality (21:2). God's gift of the new creation emerges doubly as gift in that it is constituted by praise—the new creation is a gift as is the saints' participation in bringing it to expression. Though there is no temple in the city. The city itself is temple-like. God gives to the saints the task of narrating this new creation of God in the midst of the breakdown of the Roman cosmos. In the middle of the darkening of the kingdom and throne of the beast and dragon, the church bears witness to incomparable and impenetrable light.

I have argued that the dismantling of the cosmos is not to be understood as strictly literal, that John seems to have in mind a sort of rearrangement of what is already given as creation. A strict dissolution of creation does not seem to be indicated by John's imagery. And yet I have also cautioned against the polar opposite of a literal rendering of the destruction of the cosmos. For John, the clash of worlds goes deeper than just a difference in "symbolic universes" or "worldviews." Both the judgments rendered on the world through cosmic catastrophe and the cosmic rendering of the theophanic phenomena point toward the fact that John indeed expects to see material signs that God is remaking the world. John places before his audience the dual vision of the deconstruction of the cosmic administration of eternal Rome and the way God will have it when God comes to dwell with humanity (21:3). With dramatic irony and no small amount of incarnational logic, God becomes an "inhabitant of the earth" in order to conquer the idolatry problem of all the other inhabitants of the earth. God's entrance disturbs the world order. As the cosmos Rome builds and participates in falls apart, the people who worshiped the beast are freed to pursue worship of the true God. They are freed for an alternative: to enter the heavenly city constituted by the praise of God and the Lamb.

In the new cosmic arrangement, John perceives something radically different. It is not that God simply stands at the center of a renewed creation. God and the Lamb now function as the cosmic luminaries, providing the light

---

2. Brian Brock, *Singing the Ethos of God: On the Place of Christian Ethics in Scripture* (Grand Rapids and Cambridge: Eerdmans, 2007), xvi.

for the nations in lieu of the sun and moon (21:23-24, 22:5). Strikingly, God has somehow woven Godself into the fabric of the cosmos. For a first century Jew, this must have been a startling vision. Of course, this logic is not reserved just for the vision of the new heavens and the new earth. All throughout the Apocalypse, John's imagery has hinted at the fact that God, and the Lamb, and God's angelic servants function not just as controlling administrators of the new creation, but also as cosmic bodies themselves. The one on the throne is encircled by a rainbow. Christ's face is described as shining like the sun in full force, and elsewhere as the Morning star. God and the Lamb are understood as the heavenly city's light rather than the sun. What are interpreters to do with this imagery?

Bruce Malina interprets this imagery to mean that John's message is one of portraying God as *pantokrator*—"the controller of everyone and everything," and the cosmic Jesus as *polokrator*—"the one who controls the fate of the cosmos."[3] Jesus is the pole of the universe, the one who holds the seven stars in his right hand. In terms of Malina's emphasis on astral prophecy, this means that Christ is in control in the audience's present situation—John does not give a vision of the future but of the present and immediately forthcoming.[4] This vision of the world is essentially vertical and "implies a perception of power wielded by celestial beings and events, with consequent control of human social living."[5] Malina's broad characterization of this cosmic imagery is that John offers a vision of "cosmic orientation." John's sky vision plumbs the depths of the universe in order to discern its deepest and most mysterious center. Malina argues that this is the takeaway for religious readers in the post-modern world. He writes, "In an uncentered cosmos people are hard put to develop the sense of cosmic well-being available to our ancestors in faith . . . Perhaps contemplation with the seer of Patmos focused on the God of the sky as the true center of the cosmos will offer insight into our proper place in creation."[6]

But this reading does not seem to satisfactorily account for the political concerns in John's cosmological vision. John's message is not about finding a sense of belonging or "at-homeness" within the cosmos for, as my argument has sought to make clear, John wrote in order to make his audience feel as little at home in the current world set-up as possible. The Apocalypse is not a revelation of the inner depth of the current cosmos, but discloses that

---

3. Bruce J. Malina, *On the Genre and Message of Revelation: Star Visions and Sky Journeys* (Peabody: Hendrickson, 1995), 261–263.
4. Malina, *Revelation*, 266–267.
5. Malina, *Revelation*, 266.
6. Malina, *Revelation*, 267.

the current configuration of the cosmos stands under judgment and is being dismantled. In its place emerges a renewed and restored creation, with God and the Lamb as the center and the governing cosmic bodies. John's cosmology is both rhetorical and political, or better yet, rhetorical because it is political—it calls the audience not just to epistemological reflection and comprehension, but participation and action. God and the Lamb are not simply depicted as having authority over the cosmos, but as the agents of transformation, as the ones who oversee the transfer of the universe from the kingdom of the world to the kingdom of the Lord and his Messiah. This regime change goes all the way through to the core of the universe, such that the new configuration of cosmology for John perceives God and the Lamb to actually function as the centering bodies of the cosmic reality—they have come to be a part of the new creation.

But this depiction of the cosmic Christ does not seem to be for John a way of enfolding God into the material reality of the new creation, either. Instead, the new creational light refers to the working out of God's promises in history. The prophecy of Isaiah 60:20 stands in the background of this image.[7] John's vision of the new creation, then, bears witness to the fact that promises that had yet to be realized are being brought to bear in history in the divine work of unmaking and making new. But John's vision doesn't stop there. His vision of God and the Lamb as the luminaries of the new creation is also a revelation and manifestation of God's being and glory. For it is possible that Psalm 104 [103 LXX] stands in the background here also. The psalmist gives praise to God the creator who is "wrapped in light as with a garment" (Ps. 104:2). This precedent may help us see that in using this metaphorical terminology John does not mean to imply that God is somehow enclosed within the new creation. It is rather that God clothes Godself in the garment of the new creation. There is now no longer any mystery or ambiguity concerning the presence of God in creation, for the foundations of the world now conform to the shape of the divine. If one seeks the deep structure of the new creation, it may be found in the concrete form of the mission of the slain Lamb. For John, then, this vision of the new creation is the full realization of the incarnational reality at the heart of the revelation of Christ. In John's Gospel the word becomes flesh and dwells (ἐσκήνωσεν, John 1:14) with humans. In the Apocalypse, the divine creative word becomes the center of the new creation and dwells with humans (σκηνώσει, Rev. 21:3).

---

7. G. K. Beale and Sean M. McDonough, "Revelation," in *Commentary on the New Testament Use of the Old Testament*, ed. G. K. Beal and D. A. Carson (Grand Rapids and Nottingham: Baker Academic and Apollos, 2007), 1153.

The new creation is saturated and irradiated with the glorious presence of God and the Lamb. Its entrance into the first creation is experienced as upheaval and its appearance to the idolatrous inhabitants of the earth is as darkness. But to the ones who bear on their bodies the seal of belonging to God, its presence is the overabundance of light. This interplay of light and darkness, glory and suffering is the paradoxical heart of John's rhetorical cosmology. Though the church's costly witness is experienced as suffering, it is, in its truest sense, a participation in the glory of the heavenly city. Though the inhabitants of the earth experience the disintegration and darkening of the world, in reality this experience is the coming of the light of the world. Margaret Barker points to an alternative understanding of God's anointed servant in the Great Isaiah Scroll at Qumran (1QIsa). Instead of a suffering servant being marred beyond all human recognition, the servant is one who has been anointed by God and takes on a glorious appearance and no longer looks like an ordinary human being (see also Isa. 52:12 LXX).[8] Perhaps John envisages a similar interplay of suffering and luminous glory with regard to the new creation. The new creation breaks into the world universally, but not everyone can see it as it is. One must see with the eyes of praise to understand it as gift and blessing. In a similar fashion, Augustine refers to the difference between knowledge of things in God and knowledge of things in self. In both ways of knowing the thing behold is the same. However, things seen in God are seen as in the daylight, whereas things beheld in themselves apart from God are seen as in twilight.[9] It is not surprising that the new creation would have this character when its progenitor carries within his body the costly witness of faithfulness unto death and the splendorous light of the heavenly city.

Prospects for Future Engagement

With John's vision of rhetorical cosmology sketched out above, the task remains to draw out some of the implications of this work for engaging recent apocalyptic political theology. Apocalyptic has recently become a significant word for theological thinking and, if the assessment of Cyril O'Regan is correct,

---

8. Margaret Barker, *The Revelation of Jesus Christ: Which God Gave Him to Show His Servants What Must Soon Take Place (Revelation 1.1)* (Edinburgh: T & T Clark, 2000), 6.

9. Augustine, *City of God*, XI.29. Dietrich Bonhoeffer also makes a distinction between the one whose eyes have been opened to the revelation of God and the one who sees apart from this revelation, writing, "The one whose eyes God has opened to see the Word beholds a wonderland. What until then appeared to me as dead is full of life, what was full of contradictions is resolved in a higher unity, the harsh demands become a gracious law," quoted in Brian Brock, *Singing the Ethos of God: On the Place of Christian Ethics in Scripture* (Grand Rapids: Eerdmans, 2007), 319.

its importance is waxing rather than waning.[10] This signals all the more the need to attend to the church's apocalyptic texts as resources in articulating a theology that witnesses to the revelatory and cosmic work of God in creation. How might this vision of rhetorical cosmology be a resource for political theology? How might it challenge other ways of thinking through theology and the political in the current postmodern climate?

First of all, an apocalyptic political theology will be an uncompromising vision for ethical reflection. Apocalyptic theologians have already characterized this facet of their thinking as being theology "without reserve." Douglas Harink argues that, "Discriminating judgments, definitions and differentiations, even 'totalizing' claims are intrinsic to the grammar of apocalyptic theology . . . as the manner in which Christian theology participates in the apocalypse of Jesus Christ."[11] We have seen this to be true for John. There is no amount of acceptable overlap between participation in the cosmological discourse of the Roman cult and economy, and participating proleptically in the coming of the new creation. Those who are marked by the beast and those who are marked by God exist in mutually exclusive groups, and indeed in mutually exclusive cosmic realities.

This means that any apocalyptic political theology resourced by John's vision cannot be simply one political option among the many available options within the political marketplace. Rather, apocalyptic theology will refuse to be historically inscribed as merely contextual and cultural. Walter Lowe argues that this theology inscribes the historical rather than being inscribed by it. An apocalyptic theology that addresses the political will see the whole of that political thought within its total vision of Christ. It will stubbornly refuse to be "returned to the relativizing embrace of history."[12] Therefore, there is a necessary element of refusal involved in John's apocalyptic theology. Edward Adams argues that the heavenly city is characterized by negation in that John lists seven elements which will not partake of the life of the city.[13] While we have seen that this is true, it is also true that Babylon is likewise characterized by a certain negation, with the absence of singing, lamp-light, artisanry, and

---

10. Cyril O'Regan, *Theology and the Spaces of Apocalyptic*, The Pére Marquette Lecture in Theology 2009 (Milwaukee: Marquette University Press, 2009).

11. Douglas Harink, *Paul Among the Postliberals: Pauline Theology Beyond Christendom and Modernity* (Grand Rapids: Brazos, 2003), 69.

12. Walter Lowe, "Prospects for a Postmodern Christian Theology: Apocalyptic Without Reserve," *Modern Theology* 15 (1999), 23.

13. Edward Adams, *The Stars Will Fall From Heaven: Cosmic Catastrophe in the New Testament and its World,* Library of New Testament Studies 347 (London and New York: T & T Clark, 2007), 249.

marriage celebrations. So while there is an aspect of negation in the politics of the city, there is also an aspect of spelling out positive content. John's politics is not a politics of pure critique and reaction. As we noted above, even the negative time and space of silence is for John evidence of the fullness of the entrance of the new creation. The silent endurance of the saints is predicated upon the thunderous sound of praise that constitutes the New Jerusalem.

Several questions arise out of this facet of the apocalyptic theology being developed here. The first is the issue of sectarian withdrawal versus political engagement. The interesting conversation between Jonathan R. Wilson and John Collins concerning Christian apocalyptic theology and the Dead Sea Scrolls sheds light on this issue. Wilson inquires whether sectarian withdrawal is a necessary outcome of apocalyptic theology given that Qumran exhibited some of the same inward focused apocalyptic theology developed by John of Patmos.[14] Given this tendency to sectarianism Wilson wonders if Qumran can provide either a positive or negative example to theologians who wish to develop an apocalyptic account of theology. In response to Wilson's question, Collins dismisses apocalyptic thought as a resource for a theological politics, arguing that such theology is, by nature, grounded upon assertion rather than persuasion and thus risks alienation, self-marginalization, and ultimately extinction. Collins argues that apocalyptic theology is appropriately labeled as sectarian and is therefore of little use in discussing theology's encounter with wider culture.[15]

But is sectarianism the necessary outcome of John's vision? Is it even the appropriate label for what John's rhetorical cosmology urges upon his audience? Is it not rather the case that John's vision conceives of a universal entrance of God's kingdom and new creation? Is this not the reason for the trauma felt by the Roman cosmological system and all who perpetuate its claims? Certainly the Roman system could handle a rival from within the arena of its own conception of power. As I argued above, John names Rome as fundamentally competitive and antagonistic, and therefore its vision of its own power and authority only grows with the emergence of rival power. John's own persuasive case for non-participation is not a call to become a rival sect, completely cut off and conceived of primarily in terms of being "against" the political establishment.

---

14. Jonathan R. Wilson, "The Dead Sea Scrolls and Christian Theology," in *Christian Beginnings and the Dead Sea Scrolls*, ed. John J. Collins and Craig A. Evans (Grand Rapids: Baker Academic, 2006), 126–128.

15. John J. Collins, "Apocalyptic Theology and the Dead Sea Scrolls: A Response to Jonathan Wilson," in *Christian Beginnings and the Dead Sea Scrolls*, ed. John J. Collins and Craig A. Evans (Grand Rapids: Baker Academic, 2006), 133.

The new creation that John envisions as already arriving in the work of God and the Lamb is not an opposing element in the world. It is itself a new world.

O'Regan's taxonomy of apocalyptic spaces might be particularly helpful here. O'Regan distinguishes between *kenomatic* and *pleromatic* apocalyptic space, with the former referring to a more irruptive and negative vision for theological politics "without fully specifying the alternatives" and the latter which "discloses a great deal about God's intention for the world and what God has done, is doing, and is going to do for it."[16] John's apocalyptic vision and rhetorical cosmology is not simply critique. It is critique via the explication of a robust ontology. For John, the dismantling of the world does not occur simply as a negation of the idolatrous world of Roman power. The world's foundations are shaken because of the entrance and emergence of God's newly creative work. The shaking of the foundations of Rome's cosmology is directly proportionate to the presence of the new creation as embodied in the saints' witness of silence and praise.

This leads to a related question of the means of conceiving and articulating this political vision within history. John's "refusal to be pragmatic" raises the question of how and where Christian political engagement is to operate. Perhaps here the question resides in the difference between the *kenomatic* and *pleromatic*. Does John have space and time for an account of secular government? What about the role of kings? Someone like John Howard Yoder approaches this text with a negative assessment. Because the world of Rome and the world emergent in the new creation are mutually exclusive, the saints are to adopt a minoritarian position within history—it is not the task of the church to make history run "the right way."[17] Nathan Kerr, in spelling out an apocalyptic theology and ecclesiology based largely on the thought of Yoder, follows this logic. Because the church exists only in exile in the world it is "politically a non-site."[18] Is this a refusal of the presence of a public church with clear and definite boundaries, as D. Stephen Long suggests?[19] Or is it perhaps a way of getting at the idea of a church that bears witness to the entrance of kingdom

---

16. O'Regan, *Theology and the Spaces of Apocalyptic*, 27–28. O'Regan also explicates a middle option, designating it the *metaxic*, but for our purposes interrogating the wider divergence between the *kenomatic* and *pleromatic* is a more productive exercise.

17. See John Howard Yoder, *The Politics of Jesus:* Vicit Agnus Noster, Second Edition (Grand Rapids and Carlisle: Eerdmans and Paternoster Press, 1994), 232–33.

18. Nathan Kerr, *Christ, History, and Apocalyptic: The Politics of Christian Mission*, Theopolitical Visions 2 (Eugene: Cascade Books, 2009), 190.

19. D. Stephen Long, *Hebrews*, Belief: A Theological Commentary on the Bible (Louisville: Westminster John Knox, 2011), 210.

in the world without accommodating its vision to any aspect of the disordered creation's politics. Whatever the case, it is certainly an instance of a *kenomatic* apocalyptic politics because it refuses to spell out in detail a positive vision of the kingdom.[20]

An alternative vision is offered by Oliver O'Donovan who sees a role for secular government and the role of judgment in the time between the announcement of the kingdom in the work of Jesus and the arrival of the kingdom at the eschaton.[21] According to O'Donovan, Christ's victory over the powers of sin and death means that Christ has been given authority over the nations. The ascension of Christ, an oft overlooked topic in Christology, makes room for earthly government, but only as it understands its temporary and limited role of judgment in the time between the times. In this vision of the political, O'Donovan rehabilitates an account of political liberalism within an account of the victory of Christ. This is a more *pleromatic* account of an apocalyptic political theology. John certainly has a role for earthly kings, as he pictures them carrying their glory into the New Jerusalem. However, John also understands that the world over which they ruled as kings stands under the dismantling judgment of God and the Lamb. Further work into John's account of earthly kingship may prove a productive area of inquiry for developing an apocalyptic political theology.

Finally, wherever one's preference lies regarding a *kenomatic* or *pleromatic* account of apocalyptic, the question arises as to how this vision of theology without reserve is to be enacted within the world of history. For even while refusing to be inscribed by history, this apocalyptic theology can only be lived out from within history and "on the ground." O'Regan helpfully reminds the *pleromatic* camp of its tendency toward triumphalism and the necessity of epistemic humility.[22] The focus of John's vision of the heavenly city is not on the saints' overpowering of the kings of the earth, but rather their practical witness embodied in silence and praise. An account of apocalyptic political theology will have much to critique and refuse as well as much to commend in the form of a robust kingdom ontology, but its gaze remains trained on the slain Lamb and follows him wherever he goes. John calls the saints to witness

---

20. See Kerr's insistence on a "dispossessed sociality that does not determine ahead of time what the kingdom's emergence will look like, *Christ, History, and Apocalyptic*, 195–196

21. This broad-based summary of Oliver O'Donovan's work is presented in a much more nuanced and thorough manner in two books: Oliver O'Donovan, *Desire of the Nations: Rediscovering the Roots of Political Theology* (Cambridge: Cambridge University Press, 1996) and Oliver O'Donovan, *The Ways of Judgment*, The Bampton Lectures 2003 (Grand Rapids and Cambridge: Eerdmans, 2005).

22. O'Regan, *Theology and the Spaces of Apocalyptic*, 125.

in silence and praise, and therefore their concern should be with developing the necessary practices and skills to perform this task. For all its gruesomeness and grotesquery, John's vision is not a call for the church's violent take-over of the world. John still expects his little reading communities to gather, with but "a little power" and read the text. The dismantling of the cosmos strikingly comes in the reading and performance of the text in the context of gathered worship, not with sword or coup. Witness therefore is not authoritarian but missional. It describes the life of the kingdom and new creation by embodying its life in the midst of the world. It does not seek to corral the world into the enclosure of the kingdom, but lets the kingdom do its work through witness.

It may therefore be beneficial to take up the Johannine idiom of "something like" when describing the way things will be in the coming kingdom, rather than idolize the conceptions of our own construction. For all of his bombast and bluster, John is a master of metaphor.[23] He takes constant care not to say too much or foreclose on the significance of his vision. His rhetoric resists overconfidence in seeing *the singular* way forward. Those interested in John's theo-political vision will do well not to get too obsessed with systems and platforms, but rather, with humility and patience, seek to develop within community the necessary practices to stand apart from violence, economic injustice, and ecological exploitation. The best apocalyptic politics might be done in the experimental mode: passionate but not ideological, not constrained to work within the given, attempting something here, not putting too much faith in this or that particular strategy and not pinning too much of one's hope on its success—the suffering witness of the Lamb ever the compass. If a course of action proves to be ineffective or ends up being co-opted by Babylon, a community is free to seek other ways of faithfulness, free to "follow the Lamb wherever he goes." John's testimony is exemplary here: one cannot receive the new until one is willing to release the old.

But John is exemplary in another way, too, which should caution against over-confidence and self-justification. Although John bears brusque witness against all idolatry and false witness, he himself is not immune to error. Twice he falls at the messenger angel's feet in order to worship and is reprimanded and redirected (Rev. 19:9-10; 22:8-9). At another time, he is jarred and amazed at the vision of the whore of Babylon, taken in by the whole spectacle, the same as those he is prophetically denouncing (17:6-7).[24] These episodes suggest that the Apocalypse does not give a God's-eye view. As much as John receives and

---

23. Throughout the Apocalypse, John bathes his vision report in the words related to ὅμοιος (20 occurrences) and ὡς (61 occurrences). His usage reminds interpreters that what he sees is eschatological, transcendent, and always refuses to be pinned down in a final, literal, or positivistic way.

gives a glimpse into the heavenly realities, he is still giving an account of his own perception of them. Just as John was prone to directing worship to the wrong destination, so too can the emergence of the true kingdom be distorted by faulty witness.[25]

Uncompromising and yet cautious, passionate and yet open to critique, this is what a rhetorical cosmological reading of the Apocalypse can offer in an engagement with apocalyptic theology. Perhaps these seemingly contradictory stances can only be preserved and enacted within the paradoxes of the Apocalypse itself: a Lamb slain yet standing, the dissonance between hearing and seeing, defeat that is victory. An ecclesial politics informed by rhetorical cosmology works against smug assumptions that one has it all figured out or that one controls access to the kingdom and new creation. If God's star witness can miss the mark, so can his readers. The key, therefore, is John's persistent logic that in order to gain (the promised new creation) one must lose (a self-orientation and self-justification). This may be what it means to follow the slain Lamb into the world made new.

---

24. See the insightful discussion of this amazement in Christopher A. Frilingos, *Spectacles of Empire: Monsters, Martyrs, and the Book of Revelation,* Divinations: Rereading Late Ancient Religion (Philadelphia: University of Philadelphia Press, 2004), 50–63.

25. See the counterintuitive thesis of Franke who argues that Apocalyptic discourse, rather than cutting off dialogue and understanding deepens it because it grounds all judgment in God. When the ground of all judgment is God, it has no basis in human instrumentalities, William Franke, *Poetry and Apocalypse: Theological Disclosures of Poetic Language* (Stanford: Stanford University Press, 2009), 91.

Bibliography

Adams, Edward. *The Stars Will Fall from Heaven: Cosmic Catastrophe in the New Testament and its World*. Library of New Testament Studies 347. London and New York: T & T Clark, 2007.

Allison, Dale C., Jr. *The Historical Christ and the Theological Jesus*. Grand Rapids: Eerdmans, 2009.

Armstrong-Reiner, David. *"You Opened the Book": An Instrumental Understanding of the Patristic Use of the Revelation to John*. Saarbrücken: VDM Verlag Dr. Müller, 2009.

Aune, David E. "The Apocalypse of John and the Problem of Genre." *Semeia* 36 (1986): 65–96.

———. "The Influence of Roman Imperial Court Ceremonial on the Apocalypse of John." *Biblical Research* 28 (1983): 5–26.

———. *The New Testament in its Literary Environment*. Library of Early Christianity. Philadelphia: Westminster, 1987.

———. *Revelation 1–5*. Word Biblical Commentary. Dallas: Word, 1997.

———. *Revelation 6–16*. Word Biblical Commentary. Nashville: Thomas Nelson, 1998.

———. *Revelation 17–22*. Word Biblical Commentary. Nashville: Thomas Nelson, 1998.

Balthasar, Hans Urs von. *Theo-Drama: Theological Dramatic Theory*. Volume 2: Dramatis Personae: *Man in God*. Translated by Graham Harrison. San Francisco: Ignatius, 1990.

———. *Theo-Drama: Theological Dramatic Theory*. Volume 4: *The Action*. Translated by Graham Harrison. San Francisco: Ignatius, 1994.

Bandy, Alan S. "The Layers of the Apocalypse: An Integrative Approach to Revelation's Macrostructure." *Journal for the Study for the New Testament* 31.4 (2009): 469–499.

———. *The Prophetic Lawsuit in the Book of Revelation*. New Testament Monographs 29. Sheffield: Sheffield Phoenix, 2010.

Barker, Margaret. *The Revelation of Jesus Christ: Which God Gave Him to Show His Servants What Must Soon Take Place (Revelation 1.1)*. Edinburgh: T & T Clark, 2000.

Barr, David L. "The Apocalypse as a Symbolic Transformation of the World: A Literary Analysis." *Interpretation* 38 (1984): 39–50.

———. "The Apocalypse of John as Oral Enactment." *Interpretation* 40 (1986): 243–256.

———. "Beyond Genre: The Expectations of Apocalypse." In *The Reality of Apocalypse: Rhetoric and Politics in the Book of Revelation*, edited by David L. Barr, 71–89. SBL Symposium Series 39. Atlanta: Society of Biblical Literature, 2007.

Bauckham, Richard. *The Climax of Prophecy: Studies on the Book of Revelation*. London and New York: T & T Clark, 1993.

———. *The Jewish World Around the New Testament*. Grand Rapids: Baker Academic, 2010.

———. *The Theology of the Book of Revelation*. New Testament Theology. Cambridge: Cambridge University Press, 1993.

Beale, G. K. *The Book of Revelation: A Commentary on the Greek Text*. Grand Rapids and Cambridge: Eerdmans and Paternoster, 1999.

Beale, G. K. and Sean M. McDonough. "Revelation." In *Commentary on the New Testament Use of the Old Testament*, edited by G. K. Beale and D. A. Carson, 1081–1161. Grand Rapids and Nottingham: Baker Academic and Apollos, 2007.

Berquist, Jon L. "Critical Spatiality and the Construction of the Ancient World." In *"Imagining" Biblical Worlds: Studies in Spatial, Social, and Historical Constructs in Honor of James W. Flanagan*, edited by David M. Gunn and Paula M. McNutt, 14–29. Journal for the Study of the Old Testament Supplement 359. London: Sheffield Academic, 2002.

———. "Theories of Space and Construction of the Ancient World." AAR/SBL Constructs of Social and Cultural Worlds of Antiquity Group, November 20, 1999.

Berry, Wendell. *The Long-Legged House*. New York: Harcourt, Brace, and World, 1965.

———. *The Way of Ignorance*. Berkeley: Shoemaker & Hoard, 2005.

Bloomquist, L. Gregory. "Methodological Criteria for Apocalyptic Rhetoric: A Suggestion for the Expanded Use of Sociorhetorical Analysis." In *Vision and Persuasion: Rhetorical Dimensions of Apocalyptic Discourse*, edited by Greg Carey and Gregory L. Bloomquist, 181–203. St. Louis: Chalice, 1999.

Blount, Brian K. *Can I Get a Witness? Reading Revelation through African American Culture*. Louisville: Westminster John Knox, 2005.

———. *Revelation: A Commentary*. New Testament Library. Louisville: Westminster John Knox, 2009.
Bockmuehl, Markus A. *Seeing the Word: Refocusing New Testament Study*. Studies in Theological Interpretation. Grand Rapids: Baker Academic, 2006.
Boll, Franz. *Aus der Offenbarung Johannis: Hellenistische Studien zum Weltbild der Apockalypse*. ΣΤΟΙΧΕΙΑ 1. Leipzig: Druck und Verlag B. G. Teubner, 1914.
Brock, Brian. *Singing the Ethos of God: On the Place of Christian Ethics in Scripture*. Grand Rapids: Eerdmans, 2007.
Brueggemann, Walter. *Israel's Praise: Doxology against Idolatry and Ideology*. Philadelphia: Fortress Press, 1988.
Caird, G. B. *A Commentary on the Revelation of St. John the Divine*. Harper's New Testament Commentaries. New York: Harper & Row, 1966.
Campbell, Gordon. "Findings, Seals, Trumpets, and Bowls: Variations Upon the Theme of Covenant Rupture and Restoration in the Book of Revelation." *Westminster Theological Journal* 66 (2004): 71–96.
Carey, Greg. "Introduction: Apocalyptic Discourse, Apocalyptic Rhetoric." In *Vision and Persuasion: Rhetorical Dimensions of Apocalyptic Discourse*, edited by Greg Carey and Gregory L. Bloomquist, 1–18. St. Louis: Chalice, 1999.
Carey, Greg and Gregory L. Bloomquist, ed. *Vision and Persuasion: Rhetorical Dimensions of Apocalyptic Discourse*. St Louis: Chalice, 1999.
Carnegie, David R. "Worthy is the Lamb: The Hymns in Revelation." In *Christ the Lord: Studies in Christology Presented to Donald Guthrie*, edited by H. H. Rowdon. Downers Grove: Inter-Varsity, 1982.
Certeau, Michel de. *The Practice of Everyday Life*. Translated by Steven Rendall. Berkeley: University of California Press, 1984.
Charles, R. H. *A Critical and Exegetical Commentary on The Revelation of St. John*. 2 vols. The International Critical Commentary. Edinburgh: T & T Clark, 1920.
Collins, John J., ed. *Apocalypse: The Morphology of a Genre*. Semeia 14. Missoula: Scholars, 1979.
———. "Apocalypse and Apocalypticism: Early Jewish Apocalypticism." In *The Anchor Bible Dictionary*, Vol. 1, edited by David Noel Freedman, 284–287. New York: Doubleday, 1992
———. *The Apocalyptic Imagination: An Introduction to Jewish Apocalyptic Literature*, 2nd ed. Grand Rapids and Livonia: Eerdmans and Dove Booksellers, 1998.

———. "Apocalyptic Theology and the Dead Sea Scrolls: A Response to Jonathan Wilson." In *Christian Beginnings and the Dead Sea Scrolls*, edited by John J. Collins and Craig A. Evans, 129–134. Grand Rapids: Baker Academic, 2006.

———. "Temporality and Politics in Jewish Apocalyptic Literature." In *Apocalyptic in History and Tradition*, edited by Christopher Rowland and John Barton, 26–43. Journal for the Study of the Pseudepigrapha Supplement Series 43. London: Sheffield Academic, 2002.

Danker, Frederick W. *Benefactor: Epigraphic Study of a Greco-Roman and New Testament Semantic Field*. St. Louis: Clayton Publishing House, 1982.

Davis, Dale Ralph. "The Relationship Between the Seals, Trumpets, and Bowls in the Book of Revelation." *Journal of the Evangelical Theological Society* 16.3 (1973): 149–158.

Davis, John J. *Moses and the Gods of Egypt*. Grand Rapids: Baker, 1971.

Day, John. "The Origin of Armageddon: Revelation 16:16 as an Interpretation of Zechariah 12:11." In *Crossing the Boundaries: Essays in Biblical Interpretation in Honour of Michael D. Goulder*, edited by Stanley E. Porter, et al, 315–326. Leiden: Brill, 1994.

deSilva, David A. *Seeing Things John's Way: The Rhetoric of the Book of Revelation*. Louisville: Westminster John Knox, 2009.

Duff, Paul B. *Who Rides the Beast? Prophetic Rivalry and the Rhetoric of Crisis in the Churches of the Apocalypse*. Oxford: Oxford University Press, 2001.

Ellul, Jacques. *Apocalypse: The Book of Revelation*. New York: Seabury, 1977.

Farrer, Austin. *A Rebirth of Images: The Making of Saint John's Apocalypse*. Boston: Beacon, 1949.

Flanagan, James W. "Ancient Perceptions of Space/Perceptions of Ancient Space." *Semeia* 87 (1999): 15–43.

Franke, William. *Poetry and Apocalypse: Theological Disclosures of Poetic Language*. Stanford: Stanford University Press, 2009.

Frei, Hans W. *The Eclipse of Biblical Narrative: A Study in Eighteenth and Nineteenth Century Hermeneutics*. New Haven and London: Yale University Press, 1974.

Freundorfer, Joseph. "Die Apokalypse des Apostels Johannes und die Hellensitische Kosmologie und Astrologie: Eine Auseinandersetzung mit den Hauptergebnissen der Untersuchung Franz Bolls: "Aus Der Offenbarung Johannis." *Biblische Studien* 23.1 (1929).

Frey, Jörg. "The Relevance of the Roman Imperial Cult for the Book of Revelation: Exegetical and Hermeneutical Reflections on the Relation

Between the Seven Letters and the Visionary Main Part of the Book." In *The New Testament and Early Christian Literature in Greco-Roman Context: Studies in Honor of David E. Aune,* edited by John Fotopoulos, 231–255. Supplements to Novum Testamentum 122. Leiden and Boston: Brill, 2006.

Friesen, Steven J. *Imperial Cults and the Apocalypse of John: Reading Revelation in the Ruins.* Oxford: Oxford University Press, 2001.

———. "Satan's Throne, Imperial Cults and the Social Settings of Revelation." *Journal for the Study of the New Testament* 27.3 (2005): 351–373.

Frilingos, Christopher A. *Spectacles of Empire: Monsters, Martyrs, and the Book of Revelation.* Divinations: Rereading Late Ancient Religion. Philadelphia: University of Pennsylvania Press, 2004.

Funk, Robert W. "The Apostolic *Parousia*: Form and Significance." In *Christian History and Interpretation: Studies Presented to John Knox,* edited by W. R. Farmer, *et al.,* 249–268 Cambridge: Cambridge University Press, 1967.

Gilbertson, Michael. *God and History in the Book of Revelation: New Testament Studies in Dialogue with Pannenberg and Moltmann.* Society for New Testament Studies Monograph Series 124. Cambridge: Cambridge University Press, 2003.

Girvin, Ernest Alexander. *Phineas F. Bresee: A Prince in Israel, A Biography.* Kansas City: Pentecostal Nazarene Publishing House, 1916.

Gowan, Donald E. "The Fall and Redemption of the Material World in Apocalyptic Literature." *Horizons in Biblical Theology* 7 (1985): 83–103.

Gowler, David B. "Socio-Rhetorical Interpretation: Textures of a Text and its Reception." *Journal for the Study of the New Testament* 33.2 (2010): 191–206.

Gradel, Ittai. *Emperor Worship and Roman Religion.* Oxford Classical Monographs. Oxford: Clarendon, 2002.

Graves, David W. *The Seven Messages of Revelation and Vassal Treaties: Literary Genre, Structure, and Function.* Gorgias Dissertations. Piscataway: Gorgias, 2009.

Hahne, Harry Alan. *The Corruption and Redemption of Creation: Nature in Romans 8.19-22 and Jewish Apocalyptic Literature.* Library of New Testament Studies 336. London and New York: T & T Clark, 2006.

Hall, Robert G. "Arguing Like an Apocalypse: Galatians and an Ancient *Topos* Outside the Greco-Roman Rhetorical Tradition." *New Testament Studies* 42 (1996): 434–453.

Hanson, Paul D. "Apocalypses and Apocalypticism: The Genre." "Introductory Overview." In *The Anchor Bible Dictionary,* Vol. 1, edited by David Noel Freedman, 279–282. New York: Doubleday, 1992.

———. "Introductory Overview." In *The Anchor Bible Dictionary*, Vol. 1, edited by David Noel Freedman, 279–282. New York: Doubleday, 1992.

———. "Biblical Apocalypticism: The Theological Dimension." *Horizons in Biblical Theology* 7.2 (1985): 1–20.

———. *The Dawn of Apocalyptic*. Philadelphia: Fortress Press, 1975.

Harink, Douglas. *Paul Among the Postliberals: Pauline Theology Beyond Christendom and Modernity*. Grand Rapids: Brazos, 2003.

Harrington, Wilfrid J. *Revelation*. Sacra Pagina 16. Collegeville: Liturgical, 1993.

Hellholm, David. "The Problem of Apocalyptic: Genre and the Apocalypse of John." *SBL 1982 Seminar Papers* 21 (1982): 157–198.

Hendrix, Holland. "Thessalonicans Honor Romans." Th.D. dissertation. Harvard University. Cambridge: Harvard, 1894.

Horsley, Richard A., ed. *Paul and the Roman Imperial Order*. Harrisburg: Trinity Press International, 2004.

Howard-Brook, Wes and Andrew Gwyther. *Unveiling Empire: Reading Revelation Then and Now*. The Bible and Liberation Series. Maryknoll: Orbis, 1999.

Humphrey, Edith M. "In Search of a Voice: Rhetoric Through Sight and Sound in Revelation 11:15—12:17." *Vision and Persuasion: Rhetorical Dimensions of Apocalyptic Discourse*, edited by Greg Carey and Gregory L. Bloomquist, 141–160. St. Louis: Chalice, 1999.

Janzen, J. Gerald. *Job*. Interpretation. Atlanta: John Knox, 1985.

de Jonge, Henk Jan. "The Apocalypse of John and the Imperial Cult." *Kykeon: Studies in Honour of H. S. Versnel,* edited by H. F. J. Horstmanshoff, *et al.,* 127–141. Religions in the Graeco-Roman World 142. Boston and Köln: Brill, 2002.

Jörns, Klaus-Peter. *Das Hymnische Evangelium: Untersuchungen zu Aufbau, Funktion und Herkunft der Hymnischen Stücke in der Johannesoffenbarung*. Studien zum Neuen Testament 5. Gütersloh: Gütersloher Verlagshaus Gerd Mohn, 1971.

Kennedy, George A. *Classical Rhetoric and its Christian and Secular Tradition from Ancient to Modern Times*, 2nd ed. Chapel Hill and London: The University of North Carolina Press, 1999.

———. *New Testament Interpretation through Rhetorical Criticism*. Chapel Hill: University of North Carolina Press, 1984.

Kerr, Nathan. *Christ, History, and Apocalyptic: The Politics of Christian Mission*. Theopolitical Visions 2. Eugene: Cascade Books, 2009.

Koch, Klaus. *The Rediscovery of Apocalyptic*. Studies in Biblical Theology, Vol. 22. London: SCM, 1972.

Kovacs, Judith and Christopher Rowland. *Revelation: The Apocalypse of Jesus Christ*. Blackwell Bible Commentaries. Malden and Oxford: Blackwell, 2004.

Kraybill, J. Nelson. *Imperial Cult and Commerce in John's Apocalypse*. Journal for the Study of the New Testament Supplement 132. Sheffield: Sheffield Academic, 1996.

Kreitzer, Larry J. "Apocalyptic, Apocalypticism." In *Dictionary of the Later New Testament and Its Developments*, edited by Ralph P. Martin and Peter H. Davids, 55–68. Downers Grove: InterVarsity, 1997.

Ladd, George Eldon. *A Commentary on the Revelation of John*. Grand Rapids: Eerdmans, 1972.

Limburg, James. "The Root [RÎB] and the Prophetic Lawsuit Speeches." *Journal of Biblical Literature*. 88.3 (1969): 291–304.

Linton, Gregory L. "Reading the Apocalypse as Apocalypse: The Limits of Genre." In *The Reality of Apocalypse: Rhetoric and Politics in the Book of Revelation*, edited by David L. Barr, 9–41. SBL Symposium Series 39. Atlanta: Society of Biblical Literature, 2007.

Long, D. Stephen. *Hebrews*. Belief: A Theological Commentary on the Bible. Louisville: Westminster John Knox, 2011.

Lowe, Walter. "Prospects for a Postmodern Christian Theology: Apocalyptic Without Reserve." *Modern Theology* 15.1 (1999): 17–24.

Lupieri, Edmondo F. *A Commentary on the Apocalypse of John*. Translated by Maria Poggi Johnson and Adam Kamesar. Grand Rapids: Eerdmans, 2006.

Maier, Harry O. *Apocalypse Recalled: The Book of Revelation after Christendom*. Minneapolis: Fortress Press, 2002.

Malina Bruce J. *On the Genre and Message of Revelation: Star Visions and Sky Journeys*. Peabody: Hendrickson, 1995.

———. "Christ and Time: Swiss or Mediterranean?" *The Catholic Biblical Quarterly* 51 (1989): 1–31.

Mangina, Joseph L. *Revelation*. Brazos Theological Commentary on the Bible. Grand Rapids: Brazos, 2010.

Martyn, J. Louis. "Events in Galatia: Modified Covenantal Nomism versus God's Invasion of the Cosmos in the Singular Gospel: A Response to J. D. G. Dunn and B. R. Gaventa." In *Pauline Theology*, Vol. 1. Edited by Jeanette Elizabeth Hanscome and Jouette M. Bassler. Minneapolis: Fortress Press, 1991.

———. *Galatians: A New Translation with Introduction and Commentary*. The Anchor Bible, 33A. New York: Doubleday, 1997.

Mazzaferri, Frederick David. *The Genre of the Book of Revelation from a Source-Critical Perspective*. Beiheft zur Zeitschrift für die neutestamentliche Wissenschaft und die Kunde der ältern Kirche 54. Berlin: de Gruyter, 1989.

McDonough, Sean M. "Revelation: The Climax of Cosmology." In *Cosmology and New Testament Theology*, edited by Jonathan T. Pennington and Sean M. McDonough, 178–188. Library of New Testament Studies 355. London and New York: T & T Clark, 2008.

McNicol, Allan J. "All Things New." *Christian Studies* 21 (2005–2006): 39–55.

———. *The Conversion of the Nations in Revelation*. Library of New Testament Studies 438. London: T & T Clark, 2011.

Minear, Paul. "The Cosmology of the Apocalypse." In *Current Issues in New Testament Interpretation: Essays in Honor of Otto A. Piper*, edited by William Klassen and Graydon F. Snyder, 23–37. New York: Harper, 1962.

Moo, Jonathan. "The Sea That Is No More: Revelation 21:1 and the Function of Sea Imagery in the Apocalypse of John." *Novum Testamentum* 51 (2009): 148–167.

Mounce, Robert H. *The Book of Revelation*. Revised Edition. New International Commentary on the New Testament. Grand Rapids: Eerdmans, 1998.

O'Connor, Flannery. *Wise Blood*. New York: Farrar, Straus, and Giroux, 1962.

O'Donovan, Oliver. *Desire of the Nations: Rediscovering the Roots of Political Theology*. Cambridge: Cambridge University Press, 1996.

———. "History and Politics in the Book of Revelation." In *Bonds of Imperfection: Christian Politics, Past and Present*, Oliver O'Donovan and Joan Lockwood O'Donovan, 25–47. Grand Rapids: Eerdmans, 2004.

———. *The Ways of Judgment*. The Bampton Lectures 2003. Grand Rapids and Cambridge: Eerdmans, 2005.

Okoye, James Chukwuma. "Power and Worship: Revelation in African Perspective." In *From Every People and Nation: The Book of Revelation in Intercultural Perspective*, edited by David Rhoads, 100–126. Minneapolis: Fortress Press, 2005.

O'Leary, Stephen D. *Arguing the Apocalypse: A Theory of Millennial Rhetoric*. New York: Oxford University Press, 1994.

O'Regan, Cyril. *Theology and the Spaces of Apocalyptic*. The Pére Marquette Lecture in Theology 2009. Milwaukee: Marquette University Press, 2009.

Orlov, Andrei. "The Flooded Arboretums: The Garden Traditions in the Slavonic Version of *3 Baruch* and *The Book of Giants*." *The Catholic Biblical Quarterly* 65.2 (2003): 184–201.

———. "'Noah's Younger Brother': The Anti-Noachic Polemics in *2 Enoch*." *Henoch* 22.2 (2000): 207–221.

Peerbolte, Bert Jan Lietaert. "To Worship the Beast: The Revelation of John and the Imperial Cult in Asia Minor." In *Zwischen den Reichen: Neues Testament und Römische Herrschaft,* 239–259. Tübingen; Basel: A. Francke, 2002.

Perelman, Chaïm and Lucie Olbrechts-Tyteca. *The New Rhetoric: A Treatise on Argumentation* Notre Dame: Notre Dame University Press, 1969.

Perry, Peter S. *The Rhetoric of Digressions: Revelation 7:1-17 and 10:1—11:13 and Ancient Communication.* Wisssenschaftliche Untersuchungen zum Neuen Testament: 2. Reihe 268. Tübingen: Mohr Siebeck, 2009.

Peterson, Eugene H. *Reversed Thunder: The Revelation of John and the Praying Imagination.* New York: HarperCollins, 1988.

Price, S. R. F. *Rituals and Power: The Roman Imperial Cult in Asia Minor.* Cambridge: Cambridge University Press, 1984.

———. "Rituals and Power." In *Paul and Empire: Religion and Power in Roman Imperial Society,* edited by Richard A. Horsley, 47–71. Harrisburg: Trinity Press International, 1997.

Resseguie, James L. *The Revelation of John: A Narrative Commentary.* Grand Rapids: Baker Academic, 2009.

Richard, Pablo. *Apocalypse: A People's Commentary on the Book of Revelation.* Translated by Phillip Berryman. The Bible & Liberation Series. Maryknoll: Orbis, 1995.

Rimmon-Kenan, Shlomith. *Narrative Fiction: Contemporary Poetics,* 2nd ed. London and New York: Routledge, 2002.

Rist, Martin. "Apocalypticism." In *The Interpreter's Dictionary of the Bible,* Vol. 1, edited by David A. Buttrick, 157–161. Nashville: Abingdon Press, 1962.

Robbins, Vernon K. "The Dialectical Nature of Early Christian Discourse," *Scriptura* 59 (1996), online: http://www.religion.emory.edu/faculty/robbins/SRS/vkr/dialect.cfm.

———. *The Invention of Christian Discourse,* Vol. 1. Rhetoric of Religious Antiquity. Blandford Forum, Dorset: Deo Publishing, 2009.

———. *Jesus the Teacher: A Socio-Rhetorical Interpretation of Mark.* Philadelphia: Fortress Press, 1984.

———. "Rhetography: A New Way of Seeing the Familiar Text." In *Words Well Spoken: George Kennedy's Rhetoric of the New Testament,* edited by C. Clifton Black and Duane F. Watson, 81–106. Studies in Rhetoric and Religion. Waco: Baylor University Press, 2008.

———. "Rhetorical Ritual: Apocalyptic Discourse in Mark 13." In *Vision and Persuasion: Rhetorical Dimensions of Apocalyptic Discourse,* edited by Greg Carey and Gregory L. Bloomquist, 95–122. St. Louis: Chalice, 1999.

———. *The Tapestry of Early Christian Discourse: Rhetoric, Society, Ideology.* London and New York: Routledge, 1996.

De Roche, Michael. "Yahweh's *Rîb* Against Israel: A Reassessment of the So-called 'Prophetic Lawsuit' in the Preexilic Prophets." *Journal of Biblical Literature* 102.4 (1983): 563–574.

Rowe, C. Kavin. *World Upside Down: Reading Acts in the Greco-Roman Age.* Oxford: Oxford University Press, 2009.

Rowland, Christopher. "Apocalypticism." In *The New Interpreter's Dictionary of the Bible.*, Vol. 1, edited by Katherine Doob Sakenfeld, 190–195. Nashville: Abingdon Press, 2006.

———. *The Open Heaven: A Study of Apocalyptic in Judaism and Early Christianity.* New York: Crossroad, 1982.

Ruiz, Jean-Pierre. "Betwixt and Between on the Lord's Day: Liturgy and the Apocalypse." In *The Reality of Apocalypse: Rhetoric and Politics in the Book of Revelation,* edited by David L. Barr, 221–241. SBL Symposium Series 39. Atlanta: Society of Biblical Literature, 2006.

Ryan, Sean Michael. *Hearing at the Boundaries of Vision: Education Informing Cosmology in Revelation 9.* Library of New Testament Studies 448. London: T & T Clark, 2012.

Saunders, Stanley P. "Between Blessing and Curse: Reading, Hearing, and Performing the Apocalypse in a World of Terror." In *Shaking Heaven and Earth: Essays in Honor of Walter Brueggemann and Charles B. Cousar,* edited by Christine R. Yoder, *et al.,* 141–155. Louisville: Westminster John Knox, 2005.

Scherrer, Steven J. "Signs and Wonders in the Imperial Cult: A New Look at a Roman Religious Institution in the Light of Rev. 13:13-15." *Journal of Biblical Literature* 103.4 (1984): 599–610.

Schüssler Fiorenza, Elisabeth. *The Book of Revelation: Justice and Judgment,* 2nd ed. Minneapolis: Fortress Press, 1998.

———. *Revelation: Vision of a Just World.* Proclamation Commentaries. Minneapolis: Fortress Press, 1991.

Scott, Bernard Brandon and Margaret E. Dean. "A Sound Map of the Sermon on the Mount." In *Treasures Old and New: Recent Contributions to Matthean Studies*, edited by David R. Bauer and Mark Allen Powell, 331–378. SBL Symposium Series 1. Atlanta, GA: Scholars, 1996.

Seal, David. "Shouting in the Apocalypse: The Influence of First-Century Acclamations on the Praise Utterances in Revelation 4:8 and 11." *Journal of the Evangelical Theologial Society* 51.2 (2008): 339–352.

Siew, Antoninus King Wai. *The War Between the Two Beasts and the Two Witnesses: A Chiastic Reading of Revelation 11:1—14:5*. Library of New Testament Studies 283. London and New York: T & T Clark, 2005.

de Souza Nogueira, Paulo Augusto. "Celestial Worship and Ecstatic-Visionary Experience." Translated by Leslie Milton. *Journal for the Study of the New Testament* 25.2 (2002): 165–184.

Stone, Michael E. "The Axis of History at Qumran." In *Pseudepigraphic Perspectives: The Apocrypha and Pseudepigrapha in Light of the Dead Sea Scrolls: Proceedings of the International Symposium of the Orion Center for the Study of the Dead Sea Scrolls and Associated Literature, 12–14 January, 1997*, edited by Esther G. Chazon, et al, 133–149. Boston, MA and Leiden: Brill, 1999.

———. "Lists of Revealed Things in the Apocalyptic Literature." In *Magnalia Dei: The Mighty Acts of God: Essays on the Bible and Archaeology in Memory of G. Ernest Wright*, edited by Frank Moore Cross, et al., 414–452. Garden City: Doubleday, 1976.

Sutterfield, Ragan. *Farming as a Spiritual Discipline*. Indianapolis: Englewood Review of Books, 2009. Kindle electronic edition.

Thomas, Robert L. "An Analysis of the Seventh Bowl of the Apocalypse." *The Masters Seminary Journal* 5.1 (1994): 73–95.

Thompson, Leonard. *The Book of Revelation: Apocalypse and Empire*. New York and Oxford: Oxford University Press, 1990.

Tóth, Franz. "Kult als Wirklichkeitskonstruktion: motiv- und religionsgeschichtliche Untersuchungen zue Kultsprache und zum Kultkonzept in der Johannesoffenbarung." PhD diss., Martin-Luther-Universität Halle-Wittenberg, 2005.

Vanni, Ugo. "Liturgical Dialogue as a Literary Form in the Book of Revelation." *New Testament Studies* 37 (1991): 348–372.

Wilder, Amos N. "The Rhetoric of Ancient and Modern Apocalyptic." *Interpretation* 25.4 (1971): 436–453.

Wilson, Jonathan R. "The Dead Sea Scrolls and Christian Theology." In *Christian Beginnings and the Dead Sea Scrolls*, edited by John J. Collins and Craig A. Evans, 121–128. Grand Rapids: Baker Academic, 2006.

Witherington III, Ben. *Revelation*. The New Cambridge Bible Commentary. New York: Cambridge University Press, 2003.

Wright, N. T. *The New Testament and the People of God*. Christian Origins and the Question of God, Vol. 1. Minneapolis: Fortress Press, 1992.

Wuellner, Wilhelm. "Hermeneutics and Rhetorics: From 'Truth and Method' to 'Truth and Power.'" *Scriptura* S 3 (1989): 1–54.

Yarbro Collins, Adela. *Cosmology and Eschatology in Jewish and Christian Apocalypticism*. Supplements to the Journal for the Study of Judaism 50. Leiden, New York, and Köln: Brill, 1996.

———. *Crisis and Catharsis: The Power of the Apocalypse*. Philadelphia: Westminster, 1984.

———. "The Early Christian Apocalypses." *Semeia* 14 (1979): 61–121.

———. "The History-of-Religions Approach to Apocalypticism and the 'Angel of the Waters' (Rev 16:4-7)." *Catholic Biblical Quarterly* 39.3 (1977): 367–381.

Yeo, K.K. (Khiok-khng). "Hope for the Persecuted, Cooperation with the State, and Meaning for the Dissatisfied: Three Readings of *Revelation* from a Chinese Context." In *From Every People and Nation: The Book of Revelation in Intercultural Perspective*, edited by David Rhoads, 200–221. Minneapolis: Fortress Press, 2005.

Yoder, John Howard. "Armaments and Eschatology." *Studies in Christian Ethics* 1.1 (1988): 43-61.

———. *The Politics of Jesus:* Vicit Agnus Noster, Second Edition. Grand Rapids and Carlisle: Eerdmans and Paternoster Press, 1994.

Zanker, Paul. *The Power of Images in the Age of Augustus*. Translated by Alan Shapiro. Ann Arbor: University of Michigan Press, 1988.

Index of Subjects and Names

Adams, Edward, 4–5, 37n132, 66, 162
Allison, Dale C., Jr., 49
altar, 39n142, 61, 90, 99–100, 102–4, 120–21, 124, 134, 137, 157
angels, 19n33, 21–23, 34, 36, 39n143, 40n149, 44, 71–72, 78, 87–88, 99, 102–4, 109, 111, 113–14, 116–20, 123–24, 132, 135–40, 148, 152n71, 159, 166
Antipas, 61, 90, 125
Apocalypse, genre, 14–17, 26, 66
apocalyptic theology, 10, 161–67
Armstrong-Reiner, David, 17n19
Aune, David E., 8n22, 20, 54n26, 57n46, 77n25, 86, 93–95, 99, 102n71, 103, 104n81, 110, 115–16, 118n45, 123n69, 123n70, 125, 128, 130, 137n16, 141, 143, 146, 152n69

Babylon, 38, 40n147, 44, 72, 79, 81n39, 84, 93, 98–99, 108, 112, 121, 130, 135, 140, 142–43, 146–53, 162, 166
Balthasar, Hans Urs von, 83, 85n7
Bandy, Alan S., 75n18
Barker, Margaret, 100n60, 161
Barr, David L., 14–16, 20, 45, 46nn179–80, 72
Bauckham, Richard, 18–22, 23n51, 62, 71, 79, 91–92, 99, 119n49, 122–23, 125, 130, 144n46, 150n61, 151
Beale, G. K., 81n38, 87, 92–93, 95, 99–102, 109–13, 115n31, 116–23, 128–30, 136, 139, 141–42, 148n56, 150, 152, 155
Berquist, Jon L., 31–32, 33n107, 33n108
Berry, Wendell, 8n21
blood, 90, 92–94, 96, 100n60, 111, 115n31, 134, 136–38, 141

Bloomquist, L. Gregory, 16, 18n25
Blount, Brian K., 87–88, 90, 99n53, 102n72, 103n79, 108n3, 110n9, 111, 117n38, 119n52, 124, 135n8, 148
Bockmuehl, Markus A., 17
Boll, Franz, 90n24, 135n10, 145n48
Bresee, Phineas, 107
Brock, Brian, 158, 161n9
Brueggemann, Walter, 7n20

Caird, G. B., 117
Campbell, Gordon, 75
Carnegie, David R., 128n87
Certeau, Michel de, 41n150, 43n166, 46nn181–82
Charles, R. H., 93, 99
Collins, John J., 14n2, 15, 21, 41n151, 43n166, 163
critical spatiality, 31–33, 36
cycles of seven, 1–3, 9, 42, 45, 66, 69–77, 80–81, 91, 94n37, 101n69, 103, 107–8, 128n87, 130, 133–35, 137, 148–49, 154; prophetic lawsuit motif, 75–77

Danker, Frederick W., 51n6
darkness, 70, 92, 94, 101, 106, 114–16, 118, 123n67, 131–32, 138–40, 148, 158, 161
Davis, Dale Ralph, 74n13, 81n39
Day, John, 144n47
de Jonge, Henk Jan, 61, 63, 64n76
De Roche, Michael, 75–76
Dean, Margaret E., 34
deSilva, David A., 6
Duff, Paul B., 90n23
Dylan, Bob, 49

earthquake. *See* theophany, theophanic phenomena
Ellul, Jacques, 35n121

Farrer, Austin, 88n15
Franke, William, 167n25
Frei, Hans W., 33n106
Frey, Jörg, 60n56
Friesen, Steven J., 38n135, 42–43, 52, 54n24, 60, 62n69, 67, 139
Frilingos, Christopher A., 40n146, 167n24

Gilbertson, Michael, 38n135, 42n157, 43n162
Gowler, David B., 28n74
Gradel, Ittai, 50, 54n25, 58, 64–65
Graves, David W., 76
Gwyther, Andrew, 120n57, 131n105

Hahne, Harry Alan, 37n131
hail. *See* theophany, theophanic phenomena
Hall, Robert G., 40n149
Hanson, Paul D., 19n31, 20
Harink, Douglas, 162
Harrington, Wilfrid J., 86n10, 105n86, 118n46, 142n35
heavenly city. *See* New Jerusalem
Hellholm, David, 15
Hendrix, Holland, 16n16
Horsley, Richard A., 52n12
hour, 98–99, 105n84, 140, 149–51; half an hour, 98–99, 102, 104
Howard-Brook, Wes, 120n57, 132n105
hymns, 1, 100n60, 127–30, 136–37, 153, 155

imperial cult, 8, 32, 40, 49, 51–65; contract with gods, 60–67; economic aspects, 9–10, 16n16, 56–60; rhetoric, 31n100, 50; sacrifice, 8–9, 50, 59, 61, 63–65, 67, 94, 128, 154; ubiquity of, 53–54, 57–58

Janzen, J. Gerald, 119
John, Gospel of, 98n52, 118n44, 139n25, 140, 146, 149–50, 160

Kennedy, George A., 28
Kerr, Nathan, 164, 165n20
Kovacs, Judith, 88n16, 104n82
Kraybill, J. Nelson, 56–62

lightning. *See* theophany, theophanic phenomena
Limburg, James, 75n16
Linton, Gregory L., 15n12, 17
liturgy, 45, 58, 74n15, 85n7, 98, 100, 134, 142n34, 151
Long, D. Stephen, vii, 164
Lowe, Walter, 162
Lupieri, Edmondo F., 85, 88n17, 113, 142

Maier, Harry O., 43n167, 44–45, 72
Malina, Bruce J., 4, 42n157, 46, 113n26, 159
Mangina, Joseph L., 73, 147n53
Martyn, J. Louis, 16n17, 24, 26n65, 29n84
Mazzaferri, Frederick David, 71
McDonough, Sean M., 2, 79n32, 84n2
McNicol, Allan J., 66n84, 119n48
Minear, Paul, 6, 13
Moo, Jonathan, 79
Mounce, Robert H., 94n38, 102–3, 110n9, 111, 117n38, 142n33, 150n64

New Jerusalem, 19, 38–39, 80, 97, 114, 124, 138, 143, 151, 153, 163, 165; heavenly city, 40, 78n27, 80, 97, 147, 153–54, 158, 159, 161–62, 165

Noah, 77–80, 115n31, 116; rainbow, 77–80, 86, 123, 159

O'Connor, Flannery, 1, 11
O'Donovan, Oliver, 62, 147n55, 157, 165
O'Leary, Stephen D., 42
O'Regan, Cyril, 161, 164–65
Okoye, James Chukwuma, 131n104
Orlov, Andrei, 78

Paul, 26n65, 37n132, 42, 52n12, 63
periodization of history, 38, 41–43, 45–47, 66
Perry, Peter S., 74n12, 7n45, 123n65
Peterson, Eugene H., 25n62, 39n142
plagues, 65, 69–71, 89, 91, 94n37, 96n44, 97, 101, 104n81, 106–11, 113–23, 126, 133–41, 145
Price, S. R. F., 51, 52n12
prodigy, 8n22, 94n37, 110–13, 115, 136, 146

rainbow. *See* Noah
Resseguie, James L., 120n53
rhetoric, 6, 9–10, 16, 18n25, 26–34, 36, 39, 40n149, 42–43, 45
rhetorical cosmology, 2–3, 7–10, 13–14
rhetorolect, 26–34, 48n186, 76; apocalyptic, 26–34; early Christian invention, 28–30; prophetic, 76; thetography, 31, 33, 48n186, 84n3; rhetology, 30–31, 33, 48n186
Richard, Pablo, 127
Rimmon-Kenan, Shlomith, 47n184
Robbins, Vernon K., 27–31, 33, 39–40, 48n186
Rowe, C. Kavin, 63n72, 152n72
Rowland, Christopher, 14n3, 18n26, 88n16
Ruiz, Jean-Pierre, 74n15, 77n24
Ryan, Sean Michael, 35n119

Saunders, Stanley P., 77n24

Scherrer, Steven J., 142n44
Schüssler Fiorenza, Elisabeth, 5–6, 16n13, 26, 89n20, 119n49, 127n82, 134
Scott, Bernard Brandon, 34
scroll, 33, 80, 83–84, 89, 93, 104n81, 106, 112, 123–24, 131n105, 134
sea, 38, 40, 56, 79–81, 112–13, 136, 149–50
Seal, David, 127n83
Siew, Antoninus King Wai, 125n74
silence, 5, 10, 97–103; absence, 98, 104, 106, 151–53, 162; judgment, 100–101; non-participation, 10, 84, 90, 104–6, 129, 151, 153–55, 157; prayer, 90, 98–99
stars, 90n24, 92–93, 113–14, 116, 159
Stone, Michael E., 3n7
Sutterfield, Ragan, 2n6
symbolic universe, 3, 5–7, 45–46, 66, 158

theophany, 71–72, 75, 81, 103, 107–9, 147, 154; as goal of history, 75, 80n37, 98, 104, 137, 146, 153–54; theophanic phenomena, 72, 80n37, 89, 91–92, 94n37, 98n50, 102–3, 110–11, 116n37, 127, 130–31, 142n34, 146–47
Thomas, Robert L., 135n9
Thompson, Leonard, 131n103
thunder. *See* theophany, theophanic phenomena
Tóth, Franz, 129n92
two witnesses, 92, 121, 123–27

Vanni, Ugo, 74n15, 77n24

Wilder, Amos N., 28, 35
Wilson, Jonathan R., 163
Witherington, Ben, III, 70n1
Wright, N. T., 5, 35n121, 66
Wuellner, Wilhelm, 26n67, 28

Yarbro Collins, Adela, 7n19, 20, 135n10, 147n48

Yeo, K. K., vii, 67n88

Yoder, John Howard, 133, 164

Zanker, Paul, 54–56